Stanglin in *Ethics beyond Rules* lays bare all the pseudo-foundations of the moral relativism that has gripped our culture. Tragically, even the church has been caught in the quicksand of this moral malaise and needs a fresh vision and renewed understanding of biblical ethics. Stanglin provides it in a refreshing and compelling way, focusing on many of the most pressing issues of our day. It is engagingly written, persuasively argued, and decisively relevant. Every Christian should purchase two copies, one to read, and one to give to a friend, because this book is that good.

—***Timothy C. Tennent,*** president and professor of world Christianity, Asbury Theological Seminary

Ethics beyond Rules is the product of wide reading and careful Christian thinking. Readers will find in it both the sorts of considerations that matter in moral reasoning and a discussion of many of the ethical issues that are central to human life—all of this done in a way that takes seriously not only natural reason but also Christian Scripture and tradition. Stanglin approaches disputed moral problems in thoughtful, often imaginative ways that will be accessible to many sorts of readers.

—***Gilbert Meilaender,*** senior research professor of theology, Valparaiso University

Kudos to Keith Stanglin for the courage, intelligence, and love it took to write this crucial tract for the times. It is full of Christian wisdom about how we ought to live and interact with one another in nearly every sphere of life. I applaud the way it orients our ethical reflection in relation to the question, "What does real love require?" If more of us attended to that question more regularly, deeply, and honestly, our world would be a much better place.

—***Douglas A. Sweeney,*** dean and professor of divinity, Beeson Divinity School

Ethics beyond Rules is exactly the right book in exactly the right moment for every Christian, especially in a world increasingly untethered from biblical faith. Beautifully written and intensely engaging, it examines the contentious issues of our time through the only lens that matters: What does Christian love require? Here is a book for every man and woman of faith—but also for those of no faith, because its decency and compassion refute once and for all the anti-Christian caricatures of our time.

—***Mary Eberstadt***, Panula Chair in Christian Culture, Catholic Information Center, Washington, DC, author of *Primal Screams* and *How the West Really Lost God*

Ethics beyond Rules is a clarion call to wake up a sleepy Church and to exhort Christians to become "loving resistance fighters." Drawing from Scripture, tradition, history, science, and human experience, Stanglin offers an articulate defense of the church's ageless teaching and challenges Christians everywhere to sanctify rather than submit to an increasingly secular culture.

—***DeAnn Stuart***, associate director of curriculum, Austin Institute for the Study of Family and Culture

Stanglin brings his keen mind, Christian rootedness, and lucid writing to this pointed overview of Christian ethics. A wonderfully ordered and accessibly presented discussion of the foundations of the gospel's love ethic that is then applied to a series of key issues, Stanglin pulls no punches, providing a responsible Scriptural lens on matters ranging from sexuality and race to technology and politics. Wearing its learning lightly and delving into the concrete challenges of Christian life in the world, this illuminating volume will deepen the faith and practice of any serious disciple. It deserves a wide reading throughout the church.

—***Ephraim Radner***, professor of historical theology, Wycliffe College, University of Toronto

Ethics beyond Rules is deceptively easy to read, but the discerning reader will notice the way in which Keith Stanglin has taken the ethical insights of such luminaries as Aristotle, Plato, Augustine of Hippo, and Thomas Aquinas and made them accessible to everyone, while also fully integrating this history of ethics with the inspired teaching of the Christian Scriptures. In doing this, Stanglin has produced a much needed volume of *Christian* ethics, one that will equip pastors and laity alike in living holy lives while also guiding others toward the same. This volume is not only a corrective to the erroneous moral theology so common today but a map for those who desire to love God and their neighbor wholeheartedly.

—***Greg Peters,*** professor, Torrey Honors College, Biola University

Ethics beyond Rules is a readable, insightful book. It offers guidance for Christian disciples living in a quickly changing and increasingly morally confused culture. Keith Stanglin provides both a solid framework and grounding principles for a clear, biblically informed ethic on living wisely and well. Then with balance, courage, and grace, he applies those principles to such relevant topics as race and sexuality. Finally, he exhorts us to take our calling as salt and light seriously, engaging in the spiritual and cultural challenges of our day as "loving resistance fighters." I am very pleased to recommend this fine book.

—***Paul Copan,*** Pledger Family Chair of Philosophy and Ethics, Palm Beach Atlantic University, and author of *Loving Wisdom: A Guide to Philosophy and Christian Faith*

ETHICS BEYOND *RULES*

ETHICS BEYOND *RULES*

HOW CHRIST'S CALL TO LOVE INFORMS OUR MORAL CHOICES

KEITH D. STANGLIN

ZONDERVAN
REFLECTIVE

ZONDERVAN REFLECTIVE

Ethics beyond Rules

Requests for information should be addressed to:
Zondervan, *3900 Sparks Dr. SE, Grand Rapids, Michigan 49546*

Zondervan titles may be purchased in bulk for educational, business, fundraising, or sales promotional use. For information, please email SpecialMarkets@Zondervan.com.

ISBN 978-0-310-12092-6 (audio)

Library of Congress Cataloging-in-Publication Data

Names: Stanglin, Keith D., author.
Title: Ethics beyond rules : how Christ's call to love informs our moral choices / Keith D. Stanglin.
Description: Grand Rapids : Zondervan, 2021. | Includes bibliographical references and index.
Identifiers: LCCN 2021003551 (print) | LCCN 2021003552 (ebook) | ISBN 9780310120902 (hardcover) | ISBN 9780310120919 (ebook)
Subjects: LCSH: Christian ethics. | Christian ethics--Study and teaching.
Classification: LCC BJ1261 .S73 2021 (print) | LCC BJ1261 (ebook) | DDC 241--dc23
LC record available at https://lccn.loc.gov/2021003551
LC ebook record available at https://lccn.loc.gov/2021003552

Cover design: Studio Gearbox Design
Cover photos: Renata Sedmakova; one AND only/Shutterstock

Printed in the United States of America

---

21 22 23 24 25 26 27 28 29 30 /LSC/ 14 13 12 11 10 9 8 7 6 5 4 3 2 1

For Paul, Isaac, and Rachel

Contents

Acknowledgments

After years of training in moral theology and years of teaching Christian ethics in church, university, and seminary settings, I owe a profound debt of gratitude to my teachers, colleagues, and students over the years who have taught me much, shaping my thoughts on Christian ethics and thus the content of this book.

In addition to teaching formal ethics courses, I have had the opportunity to present different versions of some of this material in other, more informal venues. These have included faculty colloquies at Austin Graduate School of Theology, high school Sunday school classes, and "table talks" at my house. I am grateful for all the participants and for their engagement with the ideas. In fact, it was the wonderful conversations with the people in these settings that inspired me to try my hand at this book.

At the risk of inadvertently omitting some names, I want to thank those who provided valuable feedback during various stages of the manuscript. Among the participants in the colloquies who saw early drafts of the first few chapters, I am grateful for the feedback from Todd Hall, David Jones, Stephen Lawson, Jeff Peterson, Mark Shipp, and Woody Woodrow. DeAnn Stuart and Ben Peterson also helped me with some important details and steered me to relevant studies that I needed. Another group of friends read portions of a later, more complete draft. These astute readers include Kraig Martin, Mark Powell, and Logan Thompson. My hat's off especially to Matt Love and Mac Sandlin, who read a draft of the entire manuscript. These five readers returned their insightful comments to me in record time. All the readers have helped me with matters of style and content, without, of course, necessarily endorsing the final product. But it is a better book because of them.

Toward the final phase of writing, I enjoyed a productive week of work at the Lanier Theological Library. It was a lovely setting, and I thank Charles Mickey for coordinating it and Mark and Becky Lanier for their generous hospitality.

I am grateful to Stan Gundry and the entire staff at Zondervan. They have been incredibly supportive of me, and it has been a pleasure to work with them on this project. I especially appreciate senior editor Matt Estel and copyeditor Amie Vaughan for their careful reading and helpful suggestions throughout the manuscript.

As always, my thanks go especially to Amanda, Paul, Isaac, and Rachel. More than with my past books, they have directly and graciously engaged the content of this one through oral presentations and written drafts.

I wrote this book primarily for my three teenagers and, by extension, for the generation that they represent. Sadly, this current age has supplied them with plenty of Christian role models who bow to the zeitgeist. May the coming generation provide the new role models who can teach others and who, like the ancient Christian apologists, are not afraid to speak truth to power.

Keith Stanglin
Austin, Texas
November 6, 2020

Introduction

Why do you think the way you do about right and wrong? Why do you think some actions or behaviors are good and others bad? Have you ever changed your mind about what is good or bad? On what basis did you change your belief? Where do most people get their ethical beliefs, their judgments about right and wrong? For most modern Westerners—that is, those of us who live in the post-Enlightenment global West—our moral beliefs come from a complex combination of everything that makes up one's context. Moral judgments are influenced by popular culture—including television, movies, celebrities, musicians, politicians, news, social media—as well as parents and family, friends, and geographical setting. The typical American's beliefs are originally formed and continually shaped by factors like these. In the end, does culture decide what is right and wrong, or is there something deeper?

Another important question is this: How do most Americans get training in ethical reflection? Where do people go to learn how to engage in moral reasoning? High schools rarely offer a course in ethics, and most bachelor's degree programs do not require it either. There is no substantive discussion of ethics in the public square. Think of an ethical issue about which there is some disagreement in culture—say, abortion, homosexuality, or race relations. Public discussion is not deep, and it seldom goes to the level of *why* something might be right or wrong. As such, most Americans will be able to go only about as deep as the television shows they watch.

Like most Americans, many Christians also have not received much or any training in how to think about ethics and ethical issues. Many of them don't know where to start. There are not enough resources that walk them through some of the big questions of ethics and present an accessible method for drawing moral conclusions. If churches continue to ignore ethical reflection, then Christians will continue to be shaped by a culture that is openly hostile to Christian faith.

This book is a modest attempt to help change the direction. The aim is to help disciples of Christ, especially those who have had little or no exposure to moral theology, think through the basics of Christian ethics in a self-critical way. I hope that readers of all persuasions will benefit from these discussions, but the intended audience is people who believe in Christ and profess to be his students. Given this audience, the book assumes, for example, that Christ is the incarnate Word of God, the divine man who accomplished reconciliation, and the ultimate moral exemplar. It assumes the value of Scripture for ethical guidance. No attempt is made to defend these and other fundamental Christian doctrines.

The goal is to help thoughtful Christians think more objectively and reasonably about our ethical commitments, a process that is rarely taught in contemporary education or even in churches. Moral evaluation should be based on more than our subjective feelings or the received wisdom or majority opinion of our community. The ethic of love articulated in these pages may challenge some aspects of your received, embedded morality. It may reinforce others. You may not agree with every premise and conclusion offered. That's okay. My aim is that you the reader may be informed about what you believe and why you believe it.

To these ends, the first part of the book raises some of the most fundamental issues in Christian ethics. Chapter 1 asks whether there is such a thing as the good (or right and wrong) and what the consequences would be if goodness does not exist. Chapter 2 considers the goal of Christian ethics and seeks to address the questions, "Why be good?" and "What kind of life should Christians pursue?" Chapter 3 defends the perhaps provocative notion that Christian ethics is an ethics of freedom, not of laws and rules. Rules are not the real center of ethics; the reason behind the rules and the cultivation of virtues should be the focus. Chapter 4 raises the central Christian virtue—love—and suggests that the central ethical question is also a very practical question: What does love require? Chapter 5 handles the complex but (for Christians) bedrock issue of how to use the Bible in moral reasoning. The chapters in the first part of the book lay the foundations for dealing with any ethical issue that may be faced. They address preliminary matters and assumptions that ought to guide Christian responses to the moral questions of the day.

The second part of the book builds on the general principles laid out in the first part. It addresses a few particular topics that are relevant to Christians today. These chapters (6–12) should be regarded as concrete case studies that approach the respective topics through the decisively Christian principles and assumptions developed in the first five chapters. Each chapter is not so much a full academic treatment of every aspect of a topic as it is an extended reflection on a few aspects. In all cases, we will strive to listen to Scripture and the Christian tradition, especially some of the ancient Christian authors. The virtue of love will predominate. The proper understanding of love, as a unifying thread in this book and in Christian ethics, helps us arrive at the right answers and behaviors regarding these and all other topics.

Admittedly, space limits the number of topics included. The chapters do not cover every hot-button issue. The point is not to cover every issue but to lay down solid foundations, put them into the service of a few select case studies, and thus equip readers to address with greater confidence the many other ethical dilemmas they might face.

In addition, the chosen topics may not necessarily be the most significant in the sense of being most central to the gospel. And they are not necessarily the most commonly committed sins. I suspect that hate, anger, lust, pride, dishonesty, and greed, for instance, are more prevalent among Christians than abortion or homosexual practice. But most Christians know that lying is wrong, and we are told this and understand it from a young age. In many ways, the broader secular culture concurs. If we lie, we generally know we are doing wrong. Arguably, that chapter would be easy to write, though perhaps harder than we think to put into practice.

Then there are issues that are perhaps not so clear to Christians and are, for various reasons, more controversial. With some of these topics, not only does the secular culture disagree with the historic Christian teaching, but Christians themselves are coming to reject that same Christian teaching. In such cases as abortion or homosexuality, for example, less is being said in the churches about these practices, and the door is opening to viewing them as indifferent or even as practices to be endorsed. These are issues about which the church has had historic unanimity, but the changing culture has now made them urgent issues for our time. In the case of other contested topics, such as technology or politics, the issues are broad, and there is no unanimous Christian consensus on engagement. Nevertheless, they are—or should be—pressing concerns. They are notorious for leaving Christians confused. Thus we discuss them.

The chapters in part 2 function more as a diagnostic than a prescriptive manual. That is, treatment is not the focus here. The task here is more basic and logically prior to pastoral care—namely, to discern the moral status of the practices in question and, when possible, to encourage believers toward a better path. In other words, the chapters in part 2 are less about what repentance may look like and more about whether repentance is needed at all.

The third and final part of the book is an exhortation for Christians to put into practice the sometimes-hard teachings of Scripture in a world that is increasingly hostile to believers. Chapter 13 discusses the paradox of being in the world but not of it and considers how Christians might strike a balance. The goal of chapter 14 is to issue a wake-up call to American churches and Christians who still tend toward complacency and who have been hesitant to recognize and to engage in the spiritual battle.

In order to facilitate further reflection on the content and to promote conversation within a group, each chapter is followed by a set of questions that review or seek to advance the discussion of each chapter. Endnotes, which I have tried to keep to a minimum, will direct readers to a few more details, as will the suggestions for further reading.

The idea for this book began as a way of responding to a moral attitude that is increasingly common among churches and individual Christians. This attitude asserts that Christians must rethink and change their positions on important ethical issues, rejecting no conduct but embracing all in the name of love. This attitude is initially appealing, for we should absolutely be willing to scrutinize our beliefs, and everything we do should flow from love. But it raises the question of what real love is, what it requires, and on what basis Christians are to form moral judgments. So, in addition to serving as a primer on ethics, this book is leading up to, articulating, and applying love as modeled by Jesus Christ. It is a call for Christians to return to Scripture. And Scripture is best read and applied in conversation with the Christian tradition, which is why many of the epigraphs at the beginning of each chapter and supporting quotations throughout the book engage the historic tradition and reflect the rootedness of these moral reflections.

This book is for Christians who are interested in these ethical topics in particular but also want to know how to respond to any ethical concerns. Rather than succumb to the cross-pressures of our modern culture, they instead seek to be guided by Scripture and to learn from the wisdom of Christian history. These readers are people who want good reasons (biblical, historical, scientific, and so on) for holding their ethical beliefs, and they are not afraid to do so even in the face of the common cultural wisdom. They believe in order that they may understand and, having gained a better understanding, that they may equip others and pass it on to the next generation. The goal here is to provide them with an accessible guide to what ethics is, what Christians should believe and practice—and why—and to challenge the church to love as Jesus Christ loves.

FOUNDATIONS

PART 1

CHAPTER 1

Is There Such a Thing as Right and Wrong?

Therefore, having girded your loins, serve God in fear and truth, having left behind the empty and meaningless talk and the error of the crowd, having believed in the one who raised our Lord Jesus Christ from the dead and gave him glory and a throne at his right hand.
—Polycarp of Smyrna[1]

For a country, the universe,
and for law one's own free will,
and especially, the intoxicating thing:
Liberty! Liberty!
—Georges Bizet[2]

Several years ago, I was on a late-night flight back home to Austin. At some point early in our small talk, Rhonda, the elderly woman seated next to me, asked me what I do for a living. When she found out that I teach at a seminary, rather than moving on to something less controversial, as many strangers are prone to do, she pressed me with religious questions that intrigued her. She was educated and well spoken, the wife of a retired University of Texas professor. The gleam in her eyes told me that this could be an interesting discussion. As the conversation progressed, she expressed her belief that all religions are equal, that none is better than the others. It hardly needs to be said that this is a common sentiment in our culture. In fact, the equality of all religions is modern-day orthodoxy, and to doubt the sentiment would be seen by many as bigotry of the highest order.

Well, with clear eyes, but at great risk, I expressed doubt. Is the Christian faith better than the Aztec religion? Is a faith that teaches love for all people better than a religion that required human sacrifice in order to feed the sun god? What may seem like an easy question, at least to a Christian, put her in a quandary. She smiled uncomfortably. She could not answer definitively. She clearly had a hard time declaring that human sacrifice, at least as practiced in the early Mesoamerican context, is wrong. So I pressed on, turning the conversation away from religion and more explicitly toward the issue of moral evaluation. I pulled out the trump card: What about the Nazis? Again, she hesitated. Was it morally wrong to kill six million innocent people? She struggled to answer.

At this point, I was amazed. I should not have been. I had read about, heard about, and taught for many years about moral relativism. But up to that moment in my life, I had not engaged in many actual conversations with relativists about their moral beliefs. Admittedly, I would have been less surprised if these opinions had come from a college student or a philosopher. But the fact that they came from an older woman who otherwise seemed to be completely rational contributed to my disbelief. Her reluctance to offer moral evaluation is a testimony to the pervasiveness of this way of thinking in our culture.

I assume that her reticence was motivated by competing interests within her. On the one hand, the disadvantage of appearing to approve of mass human sacrifice, whether of the Aztec or the Nazi variety, is fairly obvious. On the other hand, to affirm the superiority of one religion (to be sure, not just any one religion, but Christianity) over another (specifically, a Native American religion) would, to her mind, presumably open the door to all the worst abuses of colonialism, genocide, and cultural annihilation. If any practice is deemed to be wrong, the immediate cultural fear is that the practitioners will be punished or become victims of hate. She did not express this dilemma in so many words, but this rationale lies behind much of our culture's moral relativism.

ETHICS AND RELATIVISM

The conversation that Rhonda and I had on the airplane was about ethics. Ethics is the branch of philosophy that considers the moral life and deals with character formation, decision making, and behavior. Ethics is the study and pursuit of the good, how to know what is good, and how to do good. Pursuing the good entails avoiding evil. This line of thought raises a very basic—but also very important—question anticipated by my conversation with Rhonda: Is there such a thing as good and evil, right and wrong?

To many, the answer may seem like a no-brainer. Of course, there is such a thing as good and evil! But contrary to the consensus of human history, and contrary to our common sense, our modern culture increasingly assumes that objective goodness and objective evil do not exist. Have you heard someone say, "That's good for you, but not for me," or "That may be right for their culture, but not for ours"? These expressions reflect moral relativism, which, in its strictest form, claims that all moral judgment is subjective. At best, whatever the individual or the culture believes about morality is right. Moral relativism is not a recent discovery. As the ancient Deuteronomist observes, "There was no king in Israel. Each did what was right in his own eyes" (Judg 21:25). Moral relativism saturates today's culture. We see it all over the media. We experience it more and more often in everyday life, when people shrug their shoulders and say, "Who am I to judge? As long as they don't hurt anyone else, then let people do whatever they want."

Is that correct? Is moral evaluation—assessing something as good or evil—simply a product of a historically conditioned culture that could have gone a different way? Is there absolutely no place in life for moral judgment? Before we simply give it a free pass, we should put moral relativism to the test. Before we can evaluate moral relativism, we must first seek to understand it.

First of all, not everyone who is reluctant to offer a moral judgment is necessarily a moral relativist. Sometimes we do not know enough about a situation to make a determination; in such cases, withholding judgment for or against may be the wisest move. At other times, we may know everything there is to know about the situation, but we simply cannot resolve the dilemma. At still other times, we may decide that the behavior is not strictly *obligatory* (that is, something you must do, "thou shalt") or *impermissible* (something you must not do, "thou shalt not"), but simply *permissible* (something you may or may not do). The apostle Paul judged the eating of food sacrificed to idols to be, in itself, a matter of indifference (see 1 Cor 8). To be indifferent in this way is not to be a relativist or to doubt the very reality of truth.

If objective truth is something like two plus two equals four, and if a relativist is someone who tends to doubt it, then a thoroughgoing *moral* relativist is someone who claims that there is no objective truth value to *moral* statements. The "truth" behind a moral statement is, at best, simply what our culture decides or, at worst, what I as an individual decide. If this can be called truth at all, it is truth based on something subjective.

Some philosophers claim that the moral law is grounded in one's inward feelings. For philosopher A. J. Ayer, a moral statement is nothing more than an expression of a particular, individual emotion. For example, to say, "You were wrong to eat your coworker" really means, "I don't like it that you ate your coworker!"[3] According to this view, evaluative moral judgments are not statements of objective truth but mere expressions of preference, reactions and opinions, attitudes or feelings. These emotions and the subjective moral law that they express are not naturally implanted, but they come as a result of the nurture of a specific culture and more general evolutionary development. In the opinion of a true relativist, when we say something evaluative about anything external to us, we are really saying more about our own inward feelings than about any truth that is supposedly out there.

Moral relativism is a natural corollary of atheism. If, according to atheist or naturalist narratives, there is no reality beyond the material, physical realm, and if human beings and everything else that exists are just a random collection of atoms, then good and evil, right and wrong, are mere fabrications and illusions. Moral choices amount to what I like and what I don't like. Of course, this implication does not stop most atheists from living a morally decent life and even appealing to the concept of the good, especially when they feel they have been wronged. But at the end of the day, it is difficult for atheistic naturalism to ground ethics in anything beyond individual or communal preferences, derived ultimately from the need for survival. For that matter, if the notion of objective morality arose as an evolutionary good—as it does on the naturalist account—then why would we want to discard this great idea?

To the true believer of moral relativism, then, moral judgment is nothing but an expression of cultural or individual preference, and this line of thought is becoming increasingly common. Our society has for some time been experiencing a crisis of morals. In such an environment, ethical discussions can tend to devolve into shouting matches wherein each person's mind is already made up. Morality and moral debate are often reduced to one subjective opinion against another. So those who shout the loudest or have the most power tend to win.

Given the prevalence of moral relativism, we ought to assess it as a way of determining right and wrong and as a way of living. First of all, if moral relativism is true, then there is no such thing as real evil. As such, if someone concedes that there is even one action that is always morally wrong—like torturing babies—then relativism is undermined. If just one evil action exists, then the category of real evil exists, and so does true good.

If moral relativism is true, then moral assessment is impossible. All moral evaluation is out the window. You would be left unable to take any exclusive stance or say that something is universally wrong. At most, a practice can be only culturally disapproved or inadvisable for this or that group. No cross-cultural judgment is allowed. Moral discourse is simply a description of habits. The individual or the culture becomes god, the supreme moral authority.

Additionally, if moral relativism is true, then all moral persuasion is prohibited. One cannot convince anyone or be convinced by anyone that any position is wrong. This means that moral reform or moral progress is impossible. The abolition of slavery or the work of Martin Luther King Jr. would have been unthinkable in a truly relativistic culture. Indeed, if moral relativism is true, then power wins the day. Whether a practice will be permitted depends not on truth, but on who has the numbers on their side and the power to enforce it. But it is hard to find people who speak about their own moral opinions as if they are completely subjective.

This idea that cultural preferences determine what is right is the assumption behind popular-level social ethics today. It declares that whatever the crowd or the majority believes and practices is right. In other words, simply describing what most people think and do is almost the same as recommending what people *should* think and do. Once decided, then the relativism tends to fade away.[4] The crowd can be very confident in its judgments. The implication is that, if you are in the minority, you had better get on board. This set of assumptions is constantly on display and is so pervasive that it usually goes unnoticed, even by those who would challenge the practice in question.

Here is a subtle example. On the news a couple of years ago, I saw that a linebacker in the National Football League (NFL) was released by his team after being charged with domestic assault. Another NFL team immediately acquired him for their roster. This alone did not make the story newsworthy; professional sports has long been a haven for many domestic abusers. Rather, this story made headlines because one of the new team's executives appeared to minimize the player's actions, suggesting that the accusation of domestic abuse against the player is "small potatoes" compared to what other people do.[5] On the news show that was reporting this story, the commentators at the desk visibly shook their heads in dismay. Their judgment was that the comment was inappropriate and that this executive is, as they put it, extremely "tone deaf." "Tone deaf" is frequently used to describe people—and by extension, their comments—who seem ignorant of the prevailing cultural wisdom. They are not on the right side of the current moral outrage, or they have not provided enough public evidence that they feel strongly enough about the issue. The tone is the sound given off by the prevailing crowd, or at least *a* prevailing crowd. To the news anchors, the executive's comments were wrong because they appear to be unaware that domestic abuse is, at this cultural moment, a very unpopular behavior.

Setting aside the executive's full comments and the important question of the truth of the allegations, there are two ethical standards at odds in this story. One side, represented by the football executive, assumes that exceptional ability on the football field covers a multitude of sins. The primary goal of his business is to satisfy the crowd of football fans, no matter what. Besides, he says, it is a minor offense, "small potatoes," because there are plenty of other people committing apparently "large potatoes." But the other side, represented by the media, assumes that everyone should go along with another crowd, for whom domestic violence is currently much out of favor. My point is that neither side addressed anything deeper than public opinion; instead—and this is what the opposing views had in common—both sides tacitly appealed to their respective crowds. Indeed, there are competing crowds, and they can all be very fickle. Apparently, neither the team executive nor the news anchors thought of saying, "No matter what people think or how other people behave, an innocent person made in the image of God should never be abused, and if it happened, such an evil and shameful action should come with consequences." No, you will never hear that in public discourse. Subtle examples like this one can be seen every time you turn on the television.

Other examples are more overt. No group of people is more famous for bowing to the whims of the crowd than politicians. After all, especially in a democratic republic, politics is downstream from culture. Again, many instances could be cited, but a particularly famous example is Barack Obama's change of heart on same-sex marriage. During his first term as president, he was opposed to same-sex marriage, but during the campaign for his second term in 2012, he had a public change of heart. He now supported same-sex marriage, without offering a rationale for the change or, for that matter, an apology for his years of opposing it. At the time, there was considerable debate whether this change was out of convenience or conviction. Of course, another person's motives are inscrutable, but I speculate based on knowledge of how politics typically go. Leading up to the election of 2008, the majority of Americans opposed same-sex marriage. That percentage was shifting and beginning to tilt in favor of same-sex marriage by 2012. One crowd was giving way to another. Like many politicians, Obama put his finger in the wind to check its direction. It stretches credulity to think he experienced such a significant change of personal and moral understanding on the eve of the election. More likely, he wanted "what every first-term administration wants—a second term."[6] Perhaps his personal shift was genuine, but the timing was impeccable.

These themes of the crowd, politics, and the moral question converge in a poignant scene recorded in the Gospels (e.g., Mark 15:6–15). At the moment of decision, with the life of Jesus in his hands, the governor Pontius Pilate turned to "the crowd," who shouted, "Crucify him!" Though he acknowledged Jesus' innocence, Pilate submitted to the crowd and gave him up to be crucified. After all, he had to keep the peace in order to keep his job. The majority ruled, but that didn't make it moral. The highest legal authorities pushed their agenda through, but their might did not make it right. As disciples of Christ, we have committed to following the one whom the crowd and the law vehemently opposed.

Burning Christians alive did not become morally good later in the first century when the Roman Emperor Nero, the man in power, initiated the practice. Killing Jews did not suddenly become morally good because the majority of people in Hitler's Germany supported it or were complicit. Likewise, abortion didn't suddenly become a moral good when it became legal. The same can be said for same-sex marriage or substance abuse. What the crowd says and what the government says are all irrelevant to the morality of a behavior. Yet many people, in an unreflective way, base their ethical beliefs and judgments of right and wrong on popular culture—including celebrities, news and social media, politicians, and so on.

The crowd may not always be wrong, but neither is it always right. This is a truth that many people today have a hard time understanding. If we are not careful, we can get caught up in the moment. "Everyone's for it" and "everyone's doing it" do not constitute sufficient reasons for any meaningful choice, and they are terrible reasons for thinking something is good or moral. "Get on the right side of history" may be rhetorically powerful, but it fails as an argument. In fact, whenever that line is used, one should always ask, "Whose history? When?" It bears repeating: the cultural opinion of the moment does not determine morality.

This kind of cultural relativism is in deep conflict with Scripture. The biblical passage that is most frequently usurped for the cause of moral relativism is Matthew 7:1: "Do not judge, so that you may not be judged." When taken out of its context, "judge not" might sound like all moral judgment is prohibited. But if one bothers to read on—always a good thing to do when interpreting a text—one will find that Jesus is prohibiting not moral judgment per se but only harsh, hypocritical judgment. The same measure of judgment you use will be used on you (7:2). So be careful when you make judgments. Don't try to take the splinter out of your brother's eye while you have a log in your own (7:3–4). First, Jesus says, remove the log from your own eye, and then you will see clearly to remove your brother's splinter (7:5). He does not say, leave your brother alone and judge not. The purpose of the instruction is to achieve a more objective and accurate evaluation of your brother's fault and the solution for it. Jesus doesn't say that no one has a right to evaluate another person. Rather, recognize and do your best to address your own faults before you address someone else's.

The larger context of Jesus' ministry and of Scripture confirms that making judgments is necessary. Later, in the same chapter in the Sermon on the Mount, Jesus commands his disciples to distinguish between true and false prophets by judging or evaluating the fruit they produce (Matt 7:15–20). The heart of Jesus' preaching was to urge sinners to repent and turn away from evil. Jesus is the last person who should be cited in favor of moral relativism.

If our view of right and wrong is based on custom alone or on evolutionary advantage, then ethics lacks moral force. We usually want more justification for a practice than "everyone has done it this way" or mere pragmatism. Most ethicists—and perhaps most people in general—are not satisfied fully with descriptive sociology that simply bases the right thing to do on what most people believe. They usually want to base morality on something more substantive. People should want to be persuaded to improve and to do what is good.

Not only does relativism conflict with our understanding of reality, but it is also deeply impractical to say that there is no right or wrong. The *fact* is that those who philosophically reject "ought" language nevertheless continue to act as if it is real. How can they not? So much of life is predicated on the assumption that the good transcends individual and cultural preferences. The trial of Nazis at Nuremberg, for example, could not have happened in a relativist culture. No punishment, in fact, could be justified by relativism. No cutting in line, mistreatment, lying, stealing, fraud, violence, rape, or murder would be wrong. Those who try to be consistent relativists almost always protest when they are on the receiving end of those actions. We should be thankful that those who speak like relativists usually don't behave (or want others to behave) like relativists. Consistent, thoroughgoing relativism would be a scary thing indeed—a world in which everything, no matter how vile, is permissible. For these reasons, the relativism on offer today is mostly an inconsistent relativism whose moral codes are treated as objective when the crowd says so.

Moral relativism is counterintuitive, unbiblical, and impractical. It requires quite a bit of self-deception and willful ignorance to say there is no such thing as good. Are some things relative to culture? Of course! As long as there has been interaction between cultures, humans have recognized differences in taste. Does that mean everything is relative? Of course not! If cultural rules conflict with the transcendent moral order, then it is the cultural rules that are immoral.

Moral relativism and its close cousin, nihilism (the belief in no truth or transcendence), are corollaries of atheism. It is not that all atheists are immoral. But one who does not believe in God has a very hard time establishing the moral order, especially a moral order that often calls for individual sacrifice and personal loss. Caricaturing the secularist assertion of morality without God, Vladimir Solovyov said, "Man descends from the apes, therefore we must love each other."[7] Caricature aside, it is difficult to supply the missing premise in the argument. As Fyodor Dostoevsky recognizes in *The Brothers Karamazov*, "Without God . . . all things are lawful."[8] Those "things" include not just your neighbor's sexual proclivities or marijuana habit but also an abuser's rampage or Hitler's genocide. Moral relativism, especially when unmoored from any remnant of Christian underpinnings, is a frightful thing. Christians sometimes live in a way that is inconsistent with their professed moral beliefs; this is lamentable. Atheists and relativists often live in a way that is inconsistent with their professed moral beliefs; for this we should be grateful.

Morality either reflects God's nature or human nature. For the believer, the moral order is rooted in God. This conviction arises from two angles. First of all, our unshakeable belief in God, who is goodness itself, necessitates our belief in the reality of the good and recommends our pursuit of it. At the same time, our unshakeable belief in the reality of the good, of right versus wrong, points to the reality of God as the ground of that goodness. Most of us do not need a logical argument to convince us that the good is real. It is intuitive and natural, built into creation and into us. In short, some things simply *are* wrong, and we know it. There is something to be said for the feeling of disgust in the gut. It is wrong to torture babies. It is wrong to kill six million people because of their ethnicity. Is an argument needed to confirm deep conscience? And if there is at least one thing that is objectively evil, then relativism is wrong. And if relativism is wrong, then there *is* such a thing as objective good and evil, right and wrong.

So this book is addressed primarily to those who think that there is such a thing as the good. Goodness, like truth and beauty, is an undeniable and unconditional given of existence, something that we long for and pursue, even when we fall short of the ideal. In most cases, the people who affirm the reality of goodness will ground what is good in the being and nature of God.

The question remains, even after we acknowledge the reality of the good: What is the good, how do we come to know it, and how do we pursue it?

KNOWING THE MORAL ORDER

The moral order is knowable. If it were not, then moral evaluation would be impossible. When we say that the good can be known, we are not claiming that we can comprehend everything there is to know about goodness. Nor do we imply that it is always easy to know the right thing to do in every possible situation. Some situations create real ethical dilemmas. But genuine dilemmas are rare, and they should not attract all our attention or be the driving force in a discussion of ethics. In other words, some basic things are clear.

Ethical principles are evident through a combination of two broad means. First, we humans know the good by nature. This belief is referred to as "natural law"—knowledge about God and his goodness, available within the created order itself. The apostle Paul claims as much in Romans 1:18–20, which says that knowledge about God and his moral order is plain to all people, clearly seen since the creation of the world. This natural knowledge is itself grace, a gift of God's Holy Spirit to all people. What can be known is clear enough that those who reject it have no excuse. The fact that they "suppress" or "repress" this knowledge about God and his moral order does not relieve them of responsibility. Romans 2:14–15 confirms that some people who do not have God's law still by nature do the things required by the law. Even though they were not given the law through any prophet or Scripture, the law is "written on their hearts." God has created us with a conscience that can be repressed or steered in the wrong direction by constant sin. But if affirmed and rightly trained, the conscience can be a reliable guide.[9]

Anthropologists confirm that, with acknowledgment of some variation, some basic standards or laws seem to have been pretty well universal to the human race, regardless of time or place. Take, for example, the prohibition against murder. All people believe murder to be impermissible. But what about exceptions? What about those individuals or societies, ancient or modern, who seem to approve of murder? What about the headhunters of Papua New Guinea or Hitler and his regime?

Two things should be noted in response. First, a remark that applies especially to individuals who murder: the exceptions, if they are truly exceptional, prove the rule. We can find psychopaths who do not seem to understand that murder is wrong. This dysfunctional or aberrant murderer is still departing from a recognized standard. Second, a point that applies to both individuals and larger societies: many murderers excuse their actions with some sort of rationalization. "It's okay to kill those people because . . ." they are our enemies, or they are not fully human, or the gods demand it, and so on. The killers in question would deny that they are committing illicit murder. They agree that murder is wrong. But their killing, they claim, is justified. Again, such examples are still a testimony to the universal, natural law that forbids murder. They are also a testimony that confirms what Paul said: humans are very skilled at suppressing the truth in unrighteousness (Rom 1:18), or, as we might put it, rationalizing our actions.

Natural law alone, while it reveals some innate, general truths about justice and duty toward God and toward one another, is not in every case very specific or clear. This lack of clarity is why a second means of knowing the good is necessary—namely, special revelation. Special, or specific, revelation refers to what God has revealed to specific people in specific times and places. For Christians, the primary instance of specific revelation that points us to God is Jesus Christ himself. Knowledge of God's way is mediated to us in Scripture. In some cases, Scripture may challenge what we think is natural. In most cases, however, Scripture confirms our natural knowledge of the good. Like a pair of glasses, then, Scripture focuses that natural knowledge—which on its own may be a bit blurry—and makes it clearer.[10] For example, not only is murder wrong (a thing we know innately), but as Jesus teaches, so is the hatred that is the internal wellspring of murder (Matt 5:21–22). This point might not be so clear without the specific revelation that comes through Scripture. And so, as disciples of Jesus Christ, we look first and foremost to his teachings and the teachings of his apostles for guidance in our search to think and do what is good. In other words, we come to understand the moral law, first and foremost, through Scripture.

Finally, theologically speaking, when we say that something is morally impermissible, we mean what Scripture calls sin. Sin is transgression of this knowable moral order and rebellion against God. It is a disordering of goodness, a twisting of good desires. It is to miss the mark and fall short of one's true purpose or goal, the glory of God (Rom 3:23). It is folly, the opposite of wisdom and prudence. Moral relativism, reflected in modern culture, would have us deny the reality of sin, our own culpability for it, and the effects of it. Such an approach is just as detrimental as ignoring a medical diagnosis. Not wanting to hear the bad news doesn't make it go away. In fact, it ensures that the condition will not be treated but continue to grow worse. So we value truth and wisdom in our understanding of God's revealed moral will, and we seek to conform our lives to it.

CONCLUSION

The version of ethics offered in popular culture today is moral relativism, which claims that there is no such thing as good and evil or, for that matter, truth. Your truth and your good are simply whatever you desire and assert. At first, this approach to ethics could look very attractive, especially in a society that values individual freedom above all else. On closer inspection, though, it is impractical to try to live without the categories of good and evil. It goes against the deepest moral intuitions of humanity. And it is dangerous. In real life, moral relativism turns out to be just as pushy and violent as any other moral theory, especially when one moral relativist exercising his untethered autonomy clashes with another. It is important to know what moral relativism is so that we can recognize, combat, and avoid being persuaded by it.

Good and evil cannot be determined by individual or communal preferences. Goodness transcends my momentary feelings and our culture's current opinions. Therefore, as Christians, we should never base our moral judgment simply on the way we feel or on what the majority believes and practices. "Do not follow after the many to evil" (Exod 23:2). It takes a great deal of confidence and courage to stand up to the crowd and to understand that the crowd's insistence that x is right does not make it right. When the crowd shouts for Jesus' crucifixion, it takes courage to follow him anyway. That is what it means to be in the world but not of it.

The inescapable truth that there is a right and wrong, a good and evil, points us away from moral relativism and to the source of goodness, who is goodness itself. "No one is good except one: God" (Mark 10:18). As beloved creatures of this supreme Goodness, our true end or goal is found in him.

DISCUSSION QUESTIONS

1. Have you ever changed your mind about a moral practice? What made you change your mind?
2. What would life in this world be like if we denied the reality of sin, if the very idea of right and wrong were eliminated from our vocabulary? What do you think would be the consequences if you had not been raised with the concept of sin, and if you raised your children with no concept of sin?
3. Have you heard someone say, "That's good for you, but not for me," or "That may be right for their culture, but not for ours"? What topic were they discussing?
4. If the majority opinion is the final arbiter of right and wrong, what are the implications?
5. How have you been influenced in a negative way by "the crowd"? How do you think secular culture has influenced Christians or the church in non-Christian directions? What will you do to resist these influences?

CHAPTER 2

Why Be Good?

Speak to the entire assembly of Israel and say to them: "Be holy because I, the LORD your God, am holy."
—Leviticus 19:2

"Be careful not to do your acts of righteousness in front of others, to be seen by them. If you do, you will have no reward from your Father in heaven."
—Matthew 6:1

This is true perfection: not to avoid a wicked life because like slaves we servilely fear punishment, not to do good because we hope for rewards, as if cashing in on the virtuous life by some business-like and contractual arrangement. On the contrary, disregarding all those things for which we hope and which have been reserved by promise, we regard falling from God's friendship as the only thing dreadful and we consider becoming God's friend the only thing worthy of honor and desire. This, as I have said, is the perfection of life.
—Gregory of Nyssa[1]

Without doubt, my family's favorite pet was our dog Crambone. His friends called him Cramby. Among his less-endearing traits, Cramby developed a bad habit of digging under a particular corner of the backyard fence so he could escape and enjoy the neighborhood without leash or limit. He knew he was not supposed to dig, so this behavior generally surfaced during the daytime while we were away at work and school. We would hear from neighbors, usually through posts on the neighborhood Facebook page, that the dog was out again. Hunting for the dog became a regular chore. I would fill in the hole, even with large rocks, to try to deter him. The puzzling thing is that, while we were home, he was always a good citizen. But it got to the point that, within an hour of us leaving the house, he would dig out and run off. I could take the kids to school and return home twenty minutes later to find the backyard empty.

It occurred to me that Cramby was digging out of the yard only when he assumed we were away from home. So I conducted an experiment. I went in the backyard and told him goodbye, jingled my car keys, closed the garage door in his hearing—all the things I do when I leave. But this time I stayed home and watched from inside. He came to the back door and looked in but could not see me. Then he walked around the backyard for a couple of minutes before returning to look in the back door again. Still he could not see me. Then he disappeared. As I strained to look out the kitchen window toward the corner of the fence, I could see dirt flying back. I opened the back door quietly and sneaked up behind him. He could not hear me coming because the front half of his body was down in the hole that he was frantically digging in. I yelled, "Cramby!" He immediately stopped and turned around toward me, with a look on his face that was a simultaneous mixture of shock, fear, and regret, as he realized that he was not getting away with it. Whenever we were home, he was good. When we were gone and he thought no one was looking, he misbehaved. He was being good simply to avoid immediate punishment.

Is this a sufficient motivation for good behavior—not to get caught and be punished? I am reminded of the story of Gyges. In Plato's *Republic*, Plato's brother Glaucon mentions the legend of Gyges, whose magic ring would make him invisible. The question Glaucon asks is, if you could be invisible to everyone else, would you act morally? Glaucon thinks that no one would act morally if they could not be seen and never be caught. To him, it is the fact that we are seen by others—and face their judgment and consequences—that constrains us and keeps us on the right path.[2] This point is the inspiration behind H. G. Wells's *The Invisible Man*. It is also reminiscent of the ring in J. R. R. Tolkien's *The Hobbit* and *The Lord of the Rings*, which turns the wearer invisible but also corrupts him.

The desire to sin and then to hide from the consequences is as old as the human race. The first sinful action we see in the Bible is when Adam and Eve ate the forbidden fruit. Their innocence was lost, their eyes opened, and immediately the hiding began. They hid first from one another by covering themselves (cf. Gen 2:25 with 3:7). In a further attempt to cover up, they tried to hide from God (Gen 3:8), an impossible endeavor. The blame that they cast on each other and on the Serpent is another indication of their desire to hide from the responsibility of their wrongdoing. In one sense, there is grace—a remnant of the image of God—in the fact that they felt shame at all and wanted to hide. It was not a blatant, completely unapologetic, shameless sin. The ability to feel shame is at least a dim reflection of the enduring consciousness of right and wrong.

But it does reveal that, like Gyges, Gollum, and, yes, even Cramby, the first couple did what was good until they thought they could get away with something evil. Søren Kierkegaard comments on this nearly universal human trait:

> There is no question but that a man usually acts more intelligently, shows more strength, and to all appearances more self-control, when under the scrutiny of others than when he believes himself to be unobserved. But the question is

> whether this intelligence, this strength, this self-control is real, or whether through the devotion of long-continued attention to it, it does not easily slip into the lie of simulation which kindles the unsteady blush of double-mindedness in his soul. Each one who is not more ashamed before himself than before all others, if he is placed in difficulty and much tried in life, will, in one way or another, end by becoming the slave of men. For to be more ashamed in the presence of others than when alone, what else is this than to be more ashamed of seeming than of being? And turned about, should not a man be more ashamed of what he is than of what he seems?[3]

What about us? Are we no better than the animals? Have we no more integrity than the family pet? At the least, if we are so proud of the thing we do in secret, if we think it's right and good for us, then we should be willing to let our friends and loved ones know about it. We should be willing to have that discussion with them. If it's not good for us, and we know it, then why would we do it at all, in secret or not? Isn't it better to *be* good than to *seem* to be good?

WHY BE GOOD?

For disciples of Christ, our reasons and motivations for doing the good must run deeper than the motivations that impel our household pets. That is, being good and doing the good must mean more to us than receiving a reward or avoiding punishment. So what is the purpose of Christian ethics? Why be good?

Some believers suggest that living as a Christian is the best and happiest way for anyone to live, even if one is not a believer. In other words, even if one is not concerned with the prospect of eternal salvation or condemnation, the happiest life will be one that is consistent with Christian morality. If a man is faithful to his wife and family, kind to his neighbor, and generally honest, trustworthy, generous, and loving, then he is going to have a better life, here and now, than someone who cheats on his wife, is selfish, and lacks integrity.

This connection is typically valid. For instance, consider whether honesty is the best policy, as the saying goes. Someone who lies about one thing often must multiply lies to uphold the first one. If he ever gets caught in the dishonesty, which usually happens, then trust is broken, and he is now regarded as untrustworthy. But it was the assumption of trustworthiness that enabled the lie to be effective in the first place. Now having forfeited that initial trust, not only can the liar not get away with more lies, but he will also be doubted when he is telling the truth. It is an ancient truth that one is punished by the same things by which one sins (Wis 11:16). It would have been better simply to be honest in the beginning, even if it meant suffering negative consequences then. Just as honesty is the best policy, so Christian ethics in general usually brings about the best consequences and deepest happiness.

Besides the legitimate motivation of happiness, there are weightier reasons for being good. Being good is not just about living a happy or an easy life. To be good is to be who we were made to be. It is our *telos*, or purpose. This reason goes beyond the mere pursuit of happiness. There is a big difference between doing something for the primary purpose of becoming happy and doing something because it is right and what we were made for. The usual result of being good will be happiness. It is to such thriving and happiness that we are naturally called and attracted. The driving ethical question here is, "What is human life for?"

If we know what something is made for, we will have a better, more objective idea of how to evaluate it. In grade school, I remember being taught the difference between fact and opinion, and the students were tasked with classifying declarative statements as one or the other. *Two plus two equals four* and *the sun is bright* are examples of fact. We were taught, furthermore, that evaluative judgments, such as good or bad, are a matter of taste and fall under the category of opinion. Kittens are cute is an opinion. We were implicitly trained, by extension, to regard moral evaluation of right and wrong as mere opinion, a subjective or individual judgment that has no basis in fact and is, therefore, not important.[4] If one is persuaded that all moral evaluation is simply an expression of an individual opinion and has no truth value, then one is already far down the road to moral relativism.

But are all evaluative statements mere opinions? Not if a thing's *telos*, or purpose, is known. In that case, one can offer an objective evaluation of whether that thing is good or bad. This application of teleology was ubiquitous in antiquity. For example, what is the purpose of a wristwatch?[5] We can objectively agree that a wristwatch is not for playing catch. If we were to judge it with that end in mind, we would have to call it bad. Instead, a watch is made to keep time. If it does so accurately, then we call the watch good. If it gains or loses time, then we call it bad. In light of the watch's obvious purpose or end, these evaluative judgments are not just in the eye of the beholder or a matter of taste. They are objectively true—facts, not opinions. Disagreement over whether something is good is most likely disagreement over its purpose. Whether my living room chair is good depends on what we see as its primary purpose. If aesthetics is the goal, then the chair that my wife bought is indeed good. If comfort is the goal, then it is a bad chair. A combination of both—pleasing to the eye and good for sitting—would be better and make for a *really* good chair.

What are we made for? What are we made to be? There may be many goals, but there is one ultimate end toward which every aspect of life—indeed, all creation—is pointed: God. Humans have an innate longing, a yearning for something eternal and truly fulfilling. As Augustine put it, our hearts are restless until they find rest in God.[6] God is, in the words of Peter Gabriel, "the resolution of all the fruitless searches."[7] Our end, our purpose, is union with God. As we seek God, we will come to know the good and, therefore, be happy and blessed. Pursuing the good is to become like God, and becoming like God is the true end that humans were made for. And this *end* was revealed in the *beginning*. Humans were made in the image and likeness of God (Gen 1:26–27). In other words, humans were made to be good like God.

That likeness, from which we have fallen through sin, remains the goal, as is evident throughout Scripture. When the Lord issues holiness laws to the Israelites, he prefaces the commands thus: "Be holy because I, the Lord your God, am holy" (Lev 19:2). This verse is quoted in 1 Peter and presented there as the reason for our pursuit of holiness (1 Pet 1:15–16). When God calls us to become holy, he calls us to become like him. The end goal, being like God, operates as the primary motivating factor for ethical living. We are to "have the same mind" that was also in Christ Jesus (Phil 2:5). The life of discipleship is the imitation of Christ (1 Cor 11:1). According to 2 Corinthians 3:18, we reflect the Lord's glory when we are transformed into his image "from glory to glory." Like mirrors, we look to God and begin to reflect his image from one stage of glory to the next. Becoming like God is a journey, a process, an eternal progression. The life of godliness and the continual progress in all the virtues to which God has called us are means to becoming "partakers of the divine nature" (2 Pet 1:3–11). Sanctification, the process of becoming holy, is enabled by the grace of God and by cooperation with his Spirit of holiness.

Of course, Scripture mentions other reasons for being good. As Christians, it is not for the purpose of being saved that we are to refrain from sin and pursue good works. If our continued salvation hinged on the quality or quantity of our works, then what would be the quota for salvation? There is nothing we can do to make God love us any more or less. Good works are a way to show our gratitude to God for what he has done for us in Christ. Practicing the virtues confirms our calling and election (2 Pet 1:10). By being good, we glorify God and set an example so that others may do the same (Matt 5:16).

These reasons are meaningful, however, because humans were made to become like God. This most important reason for pursuing the good can, in some ways, challenge a certain understanding of the first reason given above for being good—that living a moral life will make you happy. If the criterion for the good life is a pleasant life that makes one happy, then yes, the Christian life in general will bring this result. But as Jesus made abundantly clear, the full Christian ethic is a call to suffering. It's not a call to honesty or integrity only when it's easy. It is a call to self-sacrificial love for God and others. Could a life of suffering be a good and happy life? For a believer committed to following the way of Jesus, the way of the cross and resurrection, self-giving love is indeed the best life, even if it means taking a bullet for someone else or for your beliefs. There is nothing wrong with being happy. But let's not be deceived that followers of Christ are called to the easy, happy life, at least as the world defines it. We are being called to something so much better.

"Be perfect," Jesus said, "as your heavenly Father is perfect" (Matt 5:48). But we reflexively resist. After all, nobody's perfect! Why do we immediately object to this? What problems do we have with this command? When Jesus says "perfect," it is the Greek word *teleios*, the adjectival form of *telos* (end, purpose). Perfect means to be mature, fully developed toward the goal or purpose for which we were made.

However we may wish to qualify the call to be perfect, there is no easy way out. And we should ask ourselves, What would we rather have? Would we be satisfied if God had asked for something less? What if, after all his talk of a higher standard in Matthew 5, Jesus had said, "Don't improve at all"? Would we be happier if he had said, "Step it up a notch or two"? What would that reveal about who God is and the kind of relationship he wants with us? "Be mediocre, as your heavenly Father is . . ."? God is not a God of mediocrity. And if we approach the life of discipleship with an attitude of minimalism—what's the least I can get by with?—then we have not quite grasped what salvation is all about.

As long as we live in this body and in this age, we will be tempted by sin and even succumb to it. But knowing about a shortcoming, admitting it, and seeking forgiveness for it does not mean we settle for it or should be satisfied with it. We are called to a higher standard, and we should be thankful that we are. Perfection may not be a condition of final salvation, but the eternal desire to grow and move on to the next level surely is.

CHARACTER, CONDUCT, AND CONSEQUENCES

How should Christians pursue holiness and the goal of becoming more like God? In a way, this whole book is an attempt to answer that question from distinct but consistent perspectives.

One aspect of this larger question is the more specific question, "What makes an act good?" We can start by noting that a moral act consists of three components, or "domains." Moving in logical order, first is the moral agent or actor, second is the action itself, and third is the effect of the act. Ethicists have often focused on one of these three domains to determine the morality of an act. For a moment, let us consider these three emphases independently and discuss them each in reverse order.

Some ethicists focus almost exclusively on the effects or consequences of an action to judge whether an action is right or wrong. This is known as *consequentialist ethics*. In one famous type, attention is paid to how much human pleasure results from particular actions. The difficulty comes both in quantifying and then predicting the complex effects that may result from an action. Certainly, all things being equal, the consequences of an action should be considered. Who will benefit most from potable water? What is likely to happen if we give smartphones to children? Which decision will make the majority of people happy? These are consequentialist considerations. Jesus seems to refer to consequences in the parable of the sower, when the good soil produces an abundant harvest (Mark 4:8, 20).

Other ethical systems focus more on the conduct of the agent, that is, the action itself. This is known as *deontological ethics* (from the Greek word for "must" or "duty"), which says that actions are good if they are consistent with moral duties. Divine commands regarding external actions are clearly very important in Scripture. The most famous commands are the Ten Words, or Ten Commandments (Exod 20:1–17). Jesus issues commands throughout his teaching ministry. These and other biblical commands do not necessarily take into account consequences. They are duties to be obeyed, regardless of the outcomes.

Finally, there are ethical systems that give the most attention to the character of the agent, logically before any scenario, action, or effects. This is known as *virtue ethics* because it focuses on the virtues produced in people, the motivation behind their actions, not simply on the morality of particular acts or on unusual moral dilemmas. As with duties, Scripture reveals to Christians which traits are virtuous and should be cultivated. The so-called theological virtues of faith, hope, and love are central, with love at the top of the list (1 Cor 13:13; Matt 22:37–40). The fruit of the Spirit is another influential enumeration of Christian virtues (Gal 5:22–23; see also 2 Pet 1:5–7). These lists are consistent with the four cardinal virtues of classical philosophy—justice, temperance, courage, and prudence. The virtues are modeled, taught, and passed down most effectively in community—ideally, within nuclear families and church families.

The importance of virtues for moral living can be seen in many teachings of Jesus. In the antitheses of the Sermon on the Mount, he points his listeners to the motivations of the heart with regard to vices. The action of murder begins with hate; the action of adultery begins with lust (Matt 5:21–22, 27–28). Elsewhere, he declares that it is what flows into and out of the heart that makes one clean or unclean (Matt 15:18–20). The focus here is on the virtues or character produced in people. The question is not simply about the morality of particular acts, but about the motivation behind those acts.

One's conduct and its consequences can be good while the motives make the act sinful. In Romans 14, the apostle Paul addresses the eating of meat. The very same action can, depending on the understanding and motivation of the agent, be either permissible or impermissible. Whatever is not of faith, Paul says, is sin (Rom 14:23). In Philippians 1:15–18, Paul says that some people preach the gospel out of evil, selfish motives. Their actions are good, and so are the consequences. Christ is preached, and people are brought to salvation. But as long as their motives are evil, the preachers themselves are not pursuing the good. Therefore, it is necessary to distinguish the holy good that is done by a Christian from any act that may appear to be good. The boy who helps a little old lady across the road, though the external action appears good and the consequence is good, has done less than good if his only motivation is to get a scouting patch or to be seen by others. Virtues and motives matter. If you fast, give, and pray in order to be seen by others, Jesus said, then you have received your reward in full (Matt 6:1–18).

These domains need not be considered in isolation from one another. Clearly, character, conduct, and consequences are all important. Scripture is interested in all three components of morality. But since the actions and effects all flow from the virtues or lack thereof, Christian ethics always comes back to the virtues. If a person is truly virtuous and has the mind of Christ, then her deeds will be good, irrespective of the situation at hand. The goal is character formation, because the real goal is becoming like God and being united with God in Christ, becoming partakers of the divine nature (2 Pet 1:4). And since God is love, the chief virtue from which all Christian action should flow is love.

CONCLUSION

Enough of the image of God remains in human nature that even unbelievers generally recognize that people should be good. For Christians, though, the mandate to pursue what is good should have a deeper motivation than it can possibly have for an unbeliever. Being good is not just about conforming to social norms or pleasing the people around you. It is not about avoiding punishment or bad consequences. It is about living the best possible life and putting others before self. It is about being the people we were made to be. Being good is ultimately about the imitation of Christ crucified, being conformed to his image, and becoming like the God who created us in his image and likeness. It is a call to participate in Goodness itself, the divine nature of holy love. When we "taste and see that the Lord is good" (Ps 34:8), then we desire to partake of that goodness. The end for which we were made is to become like God. That is how we thrive.

If we are to be the people whom God invites into his eternal presence, then we should recognize the importance of beginning the formation here and now. One thing we should do is identify the dangerous obstacles that hold us back from perfection, from maturity. Name the idols and get rid of them. And then fill our lives, both individually and corporately, with the things of God. Our hearts and minds need to be transformed by the power of the Spirit, and we should pray to that end. Our character and virtues need to be shaped into the image of Christ. Virtue ethics emphasizes character over rules or consequences. To act in harmony with good character is the heart of the good life. When we grow in moral excellence and love, then good actions and, almost always, good consequences will follow. We cannot anticipate all the situations and cases that we will encounter in life that call for moral decision. But we can cultivate the virtues; we can seek the mind of Christ.

DISCUSSION QUESTIONS

1. If invisible, would you act morally? Are you more prone to do the things you know are wrong when no one is looking? Are you more likely to do *good* things when someone *is* looking?
2. What is the purpose(s) of Christian ethics?
3. What are the things and ideas that distract us from the goal?
4. Is there any way that suffering and happiness could go hand in hand?
5. Do you think that downplaying perfection leads to settling for mediocrity?
6. In what concrete ways could you become more like God?

CHAPTER 3

Ethics beyond Rules

The law is not there for the righteous person, but for the lawless ones.
—1 Timothy 1:9

When I stand before the throne,
Dressed in beauty not my own,
When I see Thee as Thou art,
Love Thee with unsinning heart—
Then, Lord, shall I fully know,
Not till then, how much I owe.
—Robert M. McCheyne[1]

It is not to make us do all things right he cares, but to make us hunger and thirst after a righteousness possessing which we shall never need to think of what is or is not good, but shall refuse the evil and choose the good by a motion of the will which is at once necessity and choice.
—George MacDonald[2]

My first paid teaching job was a two-year, part-time gig teaching middle school students. Before the first semester began, I observed how other teachers posted extensive lists of rules on their classroom walls. When I was given sample syllabi as models for mine, I also noticed many rules and behavior guidelines in their syllabi. I wanted to do things differently. I wanted to state only one rule in my syllabus. It went something like, "Respect the teacher and one another." After all, if students respect themselves, each other, and the teacher, then I don't need an extra rule prohibiting speaking out of turn, because it is implied in the rule about mutual respect. It didn't take long to find out that having only one rule would not cut it. The rule list quickly expanded, and the implications of respect had to be spelled out more thoroughly. New rule: "Keep your hands and feet to yourself," and so on. What happened? What had I missed?

I was a little naïve about the students' collective maturity level, and I quickly realized why teachers felt compelled to specify so many rules. The less mature the people are, the more rules are needed. What is true for the classroom is also true for society in general. After the movie *Bird Box* came out on Netflix at the end of 2018, some people, in imitation of the apocalyptic scenario depicted in the movie, were trying to drive their cars blindfolded. Some were having it recorded and then posting their videos online. After a blindfolded teen in Layton, Utah, crashed her pickup truck into another vehicle, a Layton police officer told the local news, "Honestly, I'm almost embarrassed to have to say, 'Don't drive with your eyes covered,' but you know, apparently, we do have to say that."[3] The principle, "Drive safely," no longer sufficed; a new rule was needed.

FREEDOM FROM RULES

As the last chapter pointed out, the goal of being good is to become like God, that is, to imitate his holiness, to regain the likeness to God in which we were created (Gen 1:26). But what does this maturing process look like? In particular, what is the relationship between Christian ethics and rules? If popular media is any indication, unbelievers often equate the Christian lifestyle with overly restrictive moral codes. Christian morality is depicted as a long list of "dos and don'ts"—and mostly don'ts. To be fair, Christians are partly to blame for this depiction. Christians have been guilty of passing on a reductionistic ethics to young people. As my granddaddy used to say, "Don't drink, cuss, or chew, or go with girls who do." That may be good advice, but is that what the Christian life is all about?

To reduce Christian morality to a set of rules is to miss the point. In fact, from a certain perspective, Christian ethics has very little to do with rules. The freedom from rules is clearly expressed by the apostle Paul: "It is for freedom that Christ has set us free. Stand firm, then, and do not let yourselves be burdened again by a yoke of slavery" (Gal 5:1). Although Paul is talking here about freedom from the law of circumcision, his point is all-encompassing, as he declares a few sentences later: "For in Christ Jesus neither circumcision nor uncircumcision has any value. The only thing that counts is faith expressing itself through love" (Gal 5:6). Elsewhere, Paul seems to endorse the Christian's freedom from rules (Col 2:16–23).

For Paul, grace frees us. It is a license, a permit. It is freedom in Christ. Does having a rule-free ethic mean you can do anything that you want? Precisely. Freedom from rules means that you are free to follow the desires of your heart.

But how can that be? Is Christian ethics really not about rules? That's right—at least not primarily. However, that does not mean immorality is permitted. Again, it comes back to maturity levels. Maturity level, one's level of progress on the road to perfection, makes all the difference in how this message is received. It is risky, in fact, to advocate Christian ethics without rules because immature people could easily misunderstand.

An immature, imperfect person hears, "No rules," and thinks, "I can do whatever I want," and what he wants is evil. It's as dangerous as a blindfolded driver. But a perfect and mature person, who God calls us to be, hears, "No rules," and thinks, "I can do whatever I want, and all I want to be and do is what is good." God gives us unlimited freedom to pursue the good, to become perfect. A mature person knows that grace frees us to live. A life of perfect love frees one to thrive. Those whose desires are in line with God's are those who should follow the desires of their own heart.

Virtue ethics alone, the kind that emphasizes character over rules, would probably work in an ideal church and an ideal world. If everyone is virtuous, then rules are unnecessary. Sadly, not everyone is virtuous, and no one is perfect yet. Until all of us have reached perfection, there will be a need for some rules. In a fallen or immature world, rules are necessary to steer us in the right direction. The law—and this goes for both civic and divine law—is good because it is a teacher for those who need it. The less perfect among us will need to fall back on the rules and be reminded of the negative consequences for disobeying them.

At the same time, even as we acknowledge everyone's imperfection, some people have clearly made more progress than others on the road to sanctification. All Christians should be making moral progress, but some are more or less mature than others. The less mature we are, the more rules we need. We are sometimes like little kids who need many rules about what to touch and not to touch, how to behave toward others, and the like.

This is probably what Paul is getting at when he talks about Christian freedom and having no need of rules. Right after he disparages rules and exalts freedom at the end of Colossians 2, he spends most of Colossians 3 spelling out moral guidelines—that is, rules. The problem with rules is the way they are being used. If they are pursued as ends in themselves or as a checklist for external compliance, if they are just a list of human teachings, and if they don't take into account the formation of virtues and the goal of becoming like God, then rules alone fall short. In their proper context, however, and for those who need to hear them, rules are necessary for Christian living.

We can compare the license that is given by grace to a license to drive. The freedom to drive comes with a great responsibility.

The driver's license liberates one to drive, but within a set of clear limits. The license—the "freedom"—comes with many rules. The limitations are intended for the thriving of the one who lives within them. If there are no boundaries, then driving becomes dangerous, leading to wrecks, injuries, and perhaps fatalities. Ironically, then, driving with no regulations or boundaries almost inevitably leads to restriction of freedom.

In the same way, in our moral lives, freedom without limits becomes slavery. Freedom without limits, enjoyed by a person with a sinful heart, is not good. It is like a spacewalker's freedom after he cuts the umbilical cable. He is untethered and free to go anywhere, but it's not going to end well. The license we are given to live entails great responsibility and some clear boundaries. And slavery to righteousness, as Paul reminds us throughout Romans 6, results in true freedom.

So it all depends on how freedom is defined and who it is that is given such freedom from rules. In every aspect of life, freedom is only for the mature. Greater freedom to go beyond the rules is for those who are growing toward maturity and perfection, for those who can handle it. All people have boundaries. For those who are less mature, those boundaries need to be named. Rules are needed to help us mature. The rules we find in Scripture are obligatory, but they are for our flourishing.

The Ten Commandments, or Decalogue (Exod 20:1–17), should have been sufficient guidelines for Israel. In fact, the early church fathers believed that these "Ten Words" were the only instructions that God intended for his people.[4] Like my middle school students, however, the Israelites showed their immaturity and needed more rules. The other six hundred or so laws in the Torah are simply expansions of the Decalogue, in the same way that "Keep your hands to yourself" is a distinct rule but also a more specific expansion of "Respect others." The Decalogue is a summary of all those laws. These Ten Words are summed up in the two greatest commands, which, rightly understood, are really the only commands for Christians: Love God and love neighbor.

The progression toward maturity is assumed and illustrated well in the *Rule of Saint Benedict*. Benedict of Nursia was the founding father of Western Christian monasticism in the sixth century, and his *Rule* is an extensive set of regulations for the life of monks in the monastery. In chapter 7, "On Humility," Benedict marks twelve steps on the way to humility. At each step, he elaborates the various instructions to be followed and virtues to be cultivated. After having scaled all the steps of humility, Benedict concludes, "The monk will soon reach God's love that 'once perfected drives out fear' [1 John 4:18], through which all things that he practiced before in fear he will begin to do without any labor and as if naturally by habit, no longer by the fear of hell, but instead by the love of Christ, by both good habits and delight in virtue."[5] All this, he says, will be accomplished by the power of the Holy Spirit.

Can you think of something you used to do only when told, but after a while, you began to do freely on your own? You came to recognize the value of the action and the reason for it. It is the same with training in morals. After being trained in the rules, the eventual goal is to transcend the rules and to do what is good without effort, not grudgingly, but as a delightful habit, a natural desire, motivated by love. The goal is for each person to recognize the higher motivations and principles behind the rules and make those her own.

THE "WHY" QUESTION

To say that Christian ethics is not concerned primarily with rules is not to say that Christians should break the rules. In other words, it's not that Christians should not follow the rules. It's that, for the mature, the rules are not the starting point or chief motivation of the moral life. What looks like "rule following" is simply the natural consequence of having properly formed virtues, and from another perspective, it is the means to the ultimate end—becoming like God.

Again, the license to drive may be an instructive analogy. The traffic laws are meant to help us get from one place to another safely and efficiently, so it is a good idea to follow them, even before knowing exactly why a particular rule is in place. Some rules may not make much sense to a new driver. For instance, on a multilane highway a sign may read, "Left lane for passing only," or "Keep right except to pass." Judging from the number of drivers who routinely ignore this law, it's safe to say that many don't know about it or don't understand the reason for it. To an inexperienced driver, it could seem arbitrary. What does it matter which lane I drive in, as long as the road is clear? Why does it matter if people pass me on the right or the left? When I went through driver's education, I remember hearing the rule, but I don't remember hearing the rationale behind it. But this practice helps traffic flow smoothly and safely. It helps traffic flow to have lanes designated for slower and faster traffic. It is reasonable for the faster lane to be on the left side, since the slower cars that enter and exit almost always do so on the right side of the highway. It is dangerous for a vehicle to hold up traffic on the left and force others to pass on the right, where the slower traffic is going.

If a new driver does not understand all the reasons immediately, she should still follow the rule, if nothing else, for fear of getting pulled over by the police. Good and just laws are instructive. Over time, with enough experience, the reasons for the rule should become obvious to any perceptive driver. Once she understands the reasons behind the rule, she will then instinctively follow the rule, even when the sign is not posted and the rule is not being enforced by the police. What began as perfunctory has become natural.

Let me try another, more stark illustration. I did not assault any of my family members today. Why didn't I? Was it because my wife gave me a list of "no-nos" that I read every morning to remind myself of the rules for proper behavior? Not exactly. Was my good behavior due to the fear that someone will call 911 and have me arrested or issue a restraining order? Or did I refrain from violence because the Bible tells me so? Although the Bible does prohibit personal violence, and a violent person could reasonably expect the police to get involved, none of this is what prevented me from doing violence today.

Instead, what prevents such outrageous behavior, or even the thought of it, is love. If I truly love my family, I would not even entertain the thought of physical assault against them, much less actually carry it out. Such violence is forbidden to me not because some rulebook says so, but because they are my loved ones. The virtue has logical and moral priority above any rule or potential consequence. In my case, the virtue of love renders specific rules that prohibit assault entirely unnecessary, even insulting, to state. Similarly, how would you feel if I invited you for dinner and asked you not to throw food?

There may be some people, though, for whom violence is not the *last* resort, but the first. For such people, a hard-and-fast rule or a threat of punishment is necessary to steer them in the right direction. They need the law and perhaps some reminder to abide by it. The threat of punishment—the likelihood of bad consequences for themselves down the road—may be the only thing that restrains some potential abusers. If the person matures, he will come to see that, regardless of the rule and regardless of whether anyone else will ever know, "love does no harm" (Rom 13:10).[6]

GROWTH TOWARD MATURITY

Who needs rules? The immature. Alas, many people are morally immature, and so we have not yet dispensed with the need for rules. We all have been negatively affected by sin. Like Adam and Eve, we are immature. We desire to discern good and evil for ourselves before we are ready. Like our first parents, we desire to be the creator, not the creature. We want to set the rules. We want the freedom not so much to be good but to determine what is good.[7] God has given sinful humanity over to following their lusts and reaping the consequences (Rom 1:18–32). The minds of unbelievers have been blinded (2 Cor 4:4). Humans, then, should not be deciding on our own what is good. We should not seek to transcend the very rules that we still need.

On our own, we can do no saving good. We don't have much hope of pulling ourselves up toward maturity. The good news is that God does not abandon us in our fallenness and immaturity. Instead, God has given us rules that are good for us and meet us in our immaturity. God's rules save us from ourselves, steering us toward a better path. What's more, God has given to believers the Holy Spirit, God's very presence, for help in living the good life. The Spirit is God's gift to his children (Rom 8:14), and he brings life and freedom from sin and death (Rom 8:2).

Just as in every aspect of life—physical, emotional, intellectual—people are also in different stages of spiritual and moral maturity. Some people are farther along than others. Some Christians are more mature than others. As disciples of Christ, we are urged to press on to maturity, to adulthood. Yes, Jesus says to be like children, but in what way? In the context, he clearly was emphasizing childlike humility over against adults who vied for greater standing among their peers (Matt 18:2–4). When Jesus said to be like "this child," he didn't mean to promote immaturity or ignorance. As we have seen, he commanded his followers to be perfect, morally mature in love (Matt 5:48). When it comes to moral, spiritual, and intellectual formation, the instruction in Scripture is always to grow up. Newborn babies crave spiritual milk, which helps them to "grow up into salvation" (1 Pet 2:2). In fact, the writer of Hebrews says that we should not still be fed on milk, like an "infant unacquainted with the teaching about righteousness." Solid food is for the "mature" or "perfect." We should leave behind the beginning word about Christ and press on to "maturity" or "perfection" (Heb 5:11–6:1). And Paul says, "Let us no longer be infants," but "mature" or "perfect" (Eph 4:13–14; see also 1 Cor 14:20).

How do you know whether you are mature? It's not always easy to know. It takes a certain level of maturity even to recognize one's own immaturity. The wholly immature are generally oblivious to their shortcomings. Indeed, it is a mark of immaturity to claim maturity, to think we are farther along the path to perfection than we really are. Similarly, the most dangerous phase of an addiction is when the addict denies having a problem. We should watch out for the people who claim they need no rules at all. Awareness of one's own level of moral maturity is an important spiritual skill to develop.

Until one is mature, until the principles behind the rules have been internalized, rules must play a vital role. Sometimes I still need to be reminded not to speed on the highway. The speed limit signs and especially the police cruiser in the median are good reminders of the goal—safety. For the immature, the rules are good, especially if one realizes that they are means to an end.

CONCLUSION

The law is our teacher (Gal 3:24), and we would do well to learn its lessons and seek the principles and ends that support God's law. But rules are limited. They cannot anticipate every possible situation that might arise. This limitation is one reason why it is important to cultivate the proper virtues, to order our love rightly, and then to face each new situation with a mature, holy love.

One question we should ask ourselves is, "Are we morally mature?" Discerning one's own maturity level requires deliberate, self-aware contemplation. Chances are that we are more mature in some areas and less so in others. We must ask, What tempts me still? Where do I most often fail morally and lose in the battle against sin? And what rules or guidelines should I impose on myself to help shape me into a more mature person? Sanctification, the process of becoming holy, is a cooperative process. God, by his grace, picks us up and carries us, and he also teaches us, inspires us for good works, and sets us on our feet to walk the path, accompanying Christ on the journey, focused on him, following in his footsteps. God puts us in communities that model and help us cultivate the virtues.

Mature Christian living is not a list of dos and don'ts. The goal is not to check items off a list. Rules are not ends in themselves, but a means to help the imperfect and immature become more perfect and mature. God calls us not to be mere rule followers, but to be like him. The purpose of being good, the reason behind the rules, is to become like God. The moral perfection that is the goal, this perfect love, is the love of a mature moral agent, a mature lover. When we become mature, or perfect, we do what is right not because we have to or have to be told to. The mature do not need to be threatened with punishment in order to do what is right. No, the mature do what is right because that is what they *want* to do. They cannot imagine doing otherwise. The truly perfected and perfect disciples act in harmony with character, virtue that is conformed to the image of Christ. They are not concerned primarily with rules or consequences. They know what is right, and they do it—without need of rules or case laws. When a new situation arises, they know just what to do.

To the fully mature, even the two greatest love commands—to love God and to love neighbor—are strictly superfluous. The mature Christian already loves and does not need to be told to do so. No one needs to tell me to love my family. Sometimes, admittedly, I do need to be reminded of the best ways to show that love. It's not a bad thing to need instruction in love, but it probably reflects some degree of immaturity. In our better moments, we realize that as long as we are in this life of testing, we don't yet love with sinless hearts.

In addition to our tendency to look out for ourselves first, other factors impede us from showing true love to others. One of those impediments is the various ways our culture teaches us to think about love. Christ commands us to love, but that love is deep and can be difficult, and it might end up looking different from what popular culture means by love. In that case, for those of us who have been shaped too much by the world's values, we must learn to love as God loves.

DISCUSSION QUESTIONS

1. Are Christians really free to do anything that they want? How can this be understood in a biblical way?
2. Can you think of something that you used to do only when told to do it, but now you do it freely without being told? Why do you do that thing on your own now?
3. Are there any areas of life where you feel like you don't need rules to do what is good? Are there any areas where you acknowledge you do need rules to do what is good?
4. What used to tempt you that no longer does? What still tempts you?

CHAPTER 4

What Does Love Require?

And he [Jesus] said to him, "You will love the Lord your God with your whole heart and with your whole soul and with your whole intellect. This is the greatest and first commandment. But the second is like it: You will love your neighbor as yourself. On these two commandments hang the whole law and the prophets."
—Matthew 22:37–40

To the question, "In what does love consist?" we continue therefore to answer with scripture: the reconciliation of human beings with God in Jesus Christ. The disunion of human beings from God, from other human beings, from the world, and from themselves has ended. Their origin has once again been given back to them as a gift.

Love thus denotes what God does to human beings to overcome the disunion in which they lived.
—Dietrich Bonhoeffer[1]

I am not allowed by Jesus to hate anyone. Our culture has accepted two huge lies: The first is that if you disagree with someone's lifestyle, you must fear them or hate them. The second is that to love someone means you agree with everything they believe or do. Both are nonsense. You don't have to compromise convictions to be compassionate.
—Rick Warren[2]

Todd was twenty-two years old when he came clean to his parents. He could no longer hold it in. The three of them were sitting around the dinner table, just polishing off the last slices of pizza, when Todd finally mustered the courage to pour his heart out. "Mom, Dad," he began, "I've been drinking again."

Honestly, this revelation was not surprising to his parents. After his first arrest for drunk driving at age seventeen, his devout Christian parents were devastated, but of course, they did their best to support him. It was not an easy road. Todd was soon arrested a second time and then, over the last five years, had been in and out of rehab and Alcoholics Anonymous meetings. Through all of it, Todd had managed to stay out of the worst trouble. Things had been stabilizing over the last few months. He was holding down a job and attending church faithfully. It seemed that he was winning the battle. But his parents had seen signs of stability and sobriety before, only to be blindsided by another minor crisis involving alcohol. This time, they were not shocked.

"I've been drinking again," he continued, "and I know I'm an alcoholic. But here's the thing . . ." And then he said something that his folks were not expecting. ". . . I've decided that, after all these years of struggling against alcohol and against who I really am, it's best for me to just accept who I am and how it makes me feel. I'm so tired of trying to say no and then failing. When it comes down to it, I don't really understand why I have to say no. I'm sick of trying to be someone that I'm not. I only feel good, I only feel satisfied and confident, when I'm drinking. Why fight it?"

His parents were puzzled. "Do you mean you won't try to quit?"

"That's right. It's legal for me now," Todd said, "and all my friends drink. It can't be all bad."

"And if your friends jumped off a cliff, would you?" his dad asked. "I'm not sure you've really thought this through. What about your faith? What about the church?"

"I don't have to stop following Jesus," Todd insisted.

His parents shook their heads. "But you know drunkenness is a sin."

"I don't know," he replied. "I read that drunkenness in ancient times had pagan connotations—people thought evil spirits took over a drunk person's body, and people would get drunk at pagan ceremonies. What the Bible really means to oppose is drunkenness in the context of pagan rituals. It's not addressing people who get drunk but still love God."

"Huh?"

"Besides," Todd continued, holding back tears, "I'm pretty sure God wants me to be happy, and this is how I can be my truest self. It's so liberating to stop the charade of sobriety. It's just not me. I feel like my authentic and real self only when I'm drinking. I can't help it. I've accepted that this is the way God made me, and you should too."

Now, how should Todd's parents respond? With love? Absolutely! Their love for Todd has never been in question, and their love for him has not diminished as a result of this news. The only question is: What does love require in this situation?

Can you imagine a scenario in which they would say, "Todd, we are so proud of you! And you're right—if God made you this way, it can't be wrong. After all, who are we to judge?"

For a number of reasons, it's unlikely that Todd's parents would respond in this way. First of all, if they are not persuaded by his attempt at biblical interpretation, then, as Christians, they cannot so easily dismiss Scripture's prohibitions against drunkenness. Furthermore, aside from the biblical point, they are wise enough to know that dependence on alcohol is, in the long run, not a healthy choice—and that goes for both physical and emotional health. What seems liberating to him at the moment will only end in slavery to the next drink. The path of affirming and embracing Todd's decision would be easier right now but, as it turns out, not very loving.

As such, although the road forward may not be exactly clear, the parents' love for their son requires something other than embracing his decision. When he reveals his intention, they beg him to get help and to try to quit, for the sake of his spiritual and physical health. When he is with them, they refuse to serve him the alcohol that he desires. But because he ignores them and keeps drinking alcohol under their roof, rather than provide sanctuary for him and rather than allow him to set a bad example for their younger son, they have made the hard choice to make him leave, in hopes that he will reconsider. For their refusal to affirm his lifestyle, Todd may complain that his parents don't love him. In fact, their actions may not be easy, but they are motivated by unwavering love.

THE CHIEF VIRTUE

This parable and the reflections about what is and what is not loving raise questions about the nature or definition of love and its place in Christian ethics.

When Christianity entered the scene in the ancient world, it brought with it a virtue not really known and not everywhere appreciated in the pre-Christian world—radical, self-giving love for all people, rooted in the story of God's creation and redemption of humanity. For early Christians, God simply is love, and the human imitation of the divine requires neighbor love (1 John 4:7–8). The apostle Paul stressed that love is the preeminent virtue, without which human works and striving are empty gestures (1 Cor 13).

Love is the greatest virtue because God is holy love. God's love was on full display in the incarnation—the life, ministry, suffering, and resurrection of Jesus Christ. The early Christian emphasis on love came from Jesus himself. When he was asked what the greatest commandment is, Jesus gave a twofold response, channeling the Torah: "You will love the Lord your God with your whole heart and with your whole soul and with your whole intellect; this is the greatest and first commandment. But the second is like it: You will love your neighbor as yourself. On these two commandments hang the whole law and the prophets" (Matt 22:37–40).

The command is quite simple in its formulation: love. Love is the foundational requirement of Christian morality. The single requirement of love is distinguished into two commands, differentiated and prioritized on the basis of the object of love. That is, love for God comes first, but this primary love is inextricably connected to neighbor love. Out of love for God necessarily flows love for neighbor. A person does not truly love God if he does not also love his neighbor (1 John 4:20–21). Showing love for neighbor is one way to demonstrate love for God and is, in some ways, actually directed toward God (Matt 25:31–46). Everything that one does ought to be out of love for God and for neighbor. Describing early Christian thought on virtue, Robert Wilken writes, "Virtue was about the ordering of one's love, and the first and greatest love, the love that animates all other loves, is the love of God."[3]

REAL LOVE

Since the fundamental virtue of Christian ethics is love, then the fundamental question of ethics is, "What does love require?"[4] The end should be clear enough. Love's ultimate aim is to reconcile the world to God in Christ. Unfortunately, the essential question about the means to get there is not always easily answered. It is not always clear how one ought to show love in every circumstance. And even when the answer is clear, it is not always easy to do.

But one of the most pressing difficulties for practicing Christian love stems from the ambiguity of the word itself and the way it is used in our culture. First of all, love is used to describe any kind of positive affection for anyone or anything. In ordinary usage, pizza and football are just as likely to be objects of love as other persons or God. That's probably okay; most of us know the difference between saying "I love pizza" and "I love my wife." We also realize that there are different kinds and degrees of love in various human relationships. There is a difference, say, between loving one's child and loving one's enemy.

In addition to those ambiguities, more confusion comes because of a misunderstanding of what love means when it is directed toward others. These days, the primary falsehood is really a twofold lie, two false claims that are two sides of the same coin. We are told, first, that opposing a given action constitutes hatred or fear of the agent. Any negative judgment or assessment of another person's action is automatically viewed as contempt toward the person. As its corollary, we are told that love entails unconditional affirmation not only of the agent but also of the action. In popular culture, love has become intertwined with tolerance of anything and everything. To let someone have their way, no matter what, is now equated with love. This dual assertion—sometimes unspoken, at other times clearly vocalized—is taken for granted in public discourse.

A moment's reflection should expose this dual lie for what it is. If we think about it, we all recognize that loving others does not always mean letting them have their way. Anyone who has raised a child knows the value of tough love and, more simply, of saying no to some desires and behaviors. Parents are not showing love to their children by allowing them to eat a half gallon of ice cream every day and watch whatever they want on television. Augustine said that you should not imagine "that you love your son when you are not administering discipline to him, or that you love your neighbor when you are not correcting him. This is not love but apathy. Let love inflame you to admonishing, to correcting."[5] Sadly, though, our present culture leaves little room for the possibility that opposition to a harmful or sinful action could be the most loving thing one can do for the agent.

Simply having a desire to act in a certain way does not make that desired behavior permissible, nor is it an indication that the desire should be followed and allowed to reign in our lives. We can probably name all kinds of disordered desires we have regularly—anger, lust, pride, greed, and so on. Being true to oneself does not mean giving in to desires if they are sinful. Much less does love require us to embrace the actions of someone who decides to follow wrong desires.

True love does not aim at merely perceived goods. As sinful humans, our perception of what is good—and especially of what is good for us—can be skewed. Like children who would live on ice cream alone, our desires are harmful to the extent that they are uninformed or sinful. Feeding those disordered desires in ourselves or in someone else is not true love. J. Budziszewski defines love as "a commitment of the will to the true good of another person."[6] That is, true love seeks the *actual* good of the other. Yes, love involves the affections and desire for the other. But true love also requires evaluation and discrimination, the ability and will to judge that some objects or behaviors are better than others.

In the same homily of Augustine cited above, he proceeded to make an important distinction regarding love and admonition. "Do not love error in the man, but [love] the man; for God made the man, but the man himself made the error. Love what God made; do not love what the man himself made."[7] Augustine is articulating what is sometimes stated as, "Love the sinner; hate the sin." Again, making such distinctions does not come naturally in a culture where we've been trained to equate negative assessment with phobia, bigotry, and hatred. But there must be a place reserved in the home for a parent telling a child no without being accused of hating the child. A place must remain in society for disagreement with certain behaviors or actions without being charged with bigotry. In other words, love can be uncomfortable and still be love.

God's nature is our model. God's holiness means both difference and participation—he cannot tolerate sin, but he also invites those who are forgiven into his fellowship. Not only is God holy, but he is also love (1 John 4:8). Because he loves us, God wants the best for us. The best thing for us is to love and obey God. Neither his holiness nor his love can exist without the other; they each inform the other. To sum up the whole biblical testimony about God, we can say that his nature is that of holy love. At the most basic level, to be like God means to be an agent of holy love. And it is by God's Spirit that we grow in this love.

JESUS' EXAMPLE

All these principles, including the distinction between loving the sinner and hating the sin, are evident in the ministry of Jesus, who is the primary model of Christian virtue, the one who reveals to us God's holy love. Jesus was infamous for the love he showed to "sinners" like tax collectors and prostitutes. But what exactly did this love look like?

When Jesus invited himself to the house of the tax collector Zacchaeus, the people began to murmur, scandalized that Jesus was willing to go to a sinner's house. For his part, Zacchaeus understood the implication of having this holy man as his guest, so he immediately announced that he would pay back the money, quadruple, to those whom he had cheated. Only after that sign of repentance did Jesus declare that salvation had come to Zacchaeus and his house (Luke 19:7–10). Zacchaeus was following the instruction for repentance given to tax collectors previously in Luke's Gospel (Luke 3:12–13).

Again, when a woman caught in the act of adultery was brought before Jesus, he refused to join in condemning her to death. Instead, he showed her mercy and reminded the accusers of their own sinfulness. But his last words to the woman should not be forgotten: "Go, and from now on sin no longer" (John 8:2–11).

In both instances, the love that Jesus showed included not only mercy for the sinner but also a call to repentance, a change of heart and mind, a turning away from the sin. This love is the way to reconciliation. He loves the person, but he does not justify or tolerate their sin, much less embrace it. These cases are not exceptions. Rather, they are the rule in Jesus' ministry. "Stop sinning," Jesus said to a man he healed, "or something worse may happen to you" (John 5:14). He welcomes sinners as they are, but he heals them. He invites them and empowers them, by his Spirit, to become something so much better: who they were created to be. He meets us in our imperfect and broken condition, and because he loves us, he never leaves us in it.

Not only do people in our society have a hard time understanding the concept of love that asks us to change our heart, but Christians influenced by this society have a hard time as well. We hear about more and more Christians who assume that love for sinners entails embracing and approving of their actions. For many Christians, "unconditional love" has become the starting point and rallying cry for something not far removed from moral relativism. Again, unconditional love, when rightly defined and practiced, should be at the center of the church's ethic. God loves sinners, no matter what. So should we. But the model for that unconditional love must be Jesus, who shows that love pursues what is actually good for the person, not necessarily that person's perception of what is good.

Following the lead of a post-Christian Western culture, many Christians seem intent on moving the standard from "love the sinner; hate the sin" (as taught by Jesus and Augustine, among others) to "love the sinner; love the sin" (as taught by popular culture). It is difficult, within a Christian context, to successfully make this transition overnight. Since they know that the change must happen gradually, they advocate an implied transitional step between the two: "love the sinner; ignore the sin." That is, defer and claim some ambiguity about the moral status of the behavior in question and then assert that love means having Christlike conversations. But how did Jesus' conversations with sinners go?

Can we imagine Jesus saying to the woman caught in adultery, "I do not condemn you. Go about your business because it's none of my business what you do in the bedroom"? This is the "enlightened" Jesus that many Christians now project into ethical discussions and onto Scripture. But the Jesus found in the pages of the Gospels was not exactly a live-and-let-live kind of guy. As he practiced love perfectly—and, in fact, *because* he practiced love perfectly—he did not defer the moral question, and he did not make anyone wonder where he stood on an issue.

It should be clear what all this means when it comes to grace and forgiveness. Love invites and welcomes, and God's grace is superabundant (Rom 5:20). If Christians only communicate half of the message—"hate the sin"—and effectively ignore the sinner, then it is not hard to understand how others, outsiders and insiders alike, could interpret it as hate toward the sinner. Love for the sinner should never be in question. No sin is beyond God's ability to forgive, and if God forgives, then who are we to withhold forgiveness from the penitent? Real love calls sin what it is and seeks to rescue people from sin's clutches, calling the sinner out of bondage to sin and into true freedom.

If we are encouraging others to continue in their sin and brokenness, then it is not real love that we are showing. The example of Jesus Christ, the embodiment of real love, shows a different way. As the Word made flesh, he is "full of grace and truth" (John 1:14). He is both grace and truth, never one without the other. Grace without truth would be a mockery of love, an easy way out, a false love based on untruth, and therefore not grace but licentiousness. Truth without grace would be cold, rigid, unattractive, hypocritical, ultimately self-condemning, and therefore not truth but falsehood. Without both grace and truth, we have neither. If we are to be like Christ, we must reflect his genuine love that is full of both grace and truth. To use Paul's words, we must speak and enact the "truth in love" (Eph 4:15).

LOVE AND VIRTUE

As we have stated previously, rules are necessary to teach and guide the not-yet-mature, but a list of rules can never be comprehensive or anticipate and directly address every possible situation in life. For this reason, we fall back on love as the central virtue and the ultimate guide. Love can speak to every unique case. The answer to the question, "What does love require?" is not always clear. Given the proper definition and nature of love, some courses of action are definitely excluded, but a broad range of actions might be possible without the one sure solution or front-runner.

A certain ambiguity is to be expected, therefore, in ethics. It is not always an exact science. Aristotle said as much: "The same exactness must not be expected in all departments of philosophy alike, any more than in all the products of the arts and crafts." Thus there is "difference and error" in moral philosophy. He concludes, "It is the mark of an educated mind to expect that amount of exactness in each kind which the nature of the particular subject admits. It is equally unreasonable to accept merely probable conclusions from a mathematician and to demand strict demonstration from an orator."[8]

In light of this inherent ambiguity, two points are worth noting. First is the importance of the virtues. Since rules don't cover everything, a person's virtuous character is sometimes the only thing that guides a decision and action. These virtues are informed by Scripture and typically shaped within communities of church and family. Second, the measure of ambiguity suggests the importance of the particular virtue of humility. Again, there are clear-cut moral cases, and ambiguity should not be unnecessarily introduced into clear situations. Humility is not the same as agnosticism. If Scripture has revealed something clearly, then Christians are obliged to submit. But when there are legitimate gray areas, especially because of unique and complex situations, we must emphasize the humble application of Christian virtues, practiced in conversation with inspired Scripture and the Spirit-led community of believers. A conscience that is rightly trained in Scripture and formed by the virtues can be a sound witness and guide in unique situations.

CONCLUSION

As disciples of Christ, our calling and duty, above all else, is to follow the way of love. We love because he first loved us. Looking to the Lord as our model, we are to lean toward love, which is to be oriented to our highest end. If love is the chief virtue of Christian living, then it is important to understand what love is. For a disciple of Jesus, there is no better example of love than that of Jesus. Love is the commitment to and pursuit of the actual good of the other. By love, we see others through the eyes of God: people who are made in the image and likeness of God, people loved by God, people for whom Christ died. Like God, we want what is best for them, and no matter what, we never stop loving them—unconditionally.

"Unconditional love," of course, looks different in different situations, depending on the context. The question of what love requires cannot bypass the question of whether a given behavior is permissible or impermissible, whether it fulfills or resists God's moral will for his people. A parent's unconditional love for a child with a learning disability may look a little different than a parent's unconditional love for a teenager who gets pulled over for reckless driving. They are entirely different situations that call for different responses. What is unconditional and absolute is the commitment to pursue the child's good. Sometimes there is acceptance and accommodation. In other situations, there must be discipline, enacted for the sake of the child learning a better way. Sometimes, love requires rules—especially for the immature or, better, the not-yet-mature, the maturing.

In imitation of Christ, we should love in such a way that our love for others cannot be reasonably doubted. But beware of the dual lie that asserts that any negative evaluation of a behavior is identical to hatred of the person and then claims that love entails embracing any and every desire and practice of others. Let love—the kind that doggedly pursues the actual good of the other—rule our thoughts, words, and deeds. A so-called love that can't say no, that can't distinguish between good and evil, and that tolerates any and every behavior, is a misnomer and is no real love at all. Only when love is properly understood can one proceed to the central question of Christian ethics: What does love require?

DISCUSSION QUESTIONS

1. How do you think the parents of Todd (the alcoholic) should show love to him?
2. What is "tough love"? Have you ever been the recipient of "tough love"? How did you respond?
3. Does love look different toward someone who repents than it looks toward someone who does not repent?
4. What do you think about the saying, "Love the sinner; hate the sin"? Does the church have a harder time with the first half or with the second half of the saying? How can we strike the balance effectively?

CHAPTER 5

The Use of the Bible in Ethics

These [books of the Old and New Testaments] are fountains of salvation, that they who thirst may be satisfied with the living words they contain. In these alone is proclaimed the doctrine of godliness. Let no man add to these, neither let him take anything from these. For concerning these the Lord put to shame the Sadducees, and said, "Ye do err, not knowing the Scriptures." And He reproved the Jews, saying, "Search the Scriptures, for these are they that testify of Me."
—Athanasius of Alexandria[1]

Neither may we in this case lightly esteem what hath been allowed as fit in the judgment of antiquity, and by the long continued practice of the whole Church; from which unnecessarily to swerve, experience hath never as yet found it safe.
—Richard Hooker[2]

We believe in and with the Church that Holy Scripture has this priority over all other writings and authorities, even those of the Church. We believe in and with the Church that Holy Scripture as the original and legitimate witness of divine revelation is itself the Word of God.
—Karl Barth[3]

As we have seen, Scripture urges disciples of Jesus to follow the way of love. Thus, the primary ethical question that a Christian should ask is, "What does love require?" In many cases, the answer to that question is clear. In some cases, though, the right thing to do is not immediately clear to us. The more that we have been shaped into the image of Christ and have grown to become like God, the clearer will be the call to action. Knowledge of Scripture is one of the main factors contributing to that growth in wisdom and goodness. Without Scripture, we are wandering without a compass. When the Sadducees came to trap Jesus with a question about the final resurrection, Jesus chastised them for not knowing the Scriptures (Matt 22:29).

Following Jesus' lead, the vast majority of Christians throughout history have agreed that Scripture is the primary authority for faith and practice. In other words, not only in matters of doctrine but also in matters of ethical living the Bible is the chief authority. Thinking about issues from a Christian perspective means, first and foremost, considering them in light of Scripture. Any time a question of doctrine or ethics is raised, a Christian's first impulse should be to ask, "What does Scripture say?"

THE BIBLE TELLS ME SO?

Christians often claim that the Bible contains all the answers to life's questions. This point seems clear enough, until one actually begins to search its pages for specific guidance regarding moral questions today. On the one hand, much of what it does address seems irrelevant to modern life. This apparent irrelevance is especially noticeable in the Old Testament, which seems so far removed from our time and place. On the other hand, the questions that are currently relevant to our lives are often missing in Scripture. If you pick up a random textbook on ethics and flip through it, you will notice a number of topics that are commonly discussed today but found by name nowhere in Scripture. Abortion, euthanasia, artificial reproductive technology, artificial intelligence, immigration law, drug use, gun control, participation in the military—the list could go on—are not explicitly addressed in the Bible.

The Bible should not be criticized for these ostensible faults. Like all writings, the individual documents that together compose the Bible are occasional—that is, they were written at a specific time and place to a specific audience in a specific culture, usually to address specific questions or problems. Not surprisingly, then, these books *include* some ethical instructions that reflect a very different setting than most modern Western readers are familiar with. For instance, Exodus 21:28–32, 35–36 includes laws that stipulate how to deal with a bull that gores people or other bulls to death. The particularity of these laws is remarkable, and their relevance to another time and place is evident. The cases that they addressed were real, ordinary occurrences. On the surface, these laws are relics from a distant past that have no significance for our lives—at least for those of us who do not own bulls.

At the same time, the Bible's *silence* about a number of issues, though frustrating to Christians who seek specific guidance, is also not surprising. The reasons for silence about a particular moral question or practice are various. First, and most obvious, the Bible is silent about issues that did not exist when it was written. For example, Scripture does not address in vitro fertilization or other artificial reproductive technologies.

Second, there are other issues and practices that were known in the ancient world but are left unaddressed for other reasons. It could be that the issue was unimportant or indifferent to Christian ethics, and there was thus no reason to mention it. For instance, the consumption of meat would fall under this category of moral indifference. It is only mentioned in Scripture because some Christians thought eating meat is impermissible; that is, they made an issue out of it, so Paul corrects their misunderstanding (Rom 14).

Alternatively, it could be that a practice was indeed important, but it simply was not necessary to address because Christians held a common understanding of the issue. The shared understanding was part of the air breathed, and it never occurred to the writer to address it. For example, the believers in Corinth did not ask about, and Paul felt no need to tell them about, his views on abortion, which was known and practiced in the ancient world. His silence does not mean that he permitted abortions or that he had no opinion about the practice, but that he did not need to address the issue for the Corinthians. Similarly, if there had not been a man in a sexual relationship with his stepmother, and if Paul had not been prompted to address that issue as he did in 1 Corinthians 5—that is, if his letter to Corinth had never mentioned it and the issue never came up in the New Testament—his hypothetical silence would not indicate that he did not care about that issue. The incestuous relationship would not have somehow been permissible if he had not addressed that specific incident.

In light of these realities related to the historical context of Scripture, a couple of preliminary observations should be immediately emphasized. First, silence is neither always prohibitive nor always permissive. Historical and literary contexts, including the human author's intentions and the audience's needs, must be considered. It will not suffice to say, "The Bible doesn't mention euthanasia," or "Jesus never condemned abortion," so it must be permissible. No. He never condemned cannibalism either! So what? Scriptural silence alone cannot be the basis of a responsible Christian ethical code.

A second observation is that we will have to qualify how the Bible addresses our moral questions. It is true that Scripture answers our moral questions, but perhaps not in the direct and obvious way we initially expect. In cases where Scripture does not directly address our questions, we must see whether and how it indirectly addresses them. For the issues that are not explicitly addressed, and even for those that are, it is helpful to look for the principles behind the rules.

Take, for example, the passage about the goring bull, a passage that we might be tempted to ignore if we do not own a bull. Are there any relevant, applicable principles that we could elicit from these seemingly irrelevant, inapplicable rules? These laws about a violent bull address not only what to do with the bull but also the liability of the owner. If the owner was aware of the bull's violent tendencies but did not take proper action, then the owner is liable to greater punishment (Exod 21:29). Since I don't own a bull, am I to dismiss these commands as insignificant? We may not own a bull, but there is a principle here for those who own dogs. The owner of a pit bull or a rottweiler has a greater responsibility than the owner of a Chihuahua or a Havanese when he takes his dog for a walk in a crowded neighborhood. The point is that owners are responsible for the things under their oversight. More broadly, owning something that is potentially dangerous to others—whether a bull, a dog, an automobile, or a firearm—comes with great responsibility and liability. So, we may ask, does the Bible address gun ownership? From one perspective, not at all; from another perspective, yes, it addresses some aspects of it.

Other examples could be multiplied. When Jesus tells his disciples to follow his lead by washing each other's feet (John 13:14–15), we could mistake this command in two different ways. First, we could literally wash each other's feet when we enter each other's homes. Not only would this be creepy, but the action would not carry the same meaning that it had in the first century. Feet are generally not as dirty in our culture as they were in the ancient Near East, and if they are, they are generally well hidden from sight and smell. Second, because of the cultural distance reflected in the command, we could simply ignore the command and say it is not for us. Both responses—to follow the command literally and to ignore it completely—miss the mark. Instead, we must ask, "What is the theological principle behind the command?"

Jesus states the principle broadly later in the same chapter: love one another as I have loved you (John 13:34). Christ is the pattern. In light of this specific instance of showing love—namely, washing the disciples' feet—can we be more specific about the principle? In what way has Christ shown them love? To answer this question, we must understand that footwashing was seen as a necessary act of hospitality, but that it was also demeaning work reserved for a servant. The principle, then, is to do acts of kindness and love, even to the point of doing something that might seem demeaning.

Practice sacrificial service. How, then, would we apply John 13 today? Take out each other's garbage, clean the bathroom when it is not your turn, or wash someone else's car. To do such things is, in essence, to follow Jesus' command to wash feet.

This is not an elaborate system for circumventing a moral command or dismissing as "cultural" anything we don't want to practice today. There should be very good reasons, scripturally and otherwise, for not literally following a clear command. In the case of John 13, the footwashing itself is culturally specific. Jesus didn't introduce the practice of footwashing to the ancient Near East. He took a current practice of necessity and kindness and invested it with theological meaning. So, on a certain level, it would be inappropriate for us to wash each other's feet, given that *most* of us have cleaner feet than those in the first century. The practice of footwashing today (ceremonial or otherwise) attempts to replicate ancient culture, and the practice inevitably has a very different meaning.[4]

APPEALING TO SCRIPTURE

Although Scripture is our guide in ethical matters, it is not always as clear and certainly not as direct as being instructed by your parent or boss. The books of the Bible were addressed to people thousands of years ago in a different place and culture. The Bible was not written to us, but it was written for us. How then does it guide us?

I'd like to suggest that Scripture instructs us in morals in three ways.[5]

1. *Rules.* Scripture's most straightforward ethical instructions are rules intended for the readers. Rules are simply codes that regulate behavior. These norms or action guides are stated directly and often in the imperative. Rules correspond closely to the genre of law in Scripture, the "thou shalts" and "thou shalt nots." The Decalogue (Ten Commandments) instructs at the level of rules. They are duties that must be

followed and fulfilled. The rules or commands in Scripture are not arbitrary. In nearly every case, we can see that there are reasons or assumed principles behind the rules, even if they are not stated explicitly.

2. *Principles and Paradigms.* Most of the instruction given in Scripture does not come in the form of rules. We might think of principles and paradigms as a catch-all category that—like a digital, interactive map—zooms out a bit from rules.

   Principles are general moral frameworks that tend to leave the specifics to the moral agent or the situation. As a summary of the two tables of the Decalogue, the two greatest love commands—love God and love your neighbor (Matt 22:37–40)—are broad and reflect this second level. The Golden Rule is equally broad and reflects the whole Law and Prophets (Matt 7:12). Virtues such as the fruit of the Spirit (Gal 5:22–23) are also principles. These principles have the imperatival force of commands or rules, but they are stated more generally in order to be applied in other specific and perhaps unforeseen situations. As such, the boundary between rule and principle may sometimes be blurry. It may help to think of principles as emphasizing more the virtue than the rule that applies it.

   Paradigms are models of morality, usually embedded in narratives. Narratives are not direct commands to the readers, but they still instruct, conveying their moral instruction less directly. Narratival moral instruction could come in the form of a parable, such as in the prophet Nathan's rebuke of King David (2 Sam 12:1–4). Or the narrative could teach by way of approved example, as in the description of the early believers' devotion to God and to one another (Acts 2:42–47). Scripture is full of stories about characters who model either exemplary or wicked behavior. Usually, though not always, we can tell the difference between the two and know which patterns to follow and which to avoid. When Jesus tells the parable of the good Samaritan, the story itself communicates clear instructions about how to show love, apart from any need for rules. The mature and discerning should understand the implicit moral guidance, even before Jesus issued the command, "Go and do likewise" (Luke 10:37).

3. *Christian Worldview and Theological Convictions.* With this third level, we zoom the map out to the widest possible view. Worldview describes the basic convictions that are informed by Scripture and foundational Christian doctrines and that then inform our every moral choice. It is the story of redemption, the rule of faith, the bedrock Christian beliefs about God, creation, fall, redemption, and eternal life. For example, humans are created in the image and likeness of God. This is a basic theological conviction that permeates Scripture from first to last, and its implications for morality are many. Human beings are not merely material animals, and so they should be treated with more dignity than anything else in God's good creation. Worldview encompasses the entire moral order, including principles, paradigms, and rules.

These three distinct but overlapping levels inform one another and give rise to one another. With each specific rule, there is a larger principle or virtue from which it flows, as well as a foundational theological conviction on which it is grounded. The Bible informs and provides content on all three levels. As such, the most important question is often the "why" question. "Why this rule?" which is to say, "What is the principle or theological conviction behind this action guide?" Though moral rules may function sometimes as a line in the sand, they are rarely if ever merely arbitrary tests. They usually reflect higher principles and theological convictions.

By recognizing these different levels, we may more effectively discern God's will for us through Scripture, particularly regarding those questions about which Scripture is silent. When the Bible does mention an ethical issue and provides a clear judgment on it, it is comparatively easy for us to know God's moral will. In these cases, we can usually follow the rules as they are stated. But what are we to do when an issue is not mentioned? We need not throw our hands in the air and give up. Instead, we can look for principles relevant to the practice in question. In fact, this is how Jesus dealt with the Sadducees in Matthew 22. Although Scripture does not directly address their precise question about resurrection, Jesus indicated that they should have known the answer based on Scripture (Matt 22:29). He responded with a theological conviction about the nature of God—he is the God of the living and not of the dead—and used it as a basis for answering their question.

The virtues or moral principles that should guide God's people are emphasized throughout Scripture, especially in the New Testament. From the broader moral principles found in Scripture, we elicit rules that may not be explicit in Scripture. The specific rules that we do have may not explicitly state the principle behind them, but they usually point back to the moral principles and theological convictions that are mentioned elsewhere. Everything in Scripture should lead us to the love of God and neighbor.

AIDS TO BIBLICAL APPLICATION

So far, all of this concerns the use of *Scripture* in ethical reasoning. We look for rules and principles in Scripture to guide our thoughts and actions. Alongside Scripture, two additional resources aid our interpretation of the Christian faith. Together these three are the sources and norms of our teaching and practice. They help answer the question, "How do we know the good?" They are Scripture, tradition, and reason. Their order of priority is important. Although each can contribute something positive, there is also greater risk of fallibility as the list progresses. So we must always start with Scripture.

1. *Scripture.* As we have already observed, turning to Scripture as the first source of authority should be a practice that is intuitive to Christians. In the ancient, medieval, and

early modern periods, Scripture functioned as the highest standard of authority, the norm of Christian theology. Even in the sixteenth century, when Roman Catholics effectively exalted tradition alongside Scripture and some radical Anabaptists effectively eliminated the use of tradition, Scripture was still unanimously acknowledged as the preeminent authority for Christian faith and practice. Scripture is an infallible guide in matters of faith and morals. If Scripture seems misguided, it is more likely due to our misinterpretation. In most cases, the moral duties and expectations for disciples of Jesus are clearly revealed in Scripture's rules, principles, and worldview. These next sources help us in our interpretation and application of Scripture.

2. *Tradition*. Specifically, we have in mind the two-thousand-year history of the church, with heavier emphasis on the earlier beliefs and practices of our brothers and sisters who lived so close to the time of Jesus and his apostles. Further upstream to the fountains, the water is purer. The early church's rule of faith was the primary lens for interpreting Scripture.[6] With regard to ethical issues, we ask, "What has the universal church taught for the majority of its history?" If Christians from the earliest times have interpreted and applied the Bible's rules and principles uniformly, then we should heed their testimony. It doesn't mean that the great tradition is infallible. But if Christians have had 1,900 years of consensus on an issue, and we now decide they have been wrong all this time, then we had better have a really good rationale for dissenting. That rationale must go up the chain and should be based primarily on Scripture. This criterion of tradition, by the way, is the most neglected of the three. It requires something in short supply today—knowing and appreciating the history of Christian thought.
3. *Reason*. This criterion is available, in varying degrees, to all people, including those who have never encountered Scripture or Christian teaching. When it comes to moral

> questions, we might ask, "What does reason or common sense suggest? What does nature or natural law have to say about the issue in question? What is the natural purpose or design of the thing in question?" The appeal to human reason includes innate knowledge and assumes that, to a certain extent, right and wrong have been built into the natural order (Rom 1:18–32). This is a level at which a Christian can speak with non-Christians. That is, one can make cases that support Christian ethics without ever appealing to Scripture or Christian tradition. But, again, human reason is certainly fallible. It is subject to false arguments, emotions, ignorance, and other things that might cloud our judgment. Yet if Scripture seems to be saying *x*, and it is supported by Christian tradition, and it does not contradict reason, then that's a pretty solid case.

In addition to these three criteria, many Christians also commend the role of *experience* as a fourth source and judge.[7] We could take experience to mean our interpretation of the natural world, akin to what we think of as natural science. Positively, experience could also include a properly trained conscience in submission to Scripture. Broadly defined, no ethical judgments can be made apart from experience in some sense. Often it's taken today to mean "my own personal experience" of life, my individual opinions about right and wrong. If it is the latter, then it approaches moral relativism and is definitely the most unreliable criterion in this list. Our desires are often disordered and sinful. So experience, at best, means the experience of the entire church community, and it can then be only a confirming criterion. It does not teach new content, and it should never be exalted above Scripture or any of the criteria on the chain above. If it alone contradicts Scripture, tradition, and reason, then we have a big problem. To follow primarily the deliverances of one's personal experience is definitely one way to live—and one that is common in our society—but it is no longer a Christian way of life. In contrast to the often-undervalued voice of tradition, experience is now the most common moral source to which people appeal, especially when understood as "my individual feelings." Often against Scripture, Christian tradition, and reason, even Christians will exalt lived experience over the other sources. Because of its fallibility, this is problematic. Finally, Christians may also appeal to the Holy Spirit for moral guidance and think of this as experience. Such an appeal is legitimate, but the Holy Spirit may not be invoked in order to turn God's people away from Scripture. The Spirit speaks through Scripture and points us to it.

CONCLUSION

It is helpful first to put our moral questions to Scripture by appealing to its relevant rules, moral principles, and theological convictions, and then to filter the biblical interpretation and application through the confirming lenses of tradition and reason. Consider the story of Todd in the previous chapter, who said he feels happier as an alcoholic and wants to embrace the lifestyle. Scripture says drunkenness is wrong, communicating this judgment by way of commands that imply certain principles. For example, Ephesians 5:18 prohibits getting drunk on wine. Although it was written to first-century Christians, there is no obvious reason to think the instruction is irrelevant to twenty-first-century Christians. This verse also implies a moral principle: drunkenness (that is, particularly as addiction or alcoholism) can lead to wastefulness and can easily replace the truly valuable things in life, the things of the Holy Spirit. Other passages say similar things and reinforce these and other principles. So Scripture is clear. What about the other sources? Christian tradition confirms the prohibition against drunkenness. Reason tells us that excess of alcohol is harmful to a person's body and mind, to relationships, and to other persons. The communal experience of the church and of those who have struggled with alcoholism should confirm these judgments. Against the weight of these testimonies, however, Todd takes his personal experience to trump everything else. Again, that's one way to live—affirm and follow your every desire. It's not a healthy or stable way to live, and it's certainly not the way of Christ.

In light of this story, which is repeated daily a thousand times over in our own lives and in the lives of those we love, New Testament scholar Richard Hays's caution is salient: "There is always the danger that, in our complex hermeneutical deliberations about New Testament ethics, we might construct an elaborate system of rationalizations that simply justify the way we already live our lives."[8] Indeed, don't we tend to have problems with any command that challenges our status quo? But isn't that also the point of Scripture—to awaken us out of our slumber, to speak truth to an open heart, to change us?

As disciples of Christ who seek to be faithful to our calling, we find God's moral will and the way of Christ primarily in Scripture. In a day when Christians can give their opinions about hot topics for hours without any reference to Scripture, we should train ourselves to go to Scripture first and, once there, to look for both the commands and the principles behind the rules and narratives—in every genre and in every book. We must read Scripture through the lens of tradition, complemented by reason and natural law.

How can we do it? It could seem like a tall order, and it assumes interpretation by an educated person who is fully conversant with Scripture and the Christian tradition, not to mention skilled in the use of reason and application of natural knowledge. No individual knows everything. This is one reason why God has put us in community with others.

Above all, start with first things first. Read your Bible, and pray for God's Spirit to lead you to truth. Biblical illiteracy is both a cause and a symptom of the decline of Christianity in the West. May it not be so in our homes and churches. We should not pretend to know and apply the rules, principles, and worldview of Scripture if it's all only hearsay to us. For too many Christians, the Bible is something to invoke when it is convenient, to talk about or open on our phones once a week, but not to read and engage on a deep level. Only if we know the content of Scripture can we more faithfully follow its guidance. As readers of Scripture who intend to submit to its instruction, who engage its words to point us to the true Word, may God give us grace to know, love, and do the good.

DISCUSSION QUESTIONS

1. Discuss biblical passages and principles that are relevant to various ethical issues that are not specifically mentioned in Scripture, for example:
   a. gun control
   b. using marijuana
   c. euthanasia (physician-assisted suicide)
   d. sex with a fiancé
   e. speeding
   f. others?
2. Can you think of any biblical characters whose moral actions are ambiguous? How can you know whether they serve as a good example to be followed or a bad example to be avoided?

ISSUES

PART 2

CHAPTER 6

Sexual Ethics

It is to be anticipated that perhaps not everyone will easily accept this particular teaching. There is too much clamorous outcry against the voice of the Church, and this is intensified by modern means of communication. But it comes as no surprise to the Church that she, no less than her divine Founder, is destined to be a "sign of contradiction" (Lk. 2:34). She does not, because of this, evade the duty imposed on her of proclaiming humbly but firmly the entire moral law, both natural and evangelical.

Since the Church did not make either of these laws, she cannot be their arbiter—only their guardian and interpreter. It could never be right for her to declare lawful what is in fact unlawful, since that, by its very nature, is always opposed to the true good of man.

In preserving intact the whole moral law of marriage, the Church is convinced that she is contributing to the creation of a truly human civilization.

—Pope Paul VI[1]

Contrary to what we might at first surmise, the emphasis of the human person as an embodied and therefore a sexual being is more pronounced in the Christian understanding than in the basically secular anthropology widespread in Western culture today. The biblical doctrines of creation and resurrection imply that our sexuality is basic to our sense of self and foundational to our understanding of who we are as God's creatures.

—Stanley J. Grenz[2]

American feminist and social critic Camille Paglia asserts rightly that sexuality is "a paradigmatic theme and indeed obsession of modern culture."[3] Paglia's insight is not new. C. S. Lewis implied the same thing in the 1940s when he said:

> You can get a large audience together for a strip-tease act—that is, to watch a girl undress on the stage. Now suppose you came to a country where you could fill a theatre by simply bringing a covered plate on to the stage and then slowly lifting the cover so as to let every one see, just before the lights went out, that it contained a mutton chop or a bit of bacon, would you not think that in that country something had gone wrong with the appetite for food?[4]

It is almost charming that Lewis felt obliged to define striptease for his audience. If he thought Western culture was obsessed with sex in the 1940s, one wonders what he would think about the inundation of sexuality in the twenty-first century.

Sexual ethics has always been an important part of Christian moral teaching. But the church has not always done a good job of explaining sexual ethics. As musician Butch Hancock quipped, "Life in Lubbock, Texas, taught me . . . that sex is the most awful, filthy thing on earth and you should save it for someone you love."[5] Avoidance or canned responses can no longer suffice to maintain an ethic that is now so thoroughly countercultural. More than just another topic, the present culture has brought the obsession problem to the church's doorstep, and sexuality and the various matters that it touches have now become central subjects of debate. Different opinions on sexual ethics not only distinguish Christians from non-Christians, but they are increasingly dividing Christians from one another. It is therefore imperative that Christians come to a more unified understanding of God's design for human sexuality. What does virtue look like with regard to sexuality? What does love require?

SCRIPTURE

Scripture takes sexual ethics very seriously. The opening pages of Genesis (1:27–28 and 2:20–25) imply many things about the context of sex, the basics of what and who. There is a natural complementarity of the male and female body that reflects what is sometimes called the "nuptial meaning" of the body. Because these texts assume only one male and one female involved in sexual union, the Creator's intent is for a monogamous relationship. For Christians, the expectation is for celibacy (sexual abstinence) outside of marriage and sexual faithfulness in marriage.

In addition to these basic assumptions about the context of sex, we might ask about the purposes of sex. Why is there sex? Some people automatically respond that sex is "for pleasure." Our society, obsessed as it is with sex, communicates this message. But pleasure alone is not the natural purpose of sex. The purpose is obvious. It is called the reproductive system.[6] If I ask about the purpose of the respiratory system or the lungs, what would you say? It is to breathe, to oxygenate the blood. If I ask about the purpose of the excretory system, what would you say? It is to get rid of the body's waste. Now, it can be pleasurable to stand up and take a deep breath, especially after some brisk exercise. But we wouldn't say that's the purpose of the lungs—for our pleasure. After a long car ride and a lot of soda, it can feel really good to find a bathroom, but we wouldn't say that the purpose of the excretory system is pleasure. Sexual pleasure happens, of course, but biologically speaking, it serves procreation, ensuring that the species will reproduce and therefore survive. So why do some people assume that the primary purpose of sex is pleasure?

When we ask what something is for, remember that we are asking about its *telos* (goal or end). Sex has a natural function and design and purpose: to reproduce. In fact, the reproductive system is the only system in the body that requires two to function toward its proper end or goal—and not just any two, but one male and one female. If we will listen, there is instruction in this natural order.

So what do these same passages in Genesis (1:27–28; 2:20–25) teach about the purposes of sex? We can boil them down to three.

1. *Procreation.* Sexual relations are, at the most fundamental level, for reproduction. The command to the first couple is to "be fruitful and multiply" (Gen 1:27–28). When Noah took male-female pairs of animals into the ark to stock the postdiluvian world, the reason for this specific demand was so obvious that it did not need to be spelled out. This natural, biological purpose reflects what has been called the "generative meaning" of the body. Theologically, we are co-creators, participating in and reflecting the image of God.
2. *Union.* Sexual relations seal a one-flesh bond (Gen 2:23–24). This bond is first literal and physical. The body that was split into two (Gen 2:21–22) comes together again in sexual union. In addition, this physical union has social implications. It involves a leaving of one home (father and mother) and a cleaving to the new sexual partner—that is, the forming of a new social unit. Finally, this union has a deep spiritual or theological meaning. Most ancient cultures, in fact, saw sex and procreation as having a religious meaning. Marital sex is a reflection of and participation in the creative power of the natural order, which, of course, is also the divine order. For Christians, the marriage bond is sacramental, a sign of mystical union. It is a reflection of the covenantal bond between God and his people (Eph 5:32).
3. *Intimacy and enjoyment.* Sexual relationship implies sexual companionship and pleasure (Gen 2:18, 25). The spouse, as a suitable helper in many ways, is also a sexual partner. The Song of Songs, even when understood as a description of God's relationship with his people, trades in the language of erotic pleasure and thus validates it on the human level. This third purpose, broadly encompassing the physical and emotional pleasure of a proper sexual relationship, ought to be a natural result or consequence of (1) and (2) above.

These three purposes all go together. They are confirmed throughout Scripture. And no one purpose is contradictory to or exclusive of another.

When Jesus taught about sexuality, he either upheld the norms proposed in the Old Testament or, if he modified them, he modified them in a stricter direction. For instance, Jesus channels the Decalogue in assuming the impermissibility of adultery. But he also forbids divorce, which was rightly received by his disciples to be a very difficult teaching (Matt 19:3–12). He also condemns looking at a woman with lust or strong desire (Matt 5:27–30). These teachings are not easy to hear.

Following Jesus' lead, the importance of sexual ethics is also plain in Paul's letters. In 1 Thessalonians, probably the earliest letter we have from his pen, Paul spends the first three chapters discussing his relationship with the Thessalonian church and the news that he has received from Timothy about their faith. After these long personal remarks, he urges the Thessalonians to live in a way that is pleasing to God and reminds them of the ethical instructions he gave them in person (1 Thess 4:1–2). These instructions are, first of all, about sexual morality (1 Thess 4:3–8). In other words, the first specific moral exhortation in Paul's earliest extant letter has to do with sexual ethics; the placement and its actual content indicate that it was not an afterthought or a merely tangential topic for Paul. In Ephesians 5:3, he said that sexual immorality (*porneia*) should not even be named among believers. It is serious business.

Paul's most extensive discussion of sexual ethics appears in 1 Corinthians 5–7 as he addresses various problems in the church in Corinth. Particularly in 1 Corinthians 6:12–20, he forbids "fornication." Paul's word is *porneia*, which literally refers to prostitution, but he seems to use this word more broadly for any sinful sex act—specifically, outside of the husband-and-wife union—which is why it is usually translated as sexual immorality. This literal act of infidelity is reminiscent of and linked to the spiritual prostitution that Israel committed against the Lord. In this passage, Paul gives a clear and authoritative command: "Flee fornication" (1 Cor 6:18).

The idea of flight is important in its own right. Avoid even the tempting situations.

But it is important to observe that Paul provides several positive reasons for the prohibition. First, since God raised Christ's body, he will raise ours too. Bodies, therefore, are important, and what you do with the body matters. Second, our bodies are members of Christ's body, so don't unite Christ with a prostitute. Paul's argument is based on Genesis 2:24 and the physically and mystically unitive function of sexual intercourse. Third, your individual, physical body is the temple of the Holy Spirit. As such, it is God's house, a holy vessel. Fourth, Paul says, you belong to another master or lord, so glorify your Lord with your body. Rather than being slaves to sin, we are called to be slaves to the Lord. In this way, through proper sexuality, God is glorified.

Paul's handling of sexuality is instructive in many ways. Besides the actual arguments he makes, the fact that he makes theological arguments is important. As he often does in 1 Corinthians, Paul takes a (sinful) practice of the Corinthian Christians and shows the theological implications of it. Sexual immorality has deep meaning. It is spiritual prostitution, fornication, adultery. Most people want reasons why. Why not pre- or extramarital sex? Notice the arguments to which he does not appeal. Paul does not warn against sexually transmitted infections or unwanted pregnancy. He does not even raise the issue of infidelity to one's spouse, nor does he declare, "God says so," though all these things were surely important to him. His reasons tend to be a little more profound than the fear-driven reasons modern Christians sometimes emphasize. Paul presents a sexual ethic that envisions and enables true flourishing by preserving the integrity and dignity of each person who is created, body and soul, to be a holy temple for God's glory.

Finally, notice also the overturning of anything akin to individual freedom and "rights." What we do with our bodies says something; it speaks volumes. "But," we insist these days, "it's my body." Is it? Not according to Paul. The modern claim to unlimited, autonomous, personal rights over ourselves and our bodies sounds more like the misguided Corinthians than like Paul.

MODERN CHALLENGES TO SEXUAL ETHICS

Over the last century, the priorities and purposes of sexual relations have changed drastically. American secular culture has worked hard to erode the procreative and unitive purposes—purposes (1) and (2) above—in sexual relations. The first reason, procreation, has been eliminated altogether, virtually by all. The second reason, unity, has been eliminated by all except Christians. Intimacy and enjoyment have become the primary or sole reason for sex. "Intimacy" is the highest motive for sexual relations that secular culture will acknowledge. Even conservative Christian marriage now simply means a man and woman who love each other and want to be together forever. Ever since bodily pleasure and companionship, and not procreation, became the sole purpose of sexual relations, the consequences have been predictable. Marriage has come to mean (slightly more committed) coupling for sexual pleasure.

Focus for a moment on the demise of the procreative function. The eroding of the procreative function of sexual relations is a relatively recent phenomenon in society at large and among Christians in particular.[7] Historically, procreation and marriage have always been inseparable because sex and babies have usually gone together. This began to disintegrate a bit in the late Roman Empire, when abortions and exposing of children became more common, as did homosexual practice. Until the twentieth century, however, Christians maintained this connection between sexual relations and offspring. It was not just the Roman Catholic view, but the Christian view. As late as 1917, the Massachusetts Supreme Judicial Court upheld its prohibition of the use and even possession of contraceptives. Among other things, they wrote: "[The law's] plain purpose is to protect purity, to preserve chastity, to encourage continence and self-restraint, to defend the sanctity of the home, and thus to engender in the State and nation a virile and virtuous race of men and women."[8]

But things quickly changed. The first Christian group ever to approve of contraception was the Church of England in 1930, and other Protestant churches have followed suit. Only the Roman

Catholic Church has held fast to its prohibition of contraception,[9] though many Western Roman Catholics don't submit.

To aid in contraception, which most Protestant churches favored by the mid-twentieth century, the oral contraception, or birth control pill, was approved by the Food and Drug Administration (FDA) in 1960. Only in 1965 did the Supreme Court rule (*Griswold v. Connecticut*) that contraception could be legal for married couples. And in 1972, the Court (*Eisenstadt v. Baird*) legalized birth control for unmarried couples. Sexual relations now might have nothing to do with procreation. Due to its quick and widespread popularity, "the pill" effectively separated sexual intercourse from procreation. What had always been the natural outcome of sexual relations—namely, children—helped to ensure that sexual intercourse was appropriate for two people ready to start a family, and it helped to bind those partners together. But now pregnancy, which used to burden the woman (if not the man), was no longer a factor. With the widespread use of hormonal contraception, sex and babies have been effectively separated. To this fact one may add the observation that, with sperm donations and surrogacy, reproduction can now be outsourced.

Here is the challenge: Widespread contraception sealed, in the modern mind, the separation of sexual activity from the intent of procreation. Sex without babies and without marriage became cheap.[10] This idea of "free love" initiated the "sexual revolution" of the 1960s and '70s, the consequences of which we are still reaping today. From that point, sexual relations (within or without marriage) had nothing to do with procreation and everything to do with individual pleasure. These new assumptions are now part of the cultural air we breathe.

"Be fruitful and multiply" is the creation and marital mandate. To be sure, the mandate does not specify how many children to have. And the health of the woman should be taken into consideration. If a woman has had multiple C-sections, for example, pregnancies should be limited. But it is a far different thing now when a couple—even a Christian couple—marries and says, "Should we have children?"

PREMARITAL SEX

The historic Christian prohibition against premarital sexual relations has been universally jettisoned by secular society and dismissed even by many Christians. Abstinence before marriage is positively discouraged and openly mocked in popular culture. "You're a virgin?!" gasp the characters on countless TV shows and movies. This typical scenario reflects one of the most pervasive lies of modern culture, namely, that one must be sexually active to have a fulfilled life. It isn't true. Nevertheless, permissive sexual attitudes are introduced and reinforced in US public schools, where comprehensive sex education curricula rarely emphasize the option of abstinence. Instead, such programs begin with the assumption that teens cannot control their own sexual urges and that they will have sex. Recent evidence demonstrates that comprehensive sex education fails to lower rates of sexual activity, risky sexual behavior, sexually transmitted infections, and unwanted pregnancy. In many cases, comprehensive sex ed has been shown to increase these harmful effects.[11]

The Centers for Disease Control and Prevention (CDC) reports that about 42 percent of American teens age fifteen to nineteen have had sexual intercourse. That percentage has steadily declined from about 56 percent in 1988.[12] This means that the majority of teens actually do not have sexual intercourse, and—contrary to popular opinion—it's possible for those who are committed to abstinence to control themselves. The common wisdom about teens and sex—that the majority are sexually active and sex ed will help them be safer—is not necessarily true. It is also not true that sexual promiscuity is harmless emotionally. Those with more lifetime sexual partners tend to be less connected in relationships, less happy, and more depressed.[13]

Besides the clear biblical teaching, then, there are other reasons why Christians should hold fast to what has been deemed by many to be an outmoded morality. Even non-Christians should keep such considerations in mind regarding sex outside of covenant. When done apart from the mutual desire to be united in marriage, sex makes a mockery of lifelong commitment. Sex without commitment results in frustration and dissatisfaction. Sex is the ultimate gift of oneself, physically and emotionally and spiritually. If that gift is treated casually and is distributed promiscuously, like a handshake, then there is nothing left to give to a true lover and covenant partner. It actually ends in greater loneliness and feelings of isolation.

Another way to approach the matter is to ask, "Why are only married people qualified for sex?" Sex, in its proper context, is meant to signify and seal a personal life-union, and permanent marriage helps guarantee stability for the children who naturally result from that union.

CONCLUSION

What does love require? In this case, as in others, there are many correct and many incorrect ways to answer that question. First of all, in the circumstance of sex outside of nuptial commitment, the concept of love is often abused. Guys sometimes want sex so badly that they will pretend or even think they love a girl so that they can have sexual relations. Girls sometimes want love so badly that they will allow themselves to have sexual relations, thinking this compromise will persuade the guy to love her and to be committed to her. The guy uses the girl for sex, and the girl uses sex for (the goal of) love. Both instances are a clear misuse of sex and what the Bible means by "love."

The question for the not-yet-married to ask each other is not, "How *much* do you love me?" but "How *long* will you love me?" If the answer is "forever," then real love should lead the couple to wait until they can declare that lifelong commitment before God and publicly among their friends, family, and church.

Finally, love requires that churches do a better job of including single people and supporting those who desire to live a chaste life. The church should be a community that cultivates true and safe friendships and encourages sexual purity. It should also be a community of grace and forgiveness for those who have failed to keep their commitments, a people who practice true repentance and dependence on the Holy Spirit.

DISCUSSION QUESTIONS

1. When you were growing up, were you warned against premarital sex? What reasons were offered in favor of sexual purity?
2. What reasons would you give to encourage people to preserve sexual relations for marriage?
3. The topic of sex is frequently avoided in churches. What do you think is the most important but neglected thing that churches should be teaching about sexuality?
4. What are the consequences of making pleasure the sole or primary motivation for sexual relations?
5. How can churches do a better job of welcoming and incorporating single people?

CHAPTER 7

Homosexual Practice

Therefore God handed them over in the lusts of their hearts to impurity for dishonoring their bodies in them; who exchanged the truth of God for the lie and worshiped and served the creature rather than the creator, who is blessed forever, amen. Because of this God handed them over to passions of dishonor, for their females exchanged the natural function for the use against nature, and likewise the males, having left the natural function of the female, burned up in their desire for one another, males with males committing the shamefulness and receiving in themselves the reward of their error.
—Romans 1:24–27

Nowhere else is truth regarded with such horror as in the domain of our Church administration; nowhere else is there greater servility than in our spiritual hierarchy; nowhere is the "salutary falsehood" practiced on a larger scale than in the place where all falsehood should be held in detestation. Nowhere else are there admitted on the grounds of policy so many compromises which lower the dignity of the Church and rob her of her authority. The root cause of it all is the lack of a sufficient faith in the power of truth. And the most serious part of it is that, though we are aware of all these evils in our Church, we have come to terms with them and are content to live at peace. But such a shameful peace, such dishonorable compromise, can never promote the true peace of the Church; in the cause of truth it signifies defeat, if not betrayal.
—Ivan Aksakov[1]

One of the most rapid and remarkable changes related to sexual ethics has to do with societal approval of homosexual practice.[2] The decades-long rise in the social acceptability of sexual practice outside of heterosexual marriage rose to new heights with the US Supreme Court's *Obergefell v. Hodges* decision of 2015, legalizing same-sex marriage at the federal level.

We are interested here not in the legal question but in the moral question—again, distinct questions that too many people thoughtlessly conflate. Ultimately, we want to ask how best to show love to people with same-sex attraction. But logically prior to asking the important and sometimes complex pastoral question about how the church can most effectively show the love of Christ to homosexuals, we must be willing first to examine the moral status of the practice in question. It is this task that Christians often bypass on the way to unconditionally embracing not only moral agents but also all their actions. This chapter is dedicated to understanding the morality of homosexual practice, which is especially important given that Christians now fall on both sides of the debate. We will also consider the issue of transgender identity.

Sexual activity begins with desires, but our main question here concerns acting on same-sex attraction. As with other doctrinal and ethical questions, we should consult Scripture first and then run the question through the other two sources or criteria of Christian authority. In doing so, we may also discover the rationale for the increasing acceptance among Christians of homosexual practice. Have some Christians come to support homosexuality because new arguments from Scripture, tradition, and reason are so overwhelmingly convincing? Let us consider the question of homosexual practice in light of these criteria.[3] As is the case throughout the book, we also want to keep in mind what love requires and forbids.

SCRIPTURE AND TRADITION

The relevant biblical texts that reject homosexual practice are well known, and space prohibits an examination of each. In short,

Scripture deals with the question at the level of rules, principles and paradigms, and worldview, and its testimony is unanimously against homosexual practice.[4] The clearest statements are found in Leviticus 18:22; Romans 1:24–27; 1 Corinthians 6:9–11; and 1 Timothy 1:9–10. The story of Sodom and Gomorrah in Genesis 19, the most famous narrative about (attempted) homosexual practice, is an instance of attempted rape and therefore not directly relevant to consensual homosexual activity. But what the whole story implies about homosexuality is not entirely irrelevant.[5] The narrative itself and other biblical comments about the ancient city would lead us to believe that more than one thing was disordered with the morals in Sodom. Furthermore, the fact that most of the documents collected in Scripture do not expressly mention homosexuality at all does not imply that the authors were indifferent about the practice or that they regarded the question as insignificant. As we noted in chapter 5, besides indifference, there may be other reasons for silence about particular issues in these ad hoc, ancient documents.[6]

To a Christian who takes Scripture seriously, even if the message is difficult, these texts should be decisive. Despite the clarity and unanimity of the biblical witness, some Christians attempt to find wiggle room in Scripture that would favor consensual homosexual practice. Such attempts, however, are finally unconvincing to responsible interpreters, including to many who approve of homosexuality. For instance, Dan O. Via, who writes against Robert Gagnon in favor of homosexuality, admits, "Professor Gagnon and I are in substantial agreement that the biblical texts that deal specifically with homosexual practice condemn it unconditionally."[7] Similarly, Luke Timothy Johnson writes, "The task demands intellectual honesty. I have little patience with efforts to make Scripture say something other than what it says, through appeals to linguistic or cultural subtleties. The exegetical situation is straightforward: we know what the text says."[8] For writers such as Via and Johnson, it is not a question of exegesis but of hermeneutics or application of Scripture or, more bluntly, of an authority higher than Scripture. At any rate, even these proponents of homosexual practice agree: Scripture could not be clearer on its judgment of homosexual practice as impermissible.

The historic Christian tradition is not ambiguous when it comes to the question of homosexual practice. In contrast to the Greek pagan culture that accepted homosexual acts outside of marriage, the Christian moral tradition, from the Apostolic Fathers on, has followed the New Testament in its universal opposition to the practice of homosexuality.[9] This Christian consensus was held until the sexual revolution of the 1960s and '70s.[10] This ethical unanimity is Jewish as well and therefore predates Christianity.[11] We might add, in fact, that all civilizations have recognized the normality of heterosexual marriage and that many pre-Christian pagans argued against homosexual relationships for some of the same reasons that Christians have opposed them.[12] The facts are clear: for nearly two millennia, Christian tradition, echoing Scripture itself, unanimously regarded homosexual relations as morally impermissible.

REASON

Without ever invoking Christian Scripture or tradition, there are many considerations that should give us pause in our society's rush to normalize homosexual practice and enshrine it as marriage.

First of all, recall what nature teaches about the purpose of sexual relations. As noted in the previous chapter, the natural purpose of the reproductive system, of course, is procreation. It is the only bodily system that requires two people (no more, no less) to fulfill its natural function. They are not just any two people, but a male and a female. That is, the sexual act is intended naturally for one male and one female. Furthermore, the irrepressible desire of many homosexual couples to have biological offspring testifies to the natural link between marriage, sex, and procreation that is broken by same-sex relationships. The joining of male and female and the procreative fruit of this union are the gift of nature. This is not an exclusively "religious" point. Related to the natural purpose of procreation is the complementarity of the sexes, important for maintaining a lifelong relationship and for raising children.

Second, especially after the introduction of widespread contraception in the 1960s, our society has decided that procreation is not the primary purpose of sexual relations; instead, orgasmic pleasure is the sole purpose. Many things follow from this cultural assumption, one of which is that any sexual relationship is just as legitimate as any other, consent being the only requirement. Some of those relationships our society has formally approved—especially, homosexual relationships. Other such relationships it has not yet approved, but given enough time, it will.

Again, to amplify this point, if pleasure is the sole concern and purpose of sexual expression, then it doesn't really matter much where a man chooses to insert his genitalia. Anything that feels good is fine. What you do with your genitals is your own business. If the culture, and even the church, emphasizes pleasure to the exclusion of every other purpose of sexuality, then it will be increasingly difficult for the culture or the church to prohibit any expression of sexuality. What about polygamy? Consensual incest? In fact, what reason is commonly given for denying the legitimacy of incest? It is only a cultural taboo, which homosexuality had been fifty years ago. It's "wrong," but no one quite knows why.[13] Think of incest now. If we saturated the media and entertainment with "normal," nice, incestuous folks and talked about how roughly they have been treated, and so on, it wouldn't take long to normalize it. Indeed, why not bestiality? On the sole criterion of consent, why should such practices remain off limits? For decades, the American Civil Liberties Union has defended polygamy.[14] Others fight for pedophilia, arguing, among other things, that an *age* of consent is an arbitrary construct. For now, the only thing preventing incest, pedophilia, and bestiality is a residual feeling of cultural disgust. That won't be too hard to overcome.

The truth is that, if we no longer restrict legitimate sex to heterosexual relations with the end or potential for procreation, then there is no rationale for restricting any sexual expression, no matter how repulsive we may find that practice now. The legal approbation of same-sex marriage has left us with no grounds for opposing any form of consensual intercourse among adults.

The onus is on the supporter of same-sex marriage to demonstrate where the line should be drawn and why. No culture in history before ours has accepted—much less celebrated—homosexual marriage between adult men or adult women. The repercussions of this social experiment could be severe.

A third, broad point that all people should contemplate has to do with physical and emotional health, an important consideration when it comes to the question of what love requires. The negative physical consequences of anal sex, the primary sex act of homosexual males, often go unreported in the media and popular culture. In short, the anus and rectum easily bleed and were not made for intercourse; this is the root of the spread of disease and other physical complications. In addition, practicing homosexuals experience higher rates of partner violence and depression.[15] The promiscuity rates of homosexuals in supposedly committed relationships are radically higher than those in traditional heterosexual marriages.[16] This fact should not surprise, given that the sexual revolution in general, including the push to normalize homosexuality, is intended to counteract traditional notions of sexual restraint.[17]

EXPERIENCE

As noted above, some Christians appeal to experience but fail to acknowledge that experience is, for various reasons, the least authoritative and the most ambiguous of the criteria. At best, in a Christian context, experience is not so much a source for doctrine and morals as a guide to which teachings to emphasize—as Randy Maddox puts it, experience helps us "discern what to *keep* teaching!"[18] Otherwise, lived experience is simply what used to be called anecdotal evidence, which, if it contradicts the evidence from wider or more authoritative sources, is rightly to be dismissed as indecisive and finally irrelevant.

What about the innate and natural attractions of some people to members of the same sex? What if they are born that way and cannot help it? First of all, there is no "gay gene" and no scientific evidence that a homosexual is "born that way." The evidence, in fact, points to the fluidity of sexual attraction and expression, especially during one's adolescence and young adulthood; it is not set or determined.[19] Second, even if we granted that homosexual orientation is to a degree innate, it is also nurtured. There is no doubt that our society encourages homosexuality. It is now a given that part of adolescence (or even adulthood) involves discerning one's own sexual orientation. It is something to figure out and then embrace. But until figured out, it is a matter of question. And the rules for figuring it out are not clearly known.

When adolescents searching for their identity, especially those from less-than-ideal family situations, do not fit in, ours is now a culture that teaches kids to question their sexual orientation. When a boy is rejected by a cruel father or ignored by his older brothers, he will still long for male companionship. Any innocent, asexual attraction to someone of the same sex is now tainted with homosexual connotations. A teenager or young adult who is looking for an identity immediately finds it in the homosexual community. Now they are somebody distinct. Even if they're not liked by a few homophobes, they are accepted and loved by another group of people. They have found an identity, and that identity appears to be sealed. It shouldn't surprise us that a person who has a similar story sees this homosexual attraction as innate. But it is also undeniable that nurture is, in many cases, part of the equation.

We return to an important question posed earlier in this chapter: On what grounds are some Christians now supporting homosexual practice as morally permissible? If one aims to defend the permissibility of homosexual practice within the Christian faith, then Scripture and the Christian tradition, with their unequivocal opposition, are dead ends. No responsible interpreter has ever reached the conclusion that homosexual practice is morally permissible simply by reading Scripture and Christian historical sources. Reason, incorporating biological, medical, and social science, is mostly unhelpful to the advocate. No one was ever convinced, simply by thorough consideration of nature, that homosexuality is a fitting expression of the design and reflection of the natural order built into creation.

In contrast to Christians in the past who have appealed to *sola scriptura* (Scripture alone) as their primary or even sole rule of faith and practice, some contemporary believers make their appeal to *sola experientia* (experience alone) and pit it against Scripture and tradition.[20] Luke Timothy Johnson, who rightly characterizes the witness of Scripture against homosexual practice as "straightforward," goes on to say:

> I think it important to state clearly that we do, in fact, reject the straightforward commands of Scripture, and appeal instead to another authority when we declare that same-sex unions can be holy and good. And what exactly is that authority? We appeal explicitly to the weight of our own experience and the experience thousands of others have witnessed to, which tells us that to claim our own sexual orientation is in fact to accept the way in which God has created us.[21]

If *sola experientia* is to be considered an acceptable path for assessing homosexual practice, then there is no reason the method should not be universalized. And if this mode of ethical reasoning were to become the norm for Christian morality, imagine the possibilities. It would not take much to convince men, who on average are more sexually permissive and promiscuous than women,[22] that their sexual desires are all God-given and that they should, in the words of Johnson, "claim our sexual orientation" and "accept the way in which God has created us." A moment's reflection will reveal how disastrous and unloving it would be to lend credibility to moral reasoning of this sort.

When it comes to sexual ethics, progressive Christianity is clearly downstream from culture. It is no accident that some Christians have begun to question Scripture on homosexual practice just after the culture began to approve and celebrate the practice. To be sure, the influence of culture is good when culture reminds the church of what the Bible clearly teaches—for instance, that there is neither Jew nor Greek, but all are one in

Christ (Gal 3:28). But when the dictates of culture are just as clearly contrary to Scripture, Christian tradition, and reason, then faithful Christians must test the spirits and be aware of and resist the danger, not succumb to it.

TRANSGENDER IDENTITY

This is not the place to tackle every possible sexual practice that has been advocated in any given corner of society. However, because of its recent prominence and its successful attachment to the homosexual lobby (the T in "LGBT"), the issue of transgender identity is worth a brief consideration with the goal of determining what love requires in this case. It is not directly addressed in the points above, for it is not primarily a question of sexual contact with another person or of sexual orientation but of an individual's sexual identity and self-expression. Like abortion and same-sex marriage, the advance of the transgender movement was aided not by voters but by the US Supreme Court, which in 2020 extended the benefits of the Civil Rights Act to transgender people (*Bostock v. Clayton County*).

"Transgender" is an umbrella term that directly includes and indirectly touches on a number of different ideas and phenomena.[23] For our purposes, it may be helpful to make a preliminary distinction between, on the one hand, genuine gender dysphoria and, on the other hand, the cultural promotion of gender fluidity and transgender identity.

Gender dysphoria "refers to the experience of having a psychological and emotional identity as either male or female [that] . . . does not correspond to your biological sex—this perceived incongruity can be the source of deep and ongoing discomfort."[24] All would agree that the experience of gender dysphoria, as described here, could be extremely unsettling, emotionally and physically. Even if one has never experienced such a thing firsthand, one can imagine how disconcerting it must be for those who feel so uncomfortable in their own bodies and strongly desire to be a member of the opposite sex. Although it is virtually impossible for most people to relate to such experiences, it is essential that these experiences be taken seriously and that those who suffer with gender dysphoria be treated with compassion and understanding. It is a disorder and, regardless of its cause(s), love is the proper response.

The feeling of discomfort with one's body and even the desire to change one's sex or gender have now moved beyond a rare diagnosis limited to the pages of psychiatric manuals. It is now the stuff of popular culture. Once homosexuality had become accepted by mainstream society, popular culture ramped up support for its next cause, transgender identity. In 2015, the year that same-sex marriage was legalized by the US Supreme Court, Bruce Jenner called himself Caitlyn and became the new poster child for transgender identity, complete with a reality television show. In the same year, TLC network (formerly known as "The Learning Channel") began a series called *I Am Jazz*, documenting a teenage boy's transition to a girl. A long time coming, 2015 seemed to be the year of the transgender. In popular culture, unsurprisingly, this fad was not accompanied by thoughtful consideration of whether transgender identity is beneficial for those who so identify or what the consequences might be for society. The cultural message was clear: "Don't ask those questions. If you're not already on board with transgender identity, you better get that way."

This move to cultural acceptability was reflected in the fifth edition of the American Psychiatric Association's *Diagnostic and Statistical Manual of Mental Disorders* (*DSM*). Whereas *DSM-IV* referred to "gender identity disorder," *DSM-5* changed the terminology to "gender dysphoria" in an attempt to be "more descriptive" and to focus on "dysphoria as the clinical problem."[25] In other words, "disorder" carries a stigma, for it implies that the gender confusion itself is somehow wrong. The dysphoria, instead, is the mental distress that is an unnecessary symptom of the now normalized transgender experience. Thus, medical officials now work to relieve the distress, not address or treat the disorder.

The cultural embrace of transgender identity emphasizes the idea of gender fluidity, which itself is predicated on a distinction between sex and gender. Sex is biological, binary, and objective.

Gender is a more subjective set of characteristics that we think of as masculine or feminine. Gender fluidity presses the distinction to the point of separation, a breach between sex and gender, such that there is no correspondence. Gender becomes a choice, and there may be dozens of constructed genders from which one may choose. Facebook, for example, seems to have at least fifty-eight gender options.[26] The point pressed by transgender activists is that gender is not tied to biological sex. Try as they may, however, gender cannot so easily be separated from biological sex. That is, biological men who identify with the female gender are not usually content to live as men. They dress and behave as women, and often employ medical technologies to modify their bodies to look like women, up to and including sex reassignment surgeries (top and bottom). In other words, these cosmetic attempts to change the biological sex to match the desired gender reinforce the obvious link between gender and biological sex.

Theologically, what should Christians think about transgender identity? The creation accounts reveal that God created humans in his image as either male or female. Immediate observation of the physical body reveals the difference between the sexes, a difference that is confirmed by closer, technical examination of hormones and chromosomes. Sex is not assigned like a name by a presumptuous physician or parent. It is part of the sheer givenness of our existence. The unmistakable biological differences between male and female bear theological significance, especially in the context of marriage and procreation. To blur the differences or seek to eliminate or change one's sex is to reject something God-given, natural, and foundational to one's identity. The integrity of each sex is reflected throughout Scripture, even in matters such as sartorial standards (see, for example, Deut 22:5; 1 Cor 11:3–5).

Transgender identity trades on the separation of one's identity—who a person is, including gender—from the body. This separation of the will and self from the body is reflected in many aspects of secular culture. The Christian story of incarnation is very different, proclaiming that God the Son took on human nature, including the flesh, that he suffered in the flesh, and was raised and exalted in the flesh. This affirmation of the body is further reflected in the doctrine of the eternal redemption and resurrection of the body.

To acknowledge the binary nature and the integrity of each sex is not to deny the phenomenon of intersex individuals and their struggles with gender identity. It is extremely rare to be born with indeterminate organs, but it does happen. The biological anomaly, however, does not negate the biological norm or provide a justification for anyone and everyone to repudiate or seek to change their sex.

Besides biblical and theological considerations, there are many other reasons to resist the unrestrained promotion of transgender identity. First of all, it is not loving to promote a mental disorder. If a white person wants to identify as a black or Native American person, would we go along with it and even encourage him to change his skin tone?[27] But promoting transgender identity and medical intervention is what culture does, from pop entertainment to academia. It is one thing to love and have compassion for those who truly experience gender identity disorder or dysphoria. It is quite another thing to promote the confusion, to encourage the general population to question and decide their gender identity as casually as people question and decide their hairstyle.

Yet this is what is happening at an early age. Comprehensive sex education in many US public school districts begins relativizing gender distinctions as early as kindergarten. Kids spend time learning the proper definitions of "LGBTQ words."[28] Schools recommend children's books that feature transgender and nonbinary characters.[29] The public school curriculum in Austin, Texas, for instance, introduces third graders to the "Genderbread Person," pressing the "difference between biological sex and gender identity," stating that the latter is in one's brain.[30] The sixth-grade curriculum explicitly advocates gender confusion throughout, recommending that "being a boy, a girl, or in-between is mostly about how someone feels, not their body parts."[31] It is no longer uncommon to hear of parents raising gender neutral children and, in some cases, keeping the child's sex a secret for as long as possible, referring to the baby as a "theyby," all to let the child decide its gender. And the media report it and celebrate it.[32] What these schools, parents, and our society at large are doing is setting up the next generation for confusion and dysphoria, not about peripheral matters, but about matters central to one's identity, matters that should not be hard to figure out.[33]

This cultural agenda is indeed bearing fruit. In the UK, for example, the government's centralized Gender Identity Development Service saw a rapid increase in the number of referrals of minors (ages three to eighteen) experiencing gender dysphoria. Specifically, there were seventy-seven children referred to the national clinic for treatment during the fiscal year 2009–10. That number rose steadily and dramatically each year, so that a decade later, during the year 2018–19, there were 2,590 referrals. In fact, during the years 2014–15 to 2015–16, when media coverage of transgender identity seemed to increase so much, the number of referrals more than doubled (from 678 to 1,361).[34] The most significant increase was seen among adolescents.

These alarming numbers reflect what is commonly called Rapid Onset Gender Dysphoria, when a child, out of the blue, questions her gender identity or decides to identify as transgender.[35] Why are so many adolescents seeking treatment for gender dysphoria? One factor could be that, now that the stigma is lifting, more children feel safe to express their dysphoria. A more significant factor, however, is a pop culture that positively advocates doubt about gender identity. It is a YouTube phenomenon, a social contagion. The formula is not difficult: Take individuals in the midst of their adolescence, tell them that their personal and social problems are due to their sexual insecurity or any allegedly cross-gender traits, and then amplify their doubts, while the culture simultaneously revels in all things transgender. The results are predictable.

What, in fact, is the difference between normalizing gender identity disorder and other disorders in which a person does not feel at home in his body? Encouraging a person in his gender dysphoria—who thinks he is a woman trapped in a man's body—by calling him a woman and recommending surgery is like encouraging an anorexic girl in her dieting. Both of these disorders bear many similarities to body integrity identity disorder (BIID), or body dysmorphic disorder, in which an able-bodied person identifies as disabled and thus wants to amputate a perfectly healthy limb because he feels it should not be a part of his body. Interestingly, *DSM-5* mentions this disorder at the entries for both gender dysphoria and anorexia nervosa.[36] In both cases, BIID is noted as a "differential diagnosis," which is to say, the symptoms are so similar that a physician must be careful not to confuse the conditions when diagnosing someone. Nevertheless, the similarities speak for themselves and seem qualitative. What's more, research has found that males are affected with BIID more than females, and especially homosexuals and "man-to-woman transsexuals" are affected with BIID.[37] There appears to be a link.

It is difficult to tell a man suffering from BIID that he cannot have his arm surgically removed while a man suffering from gender dysphoria can have his penis removed by a physician. And those who suffer from BIID have noticed the same inconsistencies. For someone suffering from BIID, the desired move from able-bodied to disabled is analogous to that from male to female.[38] As Sabine Müller reports, "BIID support groups use the neologism *transabled* in analogy of the successful term *transgender* and explain the desire for amputation in analogy to the desire of transsexuals for surgical sex reassignment."[39] Why not change the terminology from body integrity identity *disorder* to *dysphoria* and just allow them their elective surgery to remove or change whatever they wish? Would disabling oneself then become a matter of social justice?

We don't promote the desires of those suffering with BIID for the same reason we don't encourage individuals to progress in various mental disorders: it is unhelpful. As the name suggests, confusion about one's gender almost always causes dysphoria, profound distress. Those who suffer from gender dysphoria struggle with depression, anxiety, and suicide. One might ask, though, whether the depression, anxiety, and suicidality might be alleviated if they were urged to switch to the desired sex by having sex reassignment surgery and living as the other sex. Despite many researchers' and activists' desires for this to be the case, studies have regularly shown that mental health problems persist at alarming rates after surgery. Compared to the general population, people who undergo sex reassignment surgery are three times more likely to need psychiatric hospitalization, five times more likely to attempt suicide, and nineteen times more likely to die by suicide.[40] After surveying all the relevant studies, Lawrence Mayer and Paul McHugh conclude, "The scientific evidence summarized suggests we take a skeptical view toward the claim that sex-reassignment procedures provide the hoped-for benefits or resolve the underlying issues that contribute to elevated mental health risks among the transgender population."[41] This means that when they decide to go through with suicide, they do it in a very final and effective way. Why? They went to such extreme and irreversible measures to try to feel good and get it right, and it didn't resolve their distress and depression. And now there is nothing else to try. The postoperation regret is not uncommon, but it is not something that the media reports. Nor do they report that between 80 and 95 percent of children who experience gender dysphoria will grow out of it without medical intervention.[42] Medical intervention simply does not help. Parents who unquestioningly encourage their children in their gender dysphoria and allow puberty blockers and surgeries are not helping them.[43] Parents who encourage their children to accept who they are in their own body are the ones showing them love by seeking their actual good.

A social consequence of transgender ideology is what it does to women and to feminism. The damage is evident in women's sports, in which biological females have been beaten, sometimes literally, by biological males who identify as females. Camille Paglia writes,

> Sex and gender have been redefined by ill-informed academic theorists as superficial, fictive phenomena produced by oppressive social forces, disconnected from biology. This hallucination has sowed confusion among young people and seriously damaged feminism. A gender theory without reference to biology is absurd on its face.[44]

And this from someone who goes on to say, "I certainly do not subscribe to a wholesale biological determinism."[45] Things have apparently gone too far even for Paglia, a 1960s–70s gender-bending lesbian.

CONCLUSION

Much of the difference between a secular and a Christian sexual ethic comes down to worldview and theological conviction. There is a divergent anthropology, and the two must be clearly distinguished.[46] Secularism generally sees no connection between body and identity. Christianity, by contrast, says that what we do with our bodies speaks volumes and is connected to who we are.

No one can deny that some Christians have sometimes used very hateful and spiteful rhetoric, and sometimes even violence, toward homosexuals and those who suffer with gender dysphoria. Christians too often are unable to show love beyond the borders of our moral convictions, and, in response, society broadens and dilutes its moral convictions so much so that it must accept everyone and every practice. Advocates of homosexuality have sometimes been impatient and too quick with their own moral denunciations of those who demur. The challenge that Jesus models is being able to love others with whom we truly disagree.

What does that love look like? There is no specific rulebook, but churches and individual Christians must be welcoming and caring to the point that their love for all people cannot be doubted. For those who struggle with their sexual orientation or gender identity, we need to listen to their perspective and struggles and be eager to walk with them along what might be a difficult path of redemption and sanctification. That is something we all need. But we do those we love no service by watering down the call of the gospel to sexual purity. Many Christians, regardless of their sexual orientation or their marital status, struggle heroically against sexual temptation. It does them no good to tell them they can't resist and so they should give up the battle, difficult as that battle may be. We wouldn't say that to an alcoholic, to a drug addict, or to someone who struggles with other kinds of sexual immorality. As long as they want to make progress, we journey with them, guided by the Holy Spirit, the bond of divine love.

Sexuality is in a state of disrepair and chaos. Sex is everywhere, but that does not mean people are flourishing. The church needs the Spirit's help to promote a positive model of human sexuality that reflects the biblical vision. Our children and our society desperately need to see this model being practiced.

DISCUSSION QUESTIONS

1. For those who support homosexuality, where do you think they would draw the line on acceptable sexual activity? On what ground?
2. Why do you think parents so often encourage their children in their gender dysphoria?
3. How can Christians and churches balance showing love without endorsing homosexual practice?

CHAPTER 8

Abortion

You will not murder a child by abortion
nor kill one having been born.
—Didache *2:2*

We must underline the fact that he who destroys germinating life kills a man and thus ventures the monstrous thing of decreeing concerning the life and death of a fellow-man whose life is given by God and therefore, like his own, belongs to Him. . . . The true light of the world shines already in the darkness of the mother's womb. And yet they want to kill him deliberately because certain reasons which have nothing to do with the child himself favour the view that he had better not be born! Is there any emergency which can justify this?
—Karl Barth[1]

In *Nineteen Eighty-Four*, George Orwell depicted a dystopian future in which the state, Big Brother, surveils and knows everything about its citizens. Big Brother tolerates no dissent whatsoever. Big Brother controls the narrative. It controls the thought and behavior of individuals. Part of this control is exercised through the gradual changing of the English language into the new, concocted dialect called "Newspeak." Through government-run publications and media, Newspeak eventually catches on. Much of the new dialect involves a reduction of vocabulary, especially of thoughtful words that represent abstract concepts. The purpose of changing the language was to "provide a medium of expression for the world-view and mental habits [that are] proper" to good citizens. And since thoughts are often dependent on the language we use to express them, once the language was shaped by the government's values, the ultimate goal was to make it impossible to express or even think anything that diverged from the principles that the government wished to instill and maintain.[2] In other words, even "thoughtcrime" would become a thing of the past.

The change in the language reflected the change of thought that the government imposed. "Anything could be true," as long as the government says so. Some of the government's favorite slogans are, "War is peace. Freedom is slavery. Ignorance is strength." It's hard work to believe these things, at first. As Orwell wrote, "Stupidity was as necessary as intelligence, and as difficult to attain."[3] But you will come to believe it, over time, provided enough social conditioning or, if necessary, torture. When you hear it constantly, when you are pressured to toe the line for fear of punishment, given enough time, and given the passage of a generation or two, the people will actually come to believe these falsehoods. The true test is when, at the end of the story, the body and mind of the onetime rebel, Winston, have been broken, and he doesn't just say it: he actually believes that 2 + 2 = 5.

I hope you can see the parallels in our own time. It is true that our thoughts influence our language, but it is also true that language influences the way we think. If certain words become obsolete, the result is that the concept the word represents will fade into oblivion. Popular culture indeed imposes certain phrases and virtues and narratives, and to question any of them is to invite destruction at the hands (or thumbs) of the Twitter mob.

So the language of public discourse is carefully chosen. I can think of no better Orwellian example than the language that surrounds the practice of abortion. Not a baby, but a fetus, a clump of cells. Not pro-abortion, but pro-choice. Not anti-abortion, but anti-choice. Not abortion rights, but women's health care, reproductive rights, and reproductive equality. The differences are significant. New York Senate Bill S.240, passed into law on January 9, 2019, eliminates penalties on abortions done after twenty-four weeks of pregnancy (that is, during the third trimester), allowing abortion up to the moment of birth. What was the bill called? The "Reproductive Health Act." But the whole point of the law is against reproduction, and it has very little to do with anyone's health.

Back in chapter 1, I mentioned that if there's just one thing that's wrong, then moral relativism is not correct. To illustrate, I suggested "torturing babies" as an example of something truly horrifying. When I have used that illustration in person in class settings, a few people sometimes recoil and cannot hide looks of disgust, and rightly so. But back up a few months, or weeks, or days, or even minutes *before* birth, and the torture—and worse, termination—is now socially acceptable and, for many, inviolable. It's called abortion.

WHAT IS ABORTION?

First of all, let us understand what we mean by abortion. We are talking about what is called induced abortion, an intentional medical procedure, to be distinguished from unintentional, spontaneous abortion, also known as miscarriage. According to the Centers for Disease Control and Prevention (CDC), there were 825,564 reported legal abortions in the United States in 2008.[4]

In 2013, the number had dropped to 664,435 in the United States.[5] There were 638,169 in 2015, and 619,591 in 2018, the most recent report available.[6] Abortion is on the decline.

Induced abortions are often distinguished into two types: therapeutic and elective. Therapeutic abortions are done for health reasons, broadly defined. The reason could be to save the mother's life or perhaps because of the baby's poor health, that is, defects that have been detected through ultrasound or other tests. But the criteria that determine the health of the mother or the baby are often subjective. It is hardly ever impossible to save either the baby or the mother only. When separation must occur, the baby need not be intentionally terminated, though death will certainly occur before viability. By far, the most common type of induced abortion is elective abortion, which is voluntary abortion for any reason. This most common type of abortion, performed for broadly social reasons, is the main subject of this chapter.

To concentrate in this chapter on elective abortion is in contrast to other treatments of the morality of abortion that begin with and focus on the rarest cases and most extreme dilemmas, often with the goal of introducing ambiguity into the Christian position. For instance, after describing a heartbreaking and extremely rare scenario (from 2009) in which a baby was aborted to save a mother's life, one author asserts that "this case vividly and tragically captures the competing moral claims at the heart of the debate about abortion."[7] In fact, the heart of the abortion debate has very little to do with mothers whose lives are in danger. Moreover, it is not wise to form moral judgments about common occurrences (in this case, elective abortion when the mother's life is in no danger whatsoever, done hundreds of thousands of times annually) on the basis of extreme and rare dilemmas (therapeutic abortion with the mother's life on the line).

In addition to changing the language about abortion—with smokescreens such as "reproductive justice"—pro-choice culture has also successfully kept a veil over the practice itself. Showing the procedure would go a long way toward deterring it. In a day when surgeries of all kinds are broadcast all over cable television (for education or, more likely, curiosity), no one sees abortion, so there is comparatively little popular understanding of what this common medical procedure involves.

So it is important to lift the veil. There are two main methods of abortion. First, a medical or medicinal abortion is induced by drugs. For example, the so-called "morning-after pill," approved by the FDA in 2006, may be used effectively up to three days after conception. More commonly, RU486 is the drug of choice and can be used before ten weeks of pregnancy. RU486 is actually a set of drugs that include a progesterone blocker (which kills the fetus) and a pill that causes uterine contractions (which expels the fetus days later). This treatment is often accompanied by painful cramping and excessive bleeding—these are expectations, not complications.

The second type, a surgical abortion, can be carried out early, but *must* be used after about eleven weeks' gestation. In 2018, 39 percent of abortions were early, medical abortions, effected by drugs. That means that the majority, the remaining 61 percent, were done by surgery. The main types of surgery are vacuum (for under 13 weeks) or Dilation and Extraction/Evacuation (D&E; that is, dilation of the cervix and extraction/evacuation of the baby). Since about 8 percent of all abortions are performed after 13 weeks gestation, these must be done by D&E.[8] Not mentioned in the surgery's name is what happens between the dilation and the extraction, namely, simply tearing the baby apart (four limbs, torso, and head), crushing its head, sucking it out, and then reassembling it to make sure everything came out.

Now that we have briefly described the practice of abortion, let's say we want to determine whether abortion is morally permissible or impermissible. What are some relevant questions that we should ask? There may be many, particularly regarding reasons that motivate someone to choose abortion. But an even more basic question lies at the heart of the issue: Is this fetal life a human person? And if it is, does it not have an inherent right to live, regardless of the circumstances of its conception?

SCRIPTURE

What are the relevant Scriptures or principles derived from Scripture that would help us evaluate abortion? Even though it was a practice known in the ancient world (though vastly more complicated, more risky, less effective, and therefore much less common than today), the Bible does not specifically address abortion. But what passages provide some principles worth considering?

The sixth commandment forbids killing, presumably, of an innocent person. But to cite this straightforward command, because it does not specify who counts as a person, begs the question of the personhood of the unborn baby. That is, the sixth commandment alone might not convince someone who doubts the personhood of the unborn baby. More is needed. Are there Scriptures that discuss the status of the fetus? Not in so many terms. But there are several passages that assume the personhood of the unborn baby. Psalm 139 describes how God "knit me together in my mother's womb" and "saw my unformed body." From the womb, we are "fearfully and wonderfully made" (Ps 139:13–16). The point of the psalm is God's omnipresence, and the divine presence extends to the very beginning of life. In other words, God is present with the child—and knows and relates to the child—in the mother's womb.

When Mary visited Elizabeth, Elizabeth's baby, John, leaped for joy in her womb upon hearing Mary's greeting (Luke 1:41–44). Whatever we make of this testimony, it is not just a bodily function or indigestion on the part of the expectant mother. The fetus is not just a clump of cells with no independent life or worth. The unborn baby is portrayed as an agent, the action is interpreted as joyful, and it brings joy to those present. As is the case throughout Scripture, children are a blessing from God, and that blessing begins not at birth but at conception.

In addition to these testimonies about the unborn child, broader biblical principles speak to one of the primary arguments of those who would defend abortion: a woman has autonomous rights over her body. Whenever the Corinthian Christians appealed to autonomous choice over their bodies, Paul informed them, in no uncertain terms, that their bodies are not their own to do with whatever they please. Their bodies are members of Christ, temples of the Holy Spirit, which belong also to their spouse (1 Cor 5; 6:12–20; 7:3–4). Individual autonomy and personal rights, as defined by modern culture, are not highly valued in Scripture.

On the level of worldview and broader theological convictions, Christians believe that all people are made in God's image. Human persons bear the divine image simply by virtue of being human. This point relates to the question of personhood and, thus, who is entitled to the rights of a person. What constitutes a person made in the image of God? Just as possession of the image of God by an individual does not depend on the individual's acknowledgment of that image, neither does personhood depend on one's actual or even potential ability to function at some minimal level that we arbitrate. Personhood is not contingent on what one can do. Rather, it is about what or who one is essentially—a human person made in God's image.

In the Christian worldview, which is admittedly counter to the world's standards, the heart of the gospel is self-sacrifice. Jesus says, "I voluntarily sacrifice my innocent life for you, and you should do the same." But to the baby, who did nothing to deserve death, abortion says, "You will involuntarily sacrifice your innocent life for me." It is analogous to the impulse that motivated the practice of child sacrifice so roundly condemned in the Bible.

In sum, the biblical evidence declares that Christian love is pro-life. It demands that we be hospitable to the unborn and welcome new life into the world. It seeks to protect the innocent and most vulnerable among us, regardless of the circumstances in which they were conceived.

CHRISTIAN TRADITION

Throughout the history of the church, abortion has been universally forbidden to Christians. Unlike many of their pagan counterparts, early Christians recognized the inherent dignity of the unborn.

What is implicit in Scripture is made explicit from the time of the earliest church fathers. The earliest Christian document outside the New Testament, the *Didache* (ca. AD 70), in the midst of its moral instruction, commands, "You will not murder a child by abortion nor kill one having been born."[9] The connection between abortion and infanticide is obvious and assumed by the writer. The *Didache*'s judgment is typical of early Christianity. Commenting on this text, Kurt Niederwimmer writes, "It is certain that from the beginning, Christians, following Old Testament and Jewish custom, rejected abortion. That there is no specific prohibition of it in the New Testament is accidental."[10] A century after the *Didache*, Tertullian explains:

> But, with us, murder is forbidden once for all. We are not permitted to destroy even the fetus in the womb, as long as blood is still being drawn to form a human being. To prevent the birth of a child is a quicker way to murder. It makes no difference whether one destroys a soul already born or interferes with its coming to birth. It is a human being and one that is to be a man, for the whole fruit is already present in the seed.[11]

Like the *Didache*, Tertullian assumes that there is no moral difference between prenatal and postpartum killing. It is the same human being before and after birth.

Not only did early Christians condemn abortion, but they were also known for rescuing unwanted children, especially those unwanted infants whose parents had abandoned them in the elements to die. This practice of exposing infants "to cold, hunger, and the dogs,"[12] leaving them to die or be captured for sex slavery,[13] was common in the ancient, pagan, Greco-Roman world and was a safer and surer alternative to abortion. As with abortion today, babies could be exposed for any reason whatsoever—from having a disability or deformation, to being the wrong sex, to simply being a drag on the family. Consider, by the way, the psychology of exposing children. The parents did not kill the children directly, but they let the outdoor elements and nature resolve their problem. The parents' attempt to remove themselves from the direct action of killing indicates an attempt to justify themselves. The way that they chose to kill their children is itself a testimony to deep conscience and the irrepressible feeling that something is profoundly wrong. There is a natural law being experienced but also suppressed. It is not unlike the avoidance of truth when abortion clinics hide ultrasound images from the mother.

Despite the unified voice of the tradition, some have questioned the unanimity of Christianity on this issue. Margaret Kamitsuka, for example, takes pains to cast doubt on the historic consensus of Christian thought opposed to abortion.[14] In short, she claims that the many Christian prohibitions against abortion were motivated by misogyny, and she notes that the early medieval penitential literature prescribed lighter penalties for women in difficult situations or if the fetus was considered still unformed (very early pregnancy). Yet, she admits, "The [medieval] penitentials considered abortion at any stage to be a sin."[15] Impugning the motives of early Christians and acknowledging that later Christians were aware of difficult circumstances—these rhetorical moves do not change the fact that at no time in Christian history did the institutional church teach that abortion is permissible. When the soul entered the fetus or when it was considered to be "formed" may have varied from theologian to theologian, but no Christians advocated the termination of an unborn child thought to be a person and to have a soul. As for misogyny, a better case can be made that the early Christian ethic was decidedly *not* misogynistic. In contrast to nearly every pagan ethic, Christians advocated strict chastity and monogamy not just for women but for men too, tying men to their wives and to the children they produced together. Misogynists would be more likely to support male promiscuity and the abortion of its unwanted fruit.[16]

Although not a part of the *Christian* tradition, many pagan philosophical and medical traditions forbade abortion as well. The ancient Hippocratic Oath expressly forbids physicians from prescribing abortifacients to pregnant women or fatal drugs to anyone.[17] This proscription is in keeping with the primary ethical code for physicians: first, do no harm.

This universal Christian consensus, of course, has been undermined only since the last third of the twentieth century. In the wake of *Roe v. Wade* (1973), some Christians now support abortion not only because it is protected by US law but also because they assume it is morally permissible. As in too many other areas, it seems that the popular culture is decisive in many accounts of Christian ethics.

REASON

Biologically speaking, the human individual's DNA is complete after conception. From this point on, nothing new is added that would change the genetic makeup of this human being. This fetus is the very organism that will grow into an adult human. Speaking as objectively and scientifically as possible, the unborn fetus is indubitably and inarguably a *human* being. As Tertullian recognized in the quotation cited above, whatever it is one minute after birth, it is the same thing one minute before birth. If it is a living, innocent human being, then it has as much a right to live and be loved as any other living, innocent human being.

This fact also relates to the frequent assertion that a woman is free to do whatever she wants with her body. There are many problems with this claim. First, from a Christian perspective, as noted earlier, your body actually is not your body, at least not exclusively. But what about from a secular or non-Christian perspective? Can a woman do whatever she wants with her body? We may suppose she *can*, but the law (civil and natural) does not allow just anything. In most areas of the United States, for instance, a woman is not free to shoot up on heroin, throw her body off a skyscraper onto a busy street, prostitute herself, appear naked in public, or arm her body with a gun and go on a shooting spree. Strictly speaking, all these things *can* be done, but it does not mean that they should be done or that they are allowed by legal or moral codes. In most places, the police or any good citizen will use force to stop someone from attempting such things. In other words, there are many things that a woman cannot do—or at least should not do—with her body.

But the main problem with this claim is that, though attached and dependent, the fetus is not exactly her body. It is another body, another person. The baby's individual identity as a discrete body and person is not compromised by virtue of an attached umbilical cord and protective womb. These are natural means for care and nutrition appropriate to the baby's fragile state, not a reason for terminating it.

Before modern science, advocates of abortion often depended on some version of the claim that, at a certain early stage, the fetus simply is not a person yet. Before the mother feels its movement, or before it has a soul, or when it is still "unformed," abortion was thought to be permissible or at least not as bad. With the knowledge provided by modern biology and ultrasound technology, however, it is now impossible—or at least entirely arbitrary—to claim some sort of radical or discontinuous change at any point after conception.

In light of this scientific obstacle, for most advocates of abortion, it now comes down to the simple question of whether the mother wants the baby. This is most evident in the culture's accepted language for miscarriage versus induced abortion. In both cases, it is the termination of an unborn human. But the unintentionally terminated fetus is unhesitatingly called a "baby"; the intentionally terminated fetus is usually denied that name. It is merely a "fetus." What is the difference? One was wanted; the other was not. A person who murders a pregnant woman is guilty of double homicide, while an unwanted, unborn baby is legally torn apart. There is a gap in the logic.

In fact, the only logic here is that the mother's choice determines the status of personhood. If she wants the baby, it is apparently owed all the rights that belong to any innocent human person. If she does not want it, it has none of those rights independently. By a similar logic of denying rights by fiat or wishing individuals or groups out of existence, slavery and a host of other abhorrent practices can be easily justified. But there is no scenario in which my rights or my desires justify taking the life of an innocent human.

CONCLUSION

By any reasonable account, elective abortion is sick, beastly, barbaric stuff, which is why no one wants to view it or even hear it described without the most confused euphemisms. If (and when) Western society falls, a strong case can be made, from a theological perspective, that it is a culture of death getting back in spades what it so richly deserves. A culture that has purposely tricked itself into thinking that it is immoral to hold a whale or elephant in captivity (and maybe it is) while, at the same time, it is perfectly permissible to tear a human baby out of the protective womb, literally limb from limb, from what should be the safest spot on earth, inside its mother—that culture probably should not survive for long.

But we find ourselves in this culture and often feel helpless to stem the pro-abortion tide. As in every case, we must ask, "What does love require?" What does it mean for the church to be meaningfully and concretely pro-life? The following suggestions are not an exhaustive list but a minimal starting point.

Love requires more than opposition to abortion. It requires support for the women who have an unexpected or unwanted pregnancy. They need to be affirmed in their choice for life, and that support should come in many forms: forgiveness in the case of sexual sin, financial and emotional help if needed, and counseling and walking with the woman through the options of keeping the baby or adoption. Not every individual or even every congregation is able or equipped to do this kind of work effectively. But there are many good organizations in cities around the country who are devoted to this kind of Christian service, helping women from pregnancy through adoption or keeping the baby. Pro-life Christians and churches should support these organizations financially and through volunteers.

Adoption is a notoriously difficult and expensive process in the United States. If Christians lobby and vote for the legal limitation or end of abortion, then they should also lobby and petition for ways to streamline the adoption process. If we want these babies to be born, then we need to think about how that new life will be supported. Churches could encourage adoption by putting Christian couples in contact with Christian organizations and adoption agencies. Congregations could also promote adoption by subsidizing the legal fees of church members who adopt. Again, there is no rulebook, so churches should get creative in their effort to show real love.

Finally, showing love means showing mercy and forgiveness to women who have chosen abortion in the past and to the men who forced the issue or remained complicit. Regardless of the reasons and the pressure they might have felt at the time, many women experience lingering guilt over their decision to abort. They need to know that forgiveness is possible, and that, for those who have sought it, removal of guilt is complete and permanent. It may be that these women are in the best position to serve and to lead the church in showing the love of Christ to the unborn, to their mothers, and to the families who raise vulnerable children.

DISCUSSION QUESTIONS

1. The Bible does not specifically address abortion, but what passages provide some principles for thinking about this issue?
2. Besides those mentioned in the chapter, what other reasons would you give to affirm that an unborn baby qualifies as a person?
3. Why do you think a woman would choose or be pressured by someone else to have an abortion?
4. Have you ever witnessed or seen a recording of an abortion (through ultrasound)? Did it change or reinforce what you thought about abortion?

CHAPTER 9

Wealth and Consumerism

Give me neither poverty nor riches; feed me the bread necessary for me. Or I will be full and deny you and say, "Who is the Lord?" or I will be poor and steal and profane the name of my God.
—Proverbs 30:8–9

The rich man has much wealth, but he is poor in the things for the Lord, being distracted by his wealth, and he has very little confession and intercessory prayer for the Lord, and what he has is small and weak, and they do not have power above. Therefore when the rich man approaches the poor and supplies him his necessities, he believes that what he works will find the reward with God, because the poor is rich in intercession and in confession, and his intercession has great power with God.
—Shepherd of Hermas ***51:5***[1]

In August of 2008, Robert Powell of Orange Park, Florida, won the lottery of $12 million and change. It was a dream come true. He chose the lump sum, which left him with over $6 million. What would he do with the windfall? He decided to tithe it and donate $600,000 to his church, Orange Park First Baptist. Remarkably, the church refused the donation.[2]

Now, I don't want to get into the fact that Powell was offended by the church's refusal and that he was apparently the one who took his story to the media. I'm interested instead in the *church's* story. Was this the right thing for the church to do—to refuse the donation? Many would think the church's response to be foolish. First of all, shouldn't the man be commended for his generous intent to donate, to do the right thing by tithing? More important, consider all the good that the church could have done with $600,000. Doesn't this church believe in benevolence to the poor and support for missions? How could they coldly reject this generous gift?

The answer to these questions must begin by observing that many Christians have regarded gambling to be morally impermissible. On what biblical principles would one consider gambling to be wrong? Gambling is a concrete form of greed that encourages idleness, wanting something for nothing. It undermines the value of work. With greed as its motivation, gambling is an affront to the biblical command to be content with what we have. It is, in most cases, wasteful of God-given, hard-earned resources, and thus not good stewardship. For example, the chances of winning the jackpot in a "6 from 49" (choose 6 numbers from 1 to 49) lottery are about 1 in 14 million. That means, if you bought a lottery ticket every week for your whole life, odds are that you would win the lottery once—if you live to be 269,000 years old. Most lotteries have even slimmer odds. For the Mega Millions interstate lottery, the chances of winning the jackpot are not 1 in 14 million, but 1 in 258 million. Consider also that it is the people in the lowest socioeconomic groups who purchase the majority of lottery tickets.

The education system or the church that accepts lottery winnings is profiting on the backs of the poor. Indeed, Christians have many reasons to oppose gambling.

It may be worth considering that not all gambling is equal. Arguably, there is a difference between high-stakes gambling or lottery playing versus a friendly game of poker or a fantasy football pool whose winnings are meant to go to charity. For instance, I recently came out on the wrong end of an over/under and had to buy my brother a Dr Pepper milkshake. This is something I would have gladly done anyway. It was all in good fun, and I bought myself one too. One test of whether one's gambling is a true vice may be if one is in fact happy to lose the money. In other words, rather than playing for other people's money, would you have simply given the money to the winner if he needed it? Would the many lottery losers be happy handing their money directly to the lottery winner? Probably not, and not continuously, week after week.

If a church is in principle opposed to gambling and to the lottery specifically—as the Orange Park First Baptist Church seems to be[3]—then accepting "tainted" money would undermine the message of the church. If, for example, there is a gambling addict in the church who has been taught by the church that compulsive gambling is sinful and that he can overcome it, what kind of message would it send for the church to accept money won by someone else's gambling? All the addict needs is a hint of rationalization—"I'll give my winnings to the church"—to sink back into the addictive practice.

It is true that there may be no such thing as untainted money. The money carried in each wallet and purse may have been literally involved in theft or dishonesty or part of some sinful transaction. Some of this cannot be helped. Nor should a congregation's leaders feel obliged to investigate the source and to examine the virtue of every donation. But that is different from the church knowingly and publicly receiving a tithe from a drug dealer's profit or from a stripper's tips. It doesn't mean their heart is not in the right place. Better to donate to the church than to invest in more drugs.

From the church's perspective, however, to accept such a donation sends a message that runs counter to the gospel. At the end of the day, the money was gained from a practice that the church deems immoral. The integrity of the church's message outweighs any benefit that might come from such money.

We return to the reason often cited against the Orange Park Church's decision: "Just think of the good that could be accomplished with this money!" I'm sure that the church and its pastor indeed thought of many such things. If Orange Park Church is like *every* other church I have ever known, then they were praying for more resources, more money. They wanted—needed—more funds to accomplish more good in the name of Christ. Imagine the discussions in the committee meeting, the noble wish lists alongside the not-quite-so-noble desiderata: the missionaries we've wanted to support, the pastor's raise, the benevolence ministry, the new gym we've prayed for, more comfortable chairs, a better sound system. I don't know of a minister who doesn't hope for a generous church. And then this gift fell into their lap. It had to be tempting to quietly accept it. Whatever their reason for refusing this donation, it could not have been an easy decision. Regardless of what one thinks of their decision, any honest person must applaud their integrity in the face of what surely was a powerful temptation. Indeed, it has to be one of the most countercultural things that I've ever heard of a church doing.

This account of the refused donation raises the question of money, the place of wealth in the Christian life, and what love requires with regard to money. The topic of money has an ambiguity that does not apply to the topics of the three previous chapters. With those three questions, though gray areas can be imagined, the line on what is morally impermissible is fairly clear. Sexual intercourse outside of marriage is wrong. Homosexual practice is sinful. Elective abortion is wrong. What's more, with regard to those other topics, a person can survive and even thrive without participating in them. One can go through life without having or performing an abortion and without engaging in sexual immorality. But no one can function in modern society without money. It directly affects everyone in ways the previous topics don't. Christian ethics does not forbid money. If everyone must have money to live, then where is the line? At what point does wealth become sinful? Maybe one doesn't play the lotto, but what about the person who works more hours for more money to spend it on himself or hoard it?

Previous chapters followed the method of consulting Scripture, tradition, and reason in their proper order and as fairly distinct sources of moral authority. In considering wealth here and other ethical issues in the following chapters, these sources, though still distinct, will be dispersed throughout each chapter.

THE PROBLEM OF MONEY

When it comes to money, we American Christians tend to think more like Americans than like Christians. In this case, we are inclined to think that money covers a multitude of sins and that problems can be solved and long-term goals achieved simply by throwing money their way.

I'm oversimplifying a bit, but contrast this American tendency with the attitude of the newly converted disciples in Ephesus, as recorded in Acts 19. After they turned to Christ, the new Christians took their scrolls of sorcery, which represented every vile thing in their lives prior to Christ, and they burned them. And the value of the scrolls was fifty thousand drachmas, about fifty thousand days' wages (Acts 19:19). At minimum wage, that's about $3 million today. Think of what could have been done with $3 million. Think of the fancy new worship center that the Ephesian church could have purchased. Think of how many poor people they could have helped. In fact, Paul was raising money from the gentile churches for the impoverished Jewish churches in Judea. According to his letters, this was one of his main ministry goals. "Yes," they could have reasoned, "Paul can put that money to good use! We can split it; half for Paul, half for us."

I'm not saying there would be no justification for selling the scrolls for cash. But they didn't sell the scrolls; they burned them. They seem to have been utterly unconcerned about the money.

There's no indication of Paul or anyone second-guessing the burning of the scrolls. Oh, maybe it was shortsighted, not for the money but for the historical value. Historians would love to have those scrolls. Think of the intellectual-historical treasure—what we could learn about the ancient world into which the gospel broke! That was not their concern. As long as those scrolls remained, they posed a threat and temptation to pagans and former-pagans-now-Christians. To them, these scrolls were not texts for historical curiosity or a means to financial security. The scrolls represented a real temptation to sorcery and competition for their allegiance. Burning them was a symbolic act signaling their newfound and exclusive devotion to Christ. The fact that Luke mentions the value indicates that the great value was noticed. But their resale value was subordinate to the principle at stake.

Luke does not lament the loss of potential revenue. Instead, in the very next verse—at the very point that we moderns would likely criticize these early Christian fanatics and hypothesize about how the money could have helped God's kingdom grow—he writes, "Thus mightily the word of the Lord grew and strengthened" (Acts 19:20). In other words, Luke explicitly links the increase of God's kingdom, at least in part, with the destruction of the magic scrolls. The message here, also confirmed throughout Scripture, is that the church is indeed powerful, but its power and growth are not derived from money or based on any other earthly power, but on the Holy Spirit.

This account in the book of Acts seems so counterintuitive to modern Christians. Frankly, the New Testament's view of money was equally scandalous in the ancient world, even to many followers of Jesus. The early Christian attitude about money is based on the life and teaching of Jesus himself. The testimony of his way of life is clear—he was poor and homeless. Jesus' teaching is equally clear. One famous example occurred during his final journey to Jerusalem, when he invited a rich man to sell his possessions and to come and follow him (Mark 10:17–27). The man refused. Jesus then claimed that it is easier for a camel to go through the eye of a needle than for a rich man to enter God's kingdom. This statement stunned the disciples. Like most of their contemporaries, they probably linked wealth with favor from God (or the gods). If a person is healthy and wealthy, God must have blessed him for his right living. So, they concluded, if a rich—which is to say, a good and divinely blessed—person cannot be saved, then who can? Jesus stops short of declaring the salvation of the rich to be impossible, but, he continues, it will take a divine miracle to pull it off (Mark 10:27).

Let that sink in. Try to forget all the customary strategies for evading the point. You have probably heard them. For instance, Jesus' command to sell one's possessions and give to the poor was meant only for people, like the rich man, who are too attached to their wealth. Are we not so attached? Isn't that the point of the test? What makes our refusal to obey somehow nobler or at all different from the rich man's refusal? When we revert so instinctively to the evasion and assure ourselves that the command was not intended for us, in fact it is proof that we are in good company with the rich man—and the command is precisely for us. As with other so-called hard sayings of Jesus, we are sometimes too quick to interpret away the demand of discipleship. So, before shrugging our shoulders and pretending like the instruction is for someone else, let the force of the teaching sink in.

Even allowing for some hyperbole, Jesus is making a point that should not be so easily dismissed: money can be more than just a challenge; it can be a problem. This familiar episode clarifies two points relevant to our discussion. First, wealth is not necessarily a sign of blessing, and one can be blessed and favored by God apart from wealth. This point is everywhere evident in the life of Jesus, who was the beloved Son of God yet lived in poverty and suffered the humiliating death of a criminal. Second, the problem with money is its unequaled ability to draw people away from God and command their allegiance (Matt 6:24). Rare is the wealthy person who is not enamored with her wealth and with the pursuit of more.

The disciples should not have been surprised by Jesus' teaching here; it is par for the course. The teaching about money is especially clear in the books of Luke and Acts, whose author seems to have had a particular interest in the topic. I will not list all the relevant passages, but consider the following examples unique to these books. The good Samaritan models generosity in his care for the wounded stranger (Luke 10:35). When Jesus' parables introduce a "rich man," he is usually the bad guy in the story (Luke 12:16; 16:19). Zacchaeus sins by exploiting his position to gain money, and his repentance and salvation involve returning the money with interest (Luke 19:1–10). The command to sell one's possessions and give to the poor is not meant just for one particularly greedy rich man, but for all (Luke 12:33–34). In the Gospel of Luke, it is one of the chief ways that one can show love.

What Jesus taught about money in Luke is reiterated and exemplified in the life of the church in the book of Acts (Luke, volume two). The earliest believers fulfilled the command of Jesus by selling their possessions and giving to the poor (Acts 2:44–45; 4:32–35). Barnabas is a positive example of the early church's generosity, contrasted with Ananias and Sapphira, who are struck dead because they lie about money, wanting the reputation of generosity without the actual sacrifice of being generous (Acts 4:36–5:11). Simon the sorcerer makes profit from magic, tries to buy from Peter and John the ability to distribute the Holy Spirit and the power of miracles, after which Peter curses him to hell along with his money (Acts 8:20). The church in Antioch sends alms to the church in Jerusalem because of the famine (Acts 11:27–30), thereby extending the local Christian charity to distant places. When Paul casts out a girl's evil spirit, her masters' profit is gone, which is the reason Paul and Silas are thrown in jail (Acts 16:16–24). In Ephesus, the pagan artisans make money off their idolatrous religion, and they form a mob when the possibility is raised that Paul's preaching could decrease their profit (Acts 19:23–29). In Luke-Acts, not every bad character is rich and not every rich person is bad, but there is a strong connection.

Let this quick survey of Luke-Acts on wealth suffice as illustrative of the whole Bible. Not just in these two books, but throughout Scripture, right thinking about money is of paramount importance. It is difficult to think of a vice that gets more negative attention in the New Testament and in the early church fathers than greed.

CONSUMERISM

In light of these biblical considerations, one area of self-examination relates to our culture of consumerist capitalism. If there is any society in the history of the world that could be considered wealthy and, therefore, to which all these biblical warnings are properly directed, it is ours. Money, by the way, includes not only the physical cash you carry or might never carry, but also the power, status, and influence that the ability to purchase represents. Understood in this way, money is perhaps the chief god of this age. As such, we would do well to recognize that its various temptations will be powerful and that there may be many ways that we constantly but unknowingly submit ourselves to its servitude.

Our modern world is in bondage, in a way that no other era has been, to a consumerism that touches rich and poor alike. It is based on the widely accepted lie that money and the stuff it buys bring fulfillment. In our age of pluralism and dizzying diversity, the lifestyle of consumption may be the one thing that unites nearly all Americans. As William Cavanaugh observes, we are detached from the producers and means of production of nearly every product we purchase. As Christians, we should have a certain detachment from material things, for the purpose of greater attachment to God and to neighbor.[4] As it is, though, because we have no hand in making what we buy, we have no meaningful connection to these products. Brad Gregory describes this cycle of consumption as "acquire, discard, repeat,"[5] that is, purchase the newest manufactured good, immediately become dissatisfied with said purchased good, discard this now hopelessly outdated piece, and then do it all over again. Bigger and better, limited only by your resources, your credit limit, and the quickly depleting resources of this planet. "Keeping up with the Joneses" has never been as important as it is now, when your status is determined by the kind of phone you carry and vehicle you drive. This is not the pursuit of the good life, but as Gregory says, the "goods" life. As a society, we are not freer, but more enslaved.

Nowhere is this slavery more evident than with smartphones.

If this seems like an exaggeration, then call to mind the lines that stretch for city blocks when each new iPhone is released, an event that has taken place nearly every year since 2007. The thing that people couldn't wait to have eleven months ago is now obsolete. Why, they wouldn't be caught dead with an iPhone 10! Making us discontent with our present possessions is the fuel that drives this part of the economy. And such lack of contentment is directly opposed to the teaching of Jesus and the apostles. It was Paul, writing from imprisonment, who found contentment not in his material possessions but in his relationship with Christ (Phil 4:11–13).

In a consumerist culture, marketing aims to make you discontent and want something you never dreamed of wanting. We have to hand it to the marketing and advertising departments. If the goal is to make people want today something they had no idea they even wanted yesterday, and, by tomorrow, turn that desire into a perceived necessity that they cannot live without, then the marketers have been wildly successful.

We all consume. The moral question here is what kind of consumer we are going to be.[6] Will we accept or resist the secular consumerist cycle that is so far removed from virtue? The answer lies in our thinking, habits, and especially our actual expenditures. How excited do you get when you update your gadgets? If you resist this consumerist cycle and don't drink the Kool-Aid, you will be mocked by the cultured despisers. Trust me. Try carrying around an old flip phone.

CONCERN FOR MONEY

Another test of a healthy relationship to wealth relates to the value or worth we ascribe to it and to those who have it. The commonly accepted lie on which this point is based says that money is the solution. The solution to what? To everything. Think of a problem in society, from the fairly trivial to the most wicked, that people *haven't* tried to solve by throwing more money at it. You will be hard-pressed.

The gospel accounts take pains to subvert the notion that money is a worthy concern. Wealth is not power, at least not the kind of power that is valued in the kingdom of God. When Jesus' opponents asked him about money, it is first of all interesting that he didn't even have a coin to look at; he had to ask for one. When he was handed the coin, he classified it among "the things of Caesar," contrasting it with "the things of God" (Mark 12:17). Of course, the things of Caesar would include any worldly concern, but the primary referent here is money. Similar language is used earlier in the narrative when Jesus rebukes Peter for not understanding what it means for Jesus to be the Messiah. Specifically, Jesus accuses Peter of having in mind "not the things of God but the things of men" (Mark 8:33). Peter thought that Jesus being king meant worldly prestige, power, and wealth, that is, "the things of men." His rebuke of Jesus was motivated by fear, the fear of the loss of money and prestige that he didn't even have yet. Money, it seems, is a spiritual threat inasmuch as it can easily distract from the things of God.

The idea that money is somehow godly or of special concern to God's people is challenged throughout the Old Testament Prophets and the New Testament. Another striking example is found in James 2. The writer chastens his audience for their obvious deference to the rich. "If a gold-ringed man"—James prefers memorable images—"if a gold-ringed man enters into your synagogue," and you give him the best seat in the house while you scatter the poor to sit on the floor or stand, then you show an evil favoritism (Jas 2:2–4). He then says, strikingly, that "God chose the poor in the world as rich in faith and heirs of the kingdom" (Jas 2:5).

To give special deference to the prospect of money or to those who have it is a perennial temptation. After all, money can come in very handy. But the temptation is, like Peter, to put wealth as a human concern next to godly concerns. When we face the threat of loss of income for doing what is right or speaking the truth, will we subordinate "the things of God" to "the things of men"? What about when the wealthy church member or board member threatens to withdraw funding, will we defer to the rich and say, "Have the best seat in the house"? It reminds me of Aidan, the first bishop of Lindisfarne, who was praised for his generosity and his courage in speaking truth to the wealthy and powerful. In his account of Aidan, the Venerable Bede added, "If the rich had done anything amiss, he never for the sake of honor or fear of displeasure spared to tell them of it; but with sharp rebuking he corrected them."[7] The point, of course, is not to treat the rich badly, but to treat the poor, who cannot repay in any earthly way, with equal love.

Money, of course, is necessary for survival, and certain resources are essential for effective ministry. As we have seen, in the book of Acts, the poor Christians are sustained by those generous Christians who have the means. Barnabas is singled out as a generous donor. We are commanded to be generous and thoughtful with our God-given resources. But when the question is about power and what the church depends on, it is not money. The church does not sacrifice principle or cater to the rich for a little more cash flow. "Money is power"? Not in Scripture. Not for disciples of Jesus.

THEOLOGICAL CONSIDERATIONS

Scripture and Christian theology provide bountiful resources for thinking rightly about money and using it in a godly way, more than can be described here. But the following three related themes may spur deeper reflection on the Christian's obligation with respect to wealth.

Almsgiving and Salvation

Almsgiving is one of the three practices of piety that Jesus assumes Jews engage in and that he expects his followers to continue (Matt 6:2). Although its general importance may not be difficult to discern, the connection of almsgiving to one's salvation is more frequently missed, especially among Protestants.

One reason that the connection is missed boils down to assumptions about salvation. It is a Protestant truism, after all, that human works contribute nothing to justification. Thus Protestants deny the category of works of merit altogether. I will return to this point later, for it touches on the wider point of the role of good works in the Christian life.

Another reason the connection is often missed is that linguistic subtleties get lost in translation. The word "alms" traces its roots to the Greek word for mercy, and "mercy" often connoted the specific merciful act of "almsgiving." For instance, when God says that he desires "mercy" and not sacrifice (Hos 6:6), early Christians and other readers of the Greek translation of the Old Testament more easily and specifically associated this mercy with acts of charity toward the poor.[8] Similarly, the Hebrew for "righteousness" could also mean almsgiving or charity toward the poor in late biblical usage.[9] This could make verses like Proverbs 10:2 and 11:4—"righteousness" delivers from death—a little more specific: "almsgiving" delivers from death, especially since the context of these proverbs concerns treasures and riches, respectively.

A quick survey of Jewish and early Christian literature reveals the prime importance of almsgiving and its relationship to salvation. Consider some evidence from the intertestamental book of Tobit, which provides an important window into Jewish thought in the centuries just preceding Jesus' birth. The story is set in Assyrian exile, but it was written around the third century BC. Early in the narrative, Tobit is confronted with the question, "Where are your acts of charity and your righteous deeds?" (Tob 2:14). The efficacy of almsgiving is spelled out at length in Tobit 4:5–11, in the midst of which it claims that, by almsgiving, "you will treasure up a good deposit for yourself for the day of necessity, because," in words reminiscent of Proverbs 10 and 11, "almsgiving delivers from death" (Tob 4:9–10). The rest of the book emphasizes Tobit's renewed devotion to the charitable acts of almsgiving and proper burial of the dead (for example, Tob 4:15–16; 12:8–10; 14:2, 10–11).

How does giving alms make the giver more secure? Doesn't it impoverish the giver? If not rewarded in this life, the emphasis is on the treasure in the life to come. As biblical scholar Gary Anderson explains, there is a heavenly bank, and making a deposit to this bank by almsgiving is like making a loan to God. Charity is something that God will repay. Jewish beggars in the early

Christian era would say, "Make a deposit to your heavenly treasury through me."[10] When we give, we believe (as a "creditor," from *credere*, to believe) that God will reward. Giving alms is not out of self-interest—no more than any good deed ought to be—but it makes a statement about what we believe about God and the world. In other words, as we care for others, we trust that God will take care of us.

One might ask whether the ideas of almsgiving as a saving action and a treasury in heaven are not simply a Jewish tradition that was overturned by Christ and his gospel. The answer seems to be no. Instead, the language of Jesus and the early church continues the theme. Jesus explicitly says that almsgiving, as also prayer and fasting, reaps a reward from the heavenly Father (Matt 6:2–4). Jesus goes on to say that, rather than hoarding up earthly wealth, you should, in words that echo Tobit 4:9, "treasure up for yourselves treasures in heaven" (Matt 6:20). Almsgiving, Jesus clearly states, adds to one's treasure in heaven (Luke 6:33).

The early church understood this basic connection and developed it. The earliest Christian document outside the New Testament, the *Didache* (ca. AD 70), declares that working with your own hands will give a ransom for sins and, repeating the point from Matthew 6, that giving generously will reap the reward of the good paymaster.[11] The homily known as *2 Clement* (ca. AD 100) ranks different acts of piety: "Almsgiving is good, as is repentance from sin. Fasting is better than prayer, but almsgiving better than both, and love covers a multitude of sins, but prayer from a good conscience delivers from death. Blessed is everyone who is found full in these, for almsgiving lightens the load of sin."[12] The language connecting almsgiving with other salvific actions echoes Tobit and (more remotely) Proverbs. Likewise, Polycarp of Smyrna, who wrote to the Philippian church (ca. AD 115), reiterates this tradition when he observes that "almsgiving delivers from death."[13]

The fullest treatment of this theme in the Apostolic Fathers appears in the *Shepherd of Hermas* (ca. AD 130), as quoted at the beginning of this chapter. The angelic shepherd reveals to Hermas that a rich man has much wealth but is poor in things offered to the Lord, such as confession and intercessory prayer, for he is distracted by his own riches. This generalization resonates with James 2:5 and other Scriptures. When the rich person approaches to supply a poor person's needs, he "believes" that he will "find the reward with God, because the poor is rich in intercession and in confession, and his intercession has great power with God."[14] This passage reflects the point made by Gary Anderson, that almsgiving is an act of belief or trust in God. It also indicates a loving exchange between rich and poor. The rich provide alms for the poor, while the poor pray for the rich. The poor need physical aid, and the rich need spiritual aid. Each has an obligation to fulfill and provides something that the other needs; together they "complete (*telousin*) the work."[15] That is, the work is perfected, brought to its proper *telos* or purpose. The wealthy, then, serve a crucial need for the poor, fulfilling a ministry or service that is pleasing to God.[16] This symbiotic relationship is a beautiful picture of the Christian use of wealth as a ministry. The section concludes with a final beatitude: "Blessed are those who have and who understand that they are made rich by the Lord, for the one who understands this will be able to render a good ministry."[17]

The idea expressed throughout Jewish and Christian history is that one can meet God in the face of the poor. John Chrysostom exhorted his congregation, "Whenever you see a poor believer . . . imagine that you behold an altar. Whenever you meet a beggar, don't insult him, but reverence him."[18] That is, the offering made to the beggar is made ultimately to God. This idea is consistent with Jesus' declaration that the good deeds done for "the least of these my brothers" are done for Christ (Matt 25:40).

As I mentioned earlier, some Protestants may feel a little uneasy with drawing an apparently causal connection between almsgiving and salvation. This is not the place to unpack everything about the role of good works in the Christian life. This specific connection was certainly abused when people bought indulgences without any penitence for sin. But it is no different from any other righteousness that we are called to do, and it presents no qualitatively different challenge than the many passages in Scripture that connect salvation with the call to good works. Anyone who remains concerned is invited to work it out in a non-Pelagian way. My only task here is to sum up the biblical evidence: as love covers a multitude of sins, so almsgiving delivers from death.

Economy of Grace

The most extended reflection in the New Testament on generous giving is found in 2 Corinthians 8–9. Paul urges the Corinthians to give to the poor Christians in Judea, as gratitude to the Lord. The key word throughout his discussion is "grace," the frequency of which is sadly obscured in most English translations. Grace (*charis*) appears ten times in these two chapters.[19] God gave grace to the Macedonian churches (2 Cor 8:1). Christ, out of his voluntary poverty, gave his grace to us all (2 Cor 8:9). Paul reminds the Corinthians of the spiritual grace they have received so that they might share their material gifts with others. Paul refers to this generous giving as grace (2 Cor 8:19). The Macedonian churches participated in this grace, voluntarily giving according to and even beyond their means (2 Cor 8:3). Giving will supply God's people with what they need and result in an overflow of thanksgivings to God (2 Cor 9:12). The recipients then pray for the donors, who benefit from their prayers, and return "grace" to God (2 Cor 9:14–15).

This cycle of generosity is what I call the economy of grace, and it is consistent with and illumines the exchange discussed earlier in Jewish and other early Christian writers. Giving is enabled by grace. Divine grace begins, infuses, and completes the whole process. There is first a reaping of a harvest of blessings ("grace" from God to people; 8:1, 9; 9:6, 8, 10–11). Then there is supplying the physical needs of the saints ("grace" from human donors to recipients; 8:6–7, 19; 9:8, 12). This is followed by intercession from recipients on behalf of the donors (9:14), a theme taken up, as we have seen, in the second-century church. Finally, thanksgivings and glory overflow to God ("grace" from all people to God; 8:19; 9:11–15).

All of it was a good lesson for the immature, gentile church in Corinth: to give money to people that, outside of Christ, they would have no interest in whatsoever. It shows the interdependence of Jew and gentile in the progress of the kingdom. The grace of giving unifies and brings into communion all believers with God and, through God, with one another.

A Spiritual Test

Money is not an unmitigated blessing or curse. Nor is it necessarily neutral. More often, money is a temptation, the acquisition of which becomes an obstacle for entrance into God's kingdom. It is a spiritual test. As Gary Anderson puts it with reference to Sirach 31, "Having money is tantamount to a spiritual ordeal whose outcome is determined by whether one has the courage to give it away."[20] Proverbs 30:8–9 summarizes an aspect of the test. "Give me neither poverty nor riches; feed me the bread necessary for me. Otherwise I will be full and deny you and say, 'Who is the LORD?' or I will be poor and steal and profane the name of my God." In other words, lead us not into temptation when it comes to money.

But alas! Even if we do not want to admit it, we do not fall into that middle category between poverty and riches. If we reside in the developed world and live above the poverty line, then, in comparison with the vast majority of humans throughout history, we live like kings, at least materially speaking. Even if we live paycheck to paycheck, we are the rich. We are among those who, as the proverb warns, are satiated and inclined to forget God.

The test, then, is about the love of money. It is important to recognize the distinction between money and the love of money. Strictly, it is not money per se, but greed or the love of money that is the root of all evils (1 Tim 6:10). So it is important to ask ourselves: What would greed look like today? How could we test whether we love money?

Clement of Alexandria speaks to this essential question in his treatise, *Who Is the Rich Man That Shall Be Saved?* Clement's point of departure is Mark 10:17–27, where Jesus says that it is easier for a camel to go through the eye of a needle than for a rich man to enter the kingdom of heaven. Clement admits that many rich people have despaired over this hard saying of Jesus,[21] so Clement recommends a spiritual interpretation of Jesus' hard saying. The point is not simply about the literal giving away of wealth, for there is nothing distinctly Christian about that.[22] The command to give away everything cannot be literal and universal, for if it were, how would we have anything left to share?[23] The point, rather, is not to cast away all wealth but the passions for it—that is, the love of money.[24] Poor people can be just as greedy as the rich. And if a rich person gives away everything but remains as greedy as ever, the problem has not been solved. Instead, the rich man who can be saved is the one who sees his wealth as a gift from God, uses it as a ministry of love, is not possessed by the riches, and "is able with cheerful mind to bear their removal equally with their abundance."[25] This is the person who passes the spiritual test.

If you have lived through the pandemic and market crash of 2020, during which over forty million Americans lost their jobs, then you may have experienced personal economic crisis. If nothing else, our attitude toward money has been tested perhaps in new ways. With God's help, it can be a good reminder of the true priorities in life and an opportunity to reconsider how we spend our money.

CONCLUSION

What does love require of us? Whether our income is large or small, how are we to use it for God's glory? How can we pass on to others the grace that we have received?

John Wesley, who gave so much of his life and resources to helping the poor and contending for their cause, preached a famous sermon on the use of money. Like all good sermons, it had three points. First, make all the money you can. Gain it honestly, of course, and don't harm anyone in the process. But use all your know-how to make as much as possible. An inauspicious beginning, perhaps, but he has our attention. Second, save all the money you can. Don't waste any of it on passing pleasures. But you cannot stop with these points, or it's worthless. Third, and finally, give away as much money as you can. Provide for yourself and your family first, and then for others of the household of faith, and then for all people. The logic is that you cannot give away much if you have not already gained and saved much. He concludes, "Give all ye have, as well as all ye are, a spiritual sacrifice to him who withheld not from you his Son, his only Son."[26]

The point is to limit luxury and give sacrificially, so much that it makes a difference in your own purchasing power, even to the point of inconvenience. As Anderson notes, there is a big difference between being short of money and being short of money for charity's sake.[27] Or as a friend of mine put it, give not just until it hurts but until it feels good. If we are willing, God can use us as channels of blessing to others.

DISCUSSION QUESTIONS

1. How does our society think about and use money?
2. Are Christians less materialistic than non-Christians? How would we know or be able to tell?
3. In what ways do we Christians use money well? In what ways do we use it poorly?
4. How is the act of giving a "grace"?
5. Do we give out of a feeling of guilt or of joy?

CHAPTER 10

The Use of Technology

All things considered it looks as though Utopia [in Brave New World*] were far closer to us than anyone, only fifteen years ago [1931], could have imagined. Then, I projected it six hundred years into the future. Today it seems quite possible that the horror may be upon us within a single century. That is, if we refrain from blowing ourselves to smithereens in the interval.*
—Aldous Huxley[1]

Scientists are actually preoccupied with accomplishment. So they are focused on whether they can do something. They never stop to ask if they should do something. They conveniently define such considerations as pointless. If they don't do it, someone else will. Discovery, they believe, is inevitable. So they just try to do it first. That's the game in science. Even pure scientific discovery is an aggressive, penetrative act.
—Michael Crichton[2]

Thoth was an Egyptian god who invented many *technai*, or arts, including numbers, geometry, and, most important, writing. Thoth wanted to give his arts or technologies to humankind, so he first took them to the king of Thebes, Ammon, for evaluation. When Thoth described writing, he raved about how great this invention was, for, he thought, it would make the Egyptians wiser and improve their ability to remember things. But Ammon first pointed out that the person who can create an art or technology is not usually able to give an objective judgment about its use and consequences. Second, Ammon said, writing will have the exact opposite effect that Thoth assumed. Writing, which is external to people, will produce forgetfulness, for it will discourage the use of internal memory and memorization. In short, this invention will make people dumber.

Socrates, who tells the tale, agrees with Ammon and thinks that writing is very bad.[3] I won't go into all the details of the advantages and disadvantages of writing as a tool, though Socrates was certainly correct about the ambiguity of the written word and the demise of memorization, results exacerbated by instant electronic written communication. What is also indisputable is that, even though it has become second nature to us, writing with letters is a technology whose origin we can pinpoint historically and fairly precisely, a technology that changed the human race and human interaction in profound ways. A number of technologies came before and have come along since then that have forever changed humans.

TECHNOPHILIA VERSUS TECHNOPHOBIA

The lesson that Neil Postman drew from Socrates' story was about how we evaluate technology. In *Technopoly*, Postman posited two extremes on a continuum: technophilia and technophobia. A technophile like Thoth, on the one hand, sees nothing but good in the latest technologies. The default setting is to love any new invention.

Especially if it makes a given task more efficient or enjoyable, by all means, go for it. A technophobe, on the other hand, sees nothing but bad in the latest technologies. The default setting is to hate or fear any new invention. The technophobe is more frequently known as a Luddite. Luddite was originally the self-designation (after a supposed Ned Ludd) of protesters who, beginning in 1811, destroyed the textile machines that put them out of work.[4] The original Luddites had good reason to be suspicious of technological change. For the extreme technophobe, then, all technological innovation is, by definition, bad.

On which end of the spectrum does our society fall? Are we generally inclined to accept or to reject new technologies? Inarguably, our culture is technophiliac. It was not always so. Our premodern ancestors were more suspicious of technological innovations. Ancient cultural myths abound that depict the gods or fallen angels bringing new technologies to humans—or humans stealing them from the gods—almost always to the detriment of human civilization. One ancient interpretation of Genesis 6 is that fallen angels, in addition to mating with human women, also introduced metallurgy and the forging of new weapons such as swords and shields. Increased violence was the result.[5] When I think of the Iron Age, I think first of a skillet for cooking—probably a technophiliac reaction. The ancients, however, associated iron first with new weapons and violence, more efficient ways for people to be slaughtered.

That premodern technophobia has, in modern times, transformed into an even stronger, unquestioned technophilia. One historian asks, "Today we award innovation, but where is the award for resisting innovation?"[6] Of course, there is no award for standing against something new, and there won't be anytime soon. We know on which side of the spectrum our society falls.

In a society of technophiles, technologically speaking, if something *can* be done, it *must* be done, especially if it is profitable. Before the turn of this century, no one ever thought, "What my mobile phone really needs is a camera." Telephones are for talking. But one company put a camera in there, and the rest is history—there is no looking back. Now you wouldn't be caught dead without a high-quality camera on your phone. After all, what would you do with your Instagram if you didn't have a camera at your fingertips at every waking moment? If someone were to say, "Wait a second. Hold the phone! What are the possible negative consequences of putting cameras on cell phones?" what would you think of that person? Most would think that he is probably a technophobe. To technophiles, a balanced person positioned in the middle of the continuum looks like a technophobe.

Are there negative consequences to having cameras on phones? Since we have raised the possibility, what might those be? We could rattle off a number of them: the ease of sexting, the loss of privacy, and the like. How many people have died, inattentive to their surroundings, while seeking the perfect selfie? How many servings of food have grown cold while posing for social media? More significant and far-reaching is the now ubiquitous experience of living life virtually through the lens of a camera that, ironically, causes people to miss out on the moment in the name of capturing the moment.

One can decide whether these specific considerations about camera phones should make a difference, but the point is that our technophiliac culture does not encourage these kinds of questions and considerations at all. As the character Ian Malcolm said in *Jurassic Park*, scientists "are focused on whether they can do something. They never stop to ask if they *should* do something."[7] That's an important question in ethics: Not *can* we, but *should* we? The "stop to ask" is where we as a society come up short. If someone working at Apple or Nokia in 2000 asked about the possible negative social consequences of cameras at everyone's fingertips, that person would have been ignored or fired. Like Socrates said, the people making the technology and, I would add, making money off the technology should not be the people deciding how it will be used. They are too attached to their product and to the money it brings in. Another group of people with a little more distance should decide.

One of Neil Postman's points is that there's no technological innovation that doesn't have negative consequences. The negatives may be so negligible that you can name them and then move on. But usually they're not. To be sure, not all technologies are created equal. With some, the advantages may outweigh the disadvantages; with others, the harm overshadows the benefit. Rarely, if ever, is a technology merely neutral.

Since our culture is naturally technophiliac, we need to train ourselves to consider the consequences of introducing new technologies. What are the costs—not just financial—of the new technology? What are the potential negatives? For example, will having more computers solve all our educational problems? Is there evidence that bringing computers into the classroom improves learning? The answer to both of those last questions is no, and researchers have known it for a long time.[8] Why, then, do schools continue to invest in more and more technology? Is it really out of love for children and the pursuit of their actual good? The technology committees for such programs, usually made up of people working in the tech industry (again, not the most unbiased participants), typically do not exist to stand in the way of technology or to ask whether a given technology builds virtue or is helpful long-term. The only question is how they will use it, and how much. I can personally attest to the difficulty of getting a hearing when nothing but enthusiasm is expected for the introduction of technology in K-12 education.

Despite the difficulties—or, perhaps, because it is so countercultural and neglected—it is important to ask the question about positives and negatives, and to do so with any technology. To ask the question is to break the spell. Sadly, such assessment is rarely practiced.[9] But we will attempt it here. Our concern, of course, is especially with the moral consequences of technology. How can we use technology for the glory of God?

As we proceed to some specific evaluation of technology, we want to begin with Scripture. In contrast to previous chapters, however, we are faced with a more formidable challenge. For obvious reasons, the Bible has very little to say directly about the topic of technology. The further back into history and prehistory we go, the fewer technological changes there were (think, for instance, of the ageless endurance of the hand ax). Technology as such was not a hot topic in antiquity. Furthermore, the innovations we generally think of as technology are comparatively recent and did not exist when Scripture was written. But like every other issue we have encountered, technology in general is addressed indirectly in Scripture, especially at the levels of principles and theological convictions. Specific technologies can also be assessed in light of various Scriptures. And with every technology, we should ask, does the use of this technology really help or hinder the work of the Holy Spirit in our lives?

SCREENS

As an example of ethical thinking about technology, let us consider one of the most common and invasive technologies to come on the scene in the last hundred years, one that, it is no exaggeration to say, has overtaken us. We are very familiar with it. It is not really a controversial issue, and it doesn't get discussed much in church settings, at least not as an ethical or moral question. Let's call it "screens." From television to cinema to computer to smartphone. By screens I intend to include both the gadgets themselves as well as the content they are designed to mediate, and I include it all, somewhat indiscriminately. Screens figure prominently in the dystopian futures imagined in George Orwell's *Nineteen Eighty-Four* and Ray Bradbury's *Fahrenheit 451*. Orwell's telescreens were coerced on the citizenry from above by a government that used them to spout propaganda, invade citizens' privacy, track their every move, and detect any hint of dissent. Now our telescreens do the same things, but the desire comes from below—we purchase them, carry them around in our pockets, and volunteer the intimate information.

One might object and say that the use of screens may be a question of prudence but that it is not a matter of Christian morality. Why are we discussing screens in a book on ethics? A couple of responses come to mind. First, prudence is a moral virtue, and it's not for nothing that the Bible talks quite a bit about wisdom versus folly. It is true that not all folly is sin. But almost all sin is a form of folly. The overlap between sin and folly is significant, and we would do well to lean toward the wise and virtuous courses of action.

Second, I contend that "screens"—including, but not limited to, cinema, TV, internet, social media, and smartphones—are indeed a moral issue. What ethical issues are related to the use of screens? Most people, after just a moment's thought, can come up with a few items. The use of screens can easily lead to or provide occasion for lust, greed, consumerism, time-wasting, sloth, hatred, anger, pride, envy, slander, despair, and so on. So much for the vices. Do screens also cultivate virtues? That one is harder to answer. Let us consider the moral pros and cons of various instantiations of screens. We need an assessment that will take into account virtues, duties, and consequences, when possible, in light of Scripture. The following reflections on screens and evaluating technology serve as just one case. They can be applied in similar ways to any technology.

As an example of screens, let us consider cell phones, especially in their current form—smartphones. It is difficult to remember life before cell phones. Back then, we just had to guess where people were and wonder what they were doing and ask them later when we saw them or could station ourselves at a landline. Strange. When the older half of our population tells a story that happened before the mid-1990s, we often say, "That was before cell phones." We offer this clarification not only to the younger people within earshot but also to those who are old enough to know or who were part of the story.

Before I go any further, pause and think about the significance of the fact that, in telling so many of these stories from the past, we have to remind even ourselves that such and such happened "before we had cell phones." What does it mean? First of all, it means that cell phones are such a normal part of our lives that it is hard to imagine life before them and without them. It indicates just how important they have become to us. Our anecdote may also have happened before the DVD player came along, but we don't mention that fact because it's usually irrelevant. We all have DVD players—or had them—but they don't matter to us or affect the stories of our lives like cell phones. We could justly divide recent history into pre– and post–cell phones. Cell phones must mean a lot to us.

The larger point here is how much technology changes the humans who use it. We tend to think that we are in control of the technology and not effectively changed by it, but in truth, the technology masters us. Theologian Jacob Shatzer, citing Michael Bess, discusses "the Jetsons fallacy." The Jetsons cartoon from the 1960s, like many other optimistic, postwar predictions of the future, assumed that there would be astounding technological upgrades, but that people wouldn't change all that much. As Shatzer describes it, "Gadgets will continue to evolve, but humans will stay basically the same."[10] About sixty years later, we can look back and see that something very different has happened: the technology has developed, though not nearly as drastically or as quickly as expected, but humans have been profoundly affected by the changes. The Christian version of the Jetsons fallacy says, "Discipleship is about following Christ, and we can direct any technology toward that end rather easily."[11] The denial that technological change will alter those who use it on a constant basis is an overly optimistic but widely held attitude.

To ponder how cell phones in particular have changed people, something only the older ones among us know firsthand, simply think back to when you first saw one in use or used one yourself. Think of how important it has since become and how many people cannot live a moment without their phones. Now tech companies talk about implanting smartphones into the human body.[12] That would definitely make it harder to put down and turn off the phone.

Sometime in the early or mid-2000s, once cell phones were no longer restricted to the wealthy and important, I recall seeing a TV advertisement that was marketing an innovative feature that I mentioned earlier: a phone that could take pictures and send the photographs to other phones via a message. A couple was waking up in bed, and the man took a picture of the woman and sent it to her; she then used her phone to snap a picture of him. At the time,

I couldn't imagine why someone would see that ad and think they had to have this product. But they did, and the world has been forever altered. It was an early vision of how these devices would inhibit love by creating a barrier between people who are physically present to one another, but lost in the screens.

The problems with smartphones are myriad, and to a degree, many Christians recognize it. On a number of occasions in recent years, I've had the opportunity to ask large groups of Christians a general, open-ended question about what our idols are and what things distract us most from what should be the chief goals in life. Invariably, they hold up their phones (yes, they have them in Sunday school). No one seriously hazards that these phones are helping us be better people or love the people next to us more. Instead, screens remove us from our neighbors. No one thinks that a smartphone in every hand has increased true human flourishing or the imitation of Christ. If becoming like God is the goal of the moral life, then—and this really is my main point—the use of smartphones is an ethical issue, but one that is seldom discussed or even considered in this light. Even when the problems are recognized, little action is taken.

The addictive nature of screen technologies and social media is another way that users are negatively affected. Part of the radical change of the last two decades is that the majority of the world's population now owns a smartphone and, it seems, is addicted to them. In its effects on the brain and its near-universal reach, smartphones are rather like the addictive drug "soma" from *Brave New World*.[13] And a large portion of the population appears to be addicted to social media of at least one form, if not many.

It is no accident. Social media platforms are designed to addict you. Big tech companies hire psychologists who specialize in addiction and know how to suck people in and give them what they want.[14] They are asking, "How can we get people to spend more money and time on our app?" This is what some of the brightest minds in the tech world are devoting themselves to: how to get more people addicted to the latest devices, apps, and video games, instead of researching and innovating in fields that actually help human flourishing. Many tech executives do not allow their children to have screens of any kind.[15] They are more aware than most consumers of how addicting and destructive these technologies can be. If you can't go a day or a whole weekend without it (whatever screen you have in mind), then you may be addicted. See if you can go a whole week without it. Then when you come back, see what you missed and rate how important those things are. That goes for any screen technology. If you can't go a day without it, you must see that that's a problem. Try it.

Again, are there some positives to screens? Sure, used in moderation. Direct, private communication with a friend, a picture of your child, road directions. But because the devices are so addictive, it takes extraordinary maturity to moderate one's usage.

The many problems with cell phones, and with smartphones in particular, can be boiled down to the fact that, given the way most people use them (that is, not in moderation), there is virtually nothing virtuous about them. Think of the four cardinal virtues—justice, temperance, courage, prudence. In light of typical smartphone use, is there a net gain or loss of these classic virtues? Or take the theological virtues of faith, hope, and love. Arguably, smartphones contribute to a net loss. Or, again, conduct the same experiment with the fruit of the Spirit (joy, peace, patience, kindness, self-control, and so on) or any spiritual discipline (prayer, meditation, silence, worship, study, and so on), or the two greatest commands, to love God and one's neighbor. Smartphones rarely help but almost always hinder us from cultivating these virtues and disciplines.

Let me approach another issue related to smartphones—and one that extends also to any device with internet access—by means of the following parable. "Here, thirteen-year-old boy, here is a handheld device for you. It has five buttons. With the first button you can communicate with family and friends instantaneously. The second button will help you do research for your homework and type your papers. The third button allows you to engage all social media and entertainment websites. The fourth button allows you to read your Bible. With the fifth button, you can access images and videos of naked women. Here is your device, son. You will have it with you wherever you go, 24–7. Now, don't ever press that fifth button." This temptation is too much for many adult Christian men to resist. But we give these things to children, often with minimal or no filter?

We, collectively, are a foolish people. Other potentially harmful things we forbid until a more mature age. Alcohol is prohibited before age twenty-one. But cell phones? Why tempt our children and ourselves with portable internet machines and all the filth that the online world has to offer? Would we purchase a house for our family that is situated between a liquor store and a brothel, even if it's convenient for getting to work or school? Would it be worth the risk? Giving children a phone with no limits is like storing booze in their bedrooms. Even if we tell them not to partake, we cannot be shocked when they do.

Yes, children need to have increasing freedom; they need to have space to make choices. They will have a phone on their own terms at some point. But why enable it and make the sin almost inevitable? We give phones to our kids and sometimes don't even bother to warn them. With devices, there must be limits, instruction, accountability. Setting limits is difficult, to be sure, but it is also the loving thing to do.

What about social media, which, along with pornography, gets a large share of collective internet usage? One ethical question relates to how it is used. If we use it, what kind of image are we portraying? Something that would make Jesus or our family proud? What kind of comments do we make online? Even if the comments seem justifiable, most readers will not bother to examine the larger context we may have in mind. Why are we using social media? Is it to connect with others? Or are we seeking validation from other people? Do we get a kick out of seeing people in conflict with one another?

We say that social media helps people connect. But most of the time, you don't log on to Instagram to connect with someone. If you really want to connect, you would call or text those people directly. With a limited number of exceptions, for the users, the platforms become ends in themselves. You're simply there, present to the screen, scrolling and becoming more addicted. And then all the negative consequences follow. Try connecting with the people around you instead and showing them a more embodied and connected love.

Each of us should be willing to ask, "How does going on social media negatively affect me?" What are some of those negatives? In short, social media inhibits true human flourishing. Social media relates to a long list of problems, getting clearer all the time. Physical health is one concern. For example, in children, the increased use of screens is associated with lower measures of brain matter that support language and literacy skills, as well as lower scores on cognitive assessments.[16] Another serious problem is what social media does to mental health. Americans are less happy and more depressed than ever before, and many view social media as a major factor. According to the CDC, "Suicide rates in the United States have risen nearly 30% since 1999" through 2016. "In 2016, nearly 45,000 suicides (15.6/100,000 population) occurred in the United States. . . . In addition, rates of emergency department visits for nonfatal self-harm, a main risk factor for suicide, increased 42% from 2001 to 2016."[17] These figures are statistically significant. In addition, annual deaths from (unintentional) drug overdose far outnumber suicides. It is all escape from a reality that is more and more dominated by technology. Direct causation is hard to prove, but there is definitely a correlation between the rise of social media and the rise of depression and suicide, not to mention the rise of anger and divisiveness in our society. A recent study of 3,826 adolescents showed an association between symptoms of depression and the use of social media and television, concluding, in typically guarded fashion, that screen use may enhance depression.[18] The scientific and anecdotal evidence is overwhelming and could be multiplied. The studies are showing what ought to be obvious to any objective observer. Less human interaction means less human happiness.

Of course, there are positive aspects to screens and smartphones. Obviously, I appreciate the convenience of having directions on a smartphone or being able to call for help in case of emergency. I value the ability to access a good book while away from one's home or library. But we know the advantages; it is the disadvantages that we ignore. And when we consider the many drawbacks, it is a heavy price to pay for the conveniences.

CONCLUSION

We tend to equate the progress of technological innovation with improvement. But progress is improvement only if it is change in the right direction. If the calling and pursuit of the good life is to be like God, technology provides a distorted means of getting there. Technology can be an expression of a desire to be like God, but it is seeking likeness to God in the wrong way. Genesis 11 provides an account of what humans did with the invention of brickmaking. It didn't take long for the people to jump from making bricks to making a name for themselves (Gen 11:3–4). Of course, we humans are capable, quite apart from technology, of transgressing our boundaries and becoming like God—or becoming our own gods—on our own terms (see Gen 3:5–6). But technology also seems to provide a special temptation that leads us to think that we are in control of the chaos, that we can discover or create our own fulfillment, and that we can get ourselves to God and become our own gods. The builders' infatuation with their own abilities was so dangerous that God thwarted it, and it was called Babel, or Babylon, the archetypal enemy of God and his people.

It is important to reiterate that not all technology is always bad. I am not recommending an unthinking technophobia, and the gospel grants us freedom to use technology in ways that glorify God. But we should think about the technologies we frequently accept without question. It requires thought and reasoned assessment, especially regarding the technologies that affect us so deeply on a daily basis. It's one thing to use screens now and then to unwind. But when we waste hour after hour of our lives in front of a TV watching things that can never produce anything virtuous, we have yielded the advantage to the enemy. Not that things like TV or technology are evil in and of themselves. As media or instruments, the ubiquitous technology of screens is mostly a means of delivery. Unfortunately, the content that these screens deliver does not usually promote Christian virtue. These media make our brains and our souls into passive recipients of all the worst the world has to offer—from the merely inane to the positively wicked. Even in the sacred space of our churches, we have a hard time escaping from the devices.

The reality is that we are in a new situation that will not soon be reversed. Technophilia is not going away. It is a situation analogous to that of Moses, who tried to regulate divorce for the hard-hearted. It's not what God wanted. It is like the challenge facing the apostle Paul, who tried to regulate the conduct of slave masters in a society that assumed the practice of slavery. It wasn't ideal. We must start with and accommodate the premise that almost everyone is already enslaved to their electronic devices.

The question we must ask, then, reflects the challenge faced also by Moses and Paul: How can we infuse into this less-than-ideal situation a measure of perspective and good sense? How should we regulate it? We cannot deceive ourselves into thinking that our justifications or solutions—for instance, "I can read my Bible on my phone!"—are ideal. They are not. They are terrible accommodations, and we should be clear-eyed about the extent of the enslavement. We have lost something worth restoring. How can we, through the help and wisdom from God's Spirit, pull ourselves up a level or two on the continuum of human flourishing on which smartphones threaten to drag us down?

What, then, does love require? With screens in particular, I recommend what Cal Newport calls "digital minimalism" and a process of "digital declutter."[19] We must set limits for ourselves and our families.[20] Let the phones just be what we call them: telephones, and occasional texting machines. The Christian vision of human flourishing is anything that helps us love God and neighbor (Matt 22:37–40). Screens don't usually help us love our neighbor more. They take us away from our neighbor, and they may lead us to hating our neighbor. Instead, let us use our Christian freedom to fill our lives with activities and even leisure that will help us grow in the grace and knowledge of our Lord Jesus Christ.

DISCUSSION QUESTIONS

1. In the last five years, what is the longest you have ever gone without your smartphone? Was it voluntary? How did you feel about it?
2. If you have a social media account, have you ever thought about deleting it? Why? If you don't have an account, why don't you?
3. What are the ways you use the technology around you for good and noble purposes? What percentage of the time would you say that's what you use it for?

CHAPTER 11

Politics

They dwell in their own fatherlands, but as sojourners; they share in all things as citizens, and steadfastly endure all things as foreigners; every foreign land is their fatherland, and every fatherland foreign. . . . On earth they live, but in heaven they are citizens. They obey the established laws, and in their own lives they conquer the laws.

—Epistle to Diognetus *5.5, 9–10*[1]

Now there are two kinds of law for our consideration. The one is the ultimate law of nature, which is probably derived from God, and the other the written code of cities. Where the written law does not contradict the law of God, it is good that the citizens should not be troubled by the introduction of strange laws. But where the law of nature, that is of God, enjoins precepts contradictory to the written laws, consider whether reason does not compel a man to dismiss the written code and the intention of the lawgivers far from his mind, and to devote himself to the divine Lawgiver and to choose to live according to His word, even if in doing this he must endure dangers and countless troubles and deaths and shame. . . .

We Christians, then, recognize that law is by nature king of all when it is the same as the law of God; and we try to live in accordance with it, having declared our renunciation of the laws which are no laws.

—Origen[2]

One of the more enigmatic and famous statements of Jesus, to which we alluded already in a previous chapter, is found in Mark 12:17: "Pay back to Caesar the things of Caesar and to God the things of God." Although Jesus was responding to a question primarily about money, this saying has often been taken more broadly as a statement about political matters and allegiances.[3] There is Caesar's kingdom, and there is God's kingdom. Like the original audience, we may marvel at the response—and even pay it lip service—without knowing exactly what it means. The broad ethical question that concerns us in this chapter is: What should a Christian's relationship to politics be? What is our responsibility as Christians toward the civil government? Should we even care? After all, Christians confess that Jesus, not Caesar, is Lord.

The word "politics" is derived from the Greek word *polis*, or city-state.[4] So politics, literally, refers to any matters related to the community or civilization and its flourishing. Augustine defined the political community, or "people," as "an assembled multitude of rational creatures bound together by a common agreement as to the objects of their love."[5] In *Republic*, Plato thought of the polis, the body politic, as the individual writ large.

This initial survey yields a few important points from the outset. First, the political is anything related to the public or civic sphere. Second, before we associate the political immediately and only with the largest possible instance of it, we should think first of the smaller communities that more often affect our everyday lives, such as family, neighborhood, city, and state.

Third, a civil government's task is to promote the good of its citizens. This could include many things, but presumably not everything. At the least, the government's role is to protect its citizens and their fundamental human rights. What are those basics? As any parent knows, one of the main jobs of an authority figure is to settle disputes or, to put it positively, rule justly. In the Old Testament, the elders of the people, who sat in the city gates, would render judgments. Ultimately, the king was the highest court in the land. Solomon was renowned for his wise and just judgments. For John Locke, the chief purpose of government is the preservation of each citizen's property and inalienable personal rights. The American Declaration of Independence promotes for citizens the rights of life, liberty, and the pursuit of happiness.

Taking stock thus far, there is nothing here that is per se antithetical to Christianity. To attend to the public good of our communities seems quite consistent with the Christian calling. At the same time, we cannot help but ask about the church's relationship to these civic communities. For the church is a discrete body, the body of Christ, the historical instantiation of his kingdom. Like the body politic, it is a people "bound together by a common agreement as to the objects of their love," to use Augustine's language. The church is its own—or, better, God's own—gathered community of people. In that sense, the church is inherently political, in the broad sense of the term. In this world, however, the church is an alternative, and sometimes a rival, community to the civic or political community. The church is its own "polis," or city, set on a hill to shed light around it (Matt 5:14). For citizens of God's kingdom, the church is state.

TWO EXTREMES

So how should a Christian relate to the civil government? Christians have been wrestling with this issue since the church's beginnings. Throughout Christian history, and particularly in the United States, the options regarding Christian involvement in politics have fallen along a wide spectrum. To get a handle on the available options, consider the two extreme ends of the spectrum, two archetypal ways to approach the issue.

Near one extreme is the approach that seeks a sort of union between God and country. Such an arrangement was not possible in the church's earliest days, when civil governments were generally ambivalent toward or outright hostile to Christians. But it became a possibility in the Roman Empire after the conversion of Emperor Constantine in AD 312. Before Constantine, the close, even symbiotic, relationship between the gods and the city or state had been widely taken for granted. The state funded the pagan priests, sacrifices, and festivals. After Constantine, the religion was shifting to Christianity, but the assumption remained that there would be a close relationship between religion and the empire. The fourth century thus ushered in the idea of Christendom in the global West, in which Christianity was the official religion of the state, in all its varied forms in various times and places, over the next 1,400-plus years.

By the early seventeenth century, the state churches had lost all meaningful authority in the nation-state. This reality is reflected later in the United States Constitution, which guarantees that there will be no official church denomination established at the federal level. But because the republic's founders and the great majority of the citizens were broadly and culturally Christian—whether practicing or not, orthodox or not—Christianity remained the unofficial religion of the country. From the earliest colonial days, the new land was seen as a land of religious opportunity, offering its inhabitants the freedom to worship as God desires. Thus, on the popular level, the success of true Christianity was tied up with the success of the country. God and country go hand in hand. To be a good American is to be a good Christian, and vice versa.

What I have briefly described here, in the specific context of the United States, has often been called "American civil religion." As Grant Wacker notes, it stems from a desire to give religious meaning to the nation itself.[6] It was once a prominent feature of American culture that America is God's nation, a people specifically chosen to embody Christian principles as a nation. In its extreme form, American patriotism and religious devotion are enmeshed together, nearly interchangeable, difficult to differentiate. This joining of patriotism and worship is reflected in the churches who display American flags in the sanctuary. I once heard Sean Hannity declare, "The United States is the greatest nation in the history of the world," and, more to the point, "America is God's greatest gift to humanity." This is God's country. The United States, not just the church, is the "city on a hill" (Matt 5:14).[7]

With this approach, the Christian's political involvement and support of the country's most venerable institutions are taken for granted. Such believers find their purpose in human government. To question God's good design for this country or to criticize any of the foundational principles of the republic, even their specific implementation—such as unrestrained capitalism or the military-industrial complex—would be tantamount to heresy.

At the other extreme end of the spectrum is the idea of nonparticipation. According to these believers, Christians should have little or no positive relation to human government or in any way support it. Human government, it is alleged, is founded on force. For some of these believers, it is wrong for a Christian even to vote. This broad position is inspired primarily by Anabaptist theology, that is, the thought of the Radical Reformers who advocated the separation of church and state in the sixteenth century. It has been articulated in North America especially by John Howard Yoder and, later, Stanley Hauerwas. It remains prominent in many mainline churches and free church denominations with pacifist histories.

Advocates of nonparticipation see the Constantinian shift as an entirely negative legacy in the history of the church. "Constantinianism," as Yoder and his admirers have called it, represented a kind of fall or apostasy. Before Constantine, it is alleged, the church was clearly separate from and opposed to Caesar and therefore untainted by all the wicked compromises that accompany support of and participation in human government. Thus, the early church generally provides a more ethical and godly model for Christian interaction with the government.[8]

To summarize the position on this end of the spectrum, participation in government, including voting as a citizen, is impermissible for at least three reasons. First, human government is inherently evil, a rebellion against God, typified in Scripture as Babel or Babylon. Second, according to this view, participation in human government necessarily involves or is complicit with force. Third, support of government means that one's allegiance is divided between God and something else.[9]

A major motivating assumption undergirding this position is that allegiance is a zero-sum game. One's allegiance is either to God or to the state; it cannot be to both. A person thinks and acts either as a Christian or as an American. One theologian defends the disjunction thus: "Some, of course, will object that my way of putting it here is insufficient by saying that the apparent tension can be resolved by a notion of dual citizenship in both the kingdom of God and in the nation-state of which we happen to be a part. But this is only a more complicated way of still effectively setting aside the lordship of Jesus."[10] In this account, to claim dual citizenship is to reject Christ.

Of these two extreme positions regarding a Christian's relation to the civil government and its politics, the former has, to put it mildly, become nearly obsolete. It is difficult to remember a time when people said, "America is God's country," with a straight face or without great qualification.[11] Commenting on the obsolescence of American civil religion, Sydney Ahlstrom wrote in 1972, "In the later twentieth century the mythic quality of the American saga has evaporated."[12] In most public discourse now, one cannot say anything good about the country or its historic statesmen without first acknowledging their many sins, both real and imagined. We have learned from hard experience not to trust the government. Even for those who a generation ago might have equated the intentions of the United States with those of God, now as the people and its elected officials stray ever further from historic Christian beliefs and ethics, no serious person is really tempted to see the United States as the city on a hill, a thousand points of light for the world. Rather, the current inclination, given the obvious corruption and rampant immorality that characterize the country, is, from a Christian motivation, to refuse any involvement with Babylon.

TWO CITIES

As an alternative to these extreme positions, I want to argue for what could be considered a conventional *via media*: Christians may participate in human government, without confusing it with the kingdom of God or compromising our primary allegiance to God. That is, a balance may be sought that is based on rightly ordered love. There is a great deal of middle ground between the two extremes, and this is not the place to delineate a full-scale Christian political philosophy or program. But the following reflections are intended to describe how Christians should think about matters related to civil government and about engagement in politics, all in light of Scripture and tradition, and with regard to the Holy Spirit's work in the lives of God's people.

So what does it mean to be both a citizen of God's kingdom and a citizen of an earthly kingdom? We may begin with Augustine's classic statement in *The City of God*. This volume is concerned with God's plan in relation to the decline of the Roman Empire. Pagans, of course, blamed the outside invasions—especially by Alaric's Goths in 410—on the recent abandoning of Rome's gods in favor of the Christian deity. In response, Augustine distinguishes between two cities or civilizations (*civitates*), the city of God and the city of the world, that is, God's kingdom throughout all time in contrast to the many earthly kingdoms that come and go. These two societies correspond to the two different desires that motivate people: a desire for God and a desire for the world or self or power, for anything besides God. People follow their desires. The fundamental question is whether those desires are disordered or restored and thus rightly ordered. The earthly city is characterized by primary love for anything that is not God. Not all earthly civilizations are equal. Some are more disordered than others. It is wrong to put family or friends above God. It is much worse, though, to put violence or thirst for genocide above God. Therefore, sometimes God's city and the earthly city track closely together. At other times, they are on very different wavelengths. As long as we live in the earthly city, we cannot escape it or take noninvolvement for granted. But we are primarily citizens of God's city, pilgrims on a journey to the blessedness of eternal fellowship with God.[13]

Augustine's vision offers helpful resources for challenging both ends of the extreme positions. In response to the first extreme, we insist that the city of the world and the city of God should never be confused with each other. No one should be surprised, Christians least of all, that the Roman Empire, founded on fratricide, went the way of all earthly empires. Even at their best, human institutions are sinking ships that are not, to use Paul Tillich's phrase, of "ultimate concern."[14] After the Roman emperors had shifted their religious devotion to Christ, at just the time that there would be a temptation to merge the empire with the church, Hosius, bishop of Cordova, onetime advisor to Constantine, rebuked Emperor Constantius II for his attempts to control the church:

> Intrude not yourself into Ecclesiastical matters, neither give commands unto us concerning them; but learn them from us. God has put into your hands the kingdom; to us He has entrusted the affairs of His Church; and as he who would steal the empire from you would resist the ordinance of God, so likewise fear on your part lest by taking upon yourself the government of the Church, you become guilty of a great offence. It is written, "Render unto Caesar the things that are Caesar's, and unto God the things that are God's." Neither therefore is it permitted unto us to exercise an earthly rule, nor have you, Sire, any authority to burn incense.[15]

This degree of separation between church and state, without overlap, that Hosius recommends was unheard of at the time, for Roman emperors had always had the "authority to burn incense." Julius Caesar, in addition to his civil offices, was *pontifex maximus*, the chief priest of Rome, the head of the priestly college. It was typical for emperors after him to hold this religious position. Like his predecessors, Constantine retained the priestly title, but it was clear from the beginning that the empire's relationship with the Christian church was going to be very different. Even when the distinction between the two kingdoms blurred, as it sometimes would over the next millennium, it was always formally maintained.

At the same time, to challenge the other extreme, being a citizen of heaven (Phil 3:20) does not mean that one renounces all earthly citizenship. Paul retained his Roman citizenship, invoking its benefits and protections on multiple occasions (Acts 16:37–38; 22:25–29; 25:11). How could this be? The implication of the biblical witness, spelled out by Augustine, is that objects of love and desire, and therefore allegiances, are not zero-sum games. They need not be mutually exclusive, if—and this is the key point—they are rightly ordered. Allegiance or devotion to family is good, and it remains virtuous if it remains in its proper place. It becomes a vice if it is disordered, if one puts family ahead of God. Likewise, support of a sports team is morally permissible, unless one's devotion to the team is put ahead of family. The devotion or allegiance then is disordered, and this is what makes it impermissible. To support family or one's favorite team does not mean you support everything that every representative of it says or does. Of course, there may come a point at which the team's actions are so wicked that it becomes difficult to support it at all. But subordinate love for or devotion to a created thing, in and of itself, is not wrong or incompatible with primary love for God.

In the same way, not all governments and political parties are created equal. Some are better than others. None is perfect, and none is of ultimate concern. But to recognize "a notion of dual citizenship in both the kingdom of God and in the nation-state" is not necessarily "complicated," nor is it per se a setting aside of the lordship of Jesus.[16] At least it is no more complicated than maintaining other human loves for created things in their proper order. If by dual citizenship we mean that being an American is equally important as being a Christian, then such dual citizenship is out of the question for a Christian. But has any thoughtful Christian suggested such a thing? For Christians, dual citizenship simply recognizes the inarguable fact that we live in two realms at once. If you lawfully reside in an earthly city, you are its citizen, by definition. Does a citizen have no duty to her city and fellow citizens? If earthly allegiance means "unquestioning obedience to an empire,"[17] then only God deserves that. But does any thoughtful Christian advocate "unquestioning obedience" to an earthly authority?

Allegiance to one's homeland and devotion to one's neighbors are not incompatible with primary allegiance to and worship of the true God. If they are, then devotion to family is just as compromised and dangerous, and all cheering for your child's sports team against another should be denounced as unloving. On the contrary, pre-Constantinian Christians knew the difference between earthly patriotism and divine worship and knew that they could be held together in their proper order. For instance, just before he offers prayer for civil authorities, Clement of Rome praises the Jewish heroine Judith (and, in similar language, Esther) for her "love of the fatherland (*patris*) and of the people."[18]

Proper boundaries may be crossed, of course. For example, devotion to the American flag could come to resemble the way military standards were treated in pagan Rome—namely, like idols. The line can be blurred, but it can be blurred with any love or allegiance, not just love for a country. For early Christians, the wedge of exclusive separation was not between proper patriotism and devotion to God; rather, patriotism and devotion to God were on one side, and on the other side was the worship of the state, burning incense to the genius of Caesar as a god, and declaring him to be Lord. Those practices were over the line. But paying honor to Caesar and showing love for country were not.

Thus, contrary to the historiography of Yoder and his followers, early, pre-Constantinian Christians did not think that love of country is somehow incompatible with Christian devotion. We may add that they did not avoid deferential but firm appeal to government officials on behalf of Christian principles. For example, note how the second-century apologists petitioned government officials. Justin Martyr addressed his *First Apology* to Emperor Antoninus Pius and "the sacred Senate." In it, he begged the emperor to hear his suit and pass judgment without prejudice. He demanded that the charges against Christians be investigated fairly.[19] He concluded with a warning that the emperor will be judged by God if he does not do what is right.[20] Justin wasn't exploiting any status or cooperating with evil or using coercion, but he worked within the system to effect change in a Christian direction (unsuccessful though he was in his own day). Athenagoras, in his *Plea for the Christians*, addressed the emperors Marcus Aurelius and Commodus as the "greatest of kings" (*megaloi basileon*), urging their consideration of the case against Christians.[21] Later, he described the emperors as upright and benevolent, assuring them that Christians pray for their government, that "the empire may receive increase and addition" and that all people would come under its sway, so all can live peaceably.[22] The apologist showed due honor to and attempted to cooperate with hostile, pagan rulers. It is clear that early Christians were able to speak deferentially to the pagan emperors, wish them earthly success—this sounds like allegiance—and promote love of country without compromising their ultimate love for God.

These observations from the early church are consistent with the typical picture presented in Scripture of God's people living in earthly society. Jeremiah 29:4–7 offers sound advice for the people of God who lived as aliens and strangers in Babylonian exile. Though exiles, it is not for God's people to upset the stability of the land in which they have been involuntarily located. Instead, they are to make it their homeland—build homes and settle, raise a family, and plant roots. "Seek the shalom," the well-being, of the city of the world, and pray for it. God's people will find their shalom in the city's shalom (Jer 29:7). While in exile, seek the peace and prosperity of the city, for if it prospers, its citizens, including God's people, will prosper. The earthly city, our country, our neighborhoods, filled as they are with our neighbors, are not the city of God, but they are worthy of our love and devotion. As God's people, we are called to labor for the state's peace and welfare.

Romans 13:1–7 is Paul's most well-known statement about civil government, and so it deserves attention. First of all, what does it mean for the government to be ordained by God? From the Christian perspective, Paul seems to exalt civil authority; it is from God. The civil government is God's servant; the authorities are his ministers (Rom 13:4, 6). These are the same kinds of words used to describe church workers. The authorities are ordained by God and therefore, in some sense, on God's team. What Paul means is that God is sovereign over all of it.

What are the government's responsibilities to the citizens? According to Paul in Romans 13, the governing authority is to be an avenger, a punisher of those who do wrong (Rom 13:3–4). In other words, the government is to uphold justice and punish criminals, to protect its citizens. The government's task of vengeance or just punishment is to be contrasted with Paul's point a few verses earlier—that vengeance does not belong to the individual but to God (Rom 12:19). Vengeance is not ours. It is not the task of individuals to inflict punishment. Individuals in community should never repay evil with evil. Vengeance belongs to God. His instrument or executor of that punishment? The civil government that he ordained for this purpose. Early Christians echoed Paul's point. The civil government, according to Irenaeus, is established by God to check the injustice and violence of the wicked.[23]

Back to our main question: What are the Christian's responsibilities to the government? Respect and submit. These duties are utterly reasonable when we consider the overall message of Scripture. In addition, according to 1 Timothy 2:1–2, we are to pray for those in authority (cf. Jer 29:7). We should pray for them to rule with wisdom and be guided by godly principles.

These and other biblical texts that speak to political matters flow from the command to love our neighbors and from the theological conviction that all people are made in the image of God. We are motivated by this love to seek the peace and prosperity of the city, acting on behalf of our neighbor.

CHRISTIAN INVOLVEMENT

The (over) 1,000-year experiment of joining church and state in Europe proved disastrous to Christianity on that continent. It is understandable that Christians and non-Christians alike would not want our society to repeat the abuses of power associated with Christian empires of the past. The fear of "Constantinianism" or of blurring the distinction between the two kingdoms keeps many Christians out of political matters altogether. After all, what does Washington have to do with Jerusalem? What does the worldly kingdom have to do with the kingdom of God? As Jeremiah 29 indicates, much in every way.

On the nonparticipation end of the spectrum, there seems to be a misconception about what human government is, along with a failure to notice that it is simply a partnership or community that seeks the good of the citizens or residents. It is analogous to any human organization that sets rules and boundaries. It might be helpful, then, to think about Christian involvement in political matters if we dial down our conception of government a few notches. When we think about government, and then the Christian's relationship to it, we tend to begin with the largest possible specimens, say, the US federal government. But let's start smaller.

As an entirely hypothetical analogy, imagine a neighborhood HOA (homeowners' association), run by one person who has the final decision on how to spend the homeowners' monthly dues. He has almost always been fair, to the satisfaction of nearly every homeowner (again, it's hypothetical). You are a Christian, and you live next door to him. One day, you make small talk and ask about neighborhood politics. He mentions that a few residents are petitioning him for certain extravagant amenities, and he then asks what you think. The proposed expenditures seem wasteful to you. Your judgments about these HOA affairs, as in everything you think and do, are informed by your Christian principles, and you engage him, a non-Christian, on that basis.

Our local and federal governments are analogous to the HOA. Indeed, there are many quantitative and perhaps some qualitative differences, but the subject is a community of people, paying a tax, submissive to a governing system.

The typical HOA is run not by a single director but by a board of directors who are residents, representing all the residents. Should I refuse to participate in an HOA vote, saying that it is worldly business, not the business of the church, to decide how to spend HOA funds to which I also contribute? And if such a distinction is made, now we have really segregated Christian religion from the rest of life. In other words, my opinion about the proposed amenities is informed, like every opinion I have, by my Christian principles and guidance of the Spirit. If all Christians decide not to give input, what will happen?

In a monarchy or oligarchy, a citizen could be more easily excused for nonparticipation in a system in which matters of the state lie with the king and his counsel. In a democratic republic, however, the political system is established precisely to allow citizens to have a voice. We are invited every two years to choose political officials to represent us and our concerns. Our representatives are, or should be, soliciting our opinions. We should give those opinions, in the voting booth and otherwise, in ways that reflect our Christian values. Certainly this form of government comes with a sense of opportunity, responsibility, and risk for citizens. Participation by individual Christians in this process should not be confused with the whole of one's Christian duty or witness to the world, and certainly most Christian service to the world happens outside of civic political structures. But if Christian citizens say that they will not vote or participate in the political process or run for office—because it is not God's kingdom or the choices are less than ideal—then they are at least partly to blame for having a society that constantly legislates and judges against Christian principles.

When my city's independent school district sought to implement a radical sex education program in the public school system, a grassroots organization of parents and concerned citizens, called Stand Up for Children, was formed to combat it. A few of the group's representatives were able to get an audience with a staff member from the governor's office to share their legitimate concerns about the legality and propriety of the proposed curriculum. As their meeting drew to a close, the staff member mentioned that she welcomed more communication from this group, emphasizing that representatives from the opposing perspective were there lobbying and making their case *all the time*. When Christians stand on the sidelines and assume that political action has little or nothing to do with matters related to the kingdom of God, or they don't want to "mix politics and religion," then, by default, they leave governance to all the non- and anti-Christian agendas. Not surprisingly, such agendas are not usually conducive to building and maintaining a moral or flourishing society.[24]

WHEN GOVERNMENT GOES BAD

The government, to one Christian writer and audience, may be God's servant (*diakonos*) and minister (*leitourgos*) (Rom 13:4, 6). To another Christian writer and audience, the government is the great harlot (*pornē*) (Rev 17:1). As stated above, depending on the type of government and the ones who hold power, some political entities are better than others. Some governments shirk their duty and, rather than protect their law-abiding citizens, punish them unjustly. This recognition of unique situations raises the question: If the government, though ordained by God, is run by evil rulers or makes laws contrary to Christian faith and morals, what is the Christian's responsibility then?

First, what about when the ruling class is wicked? How is a Christian to vote when the choice is between two corrupt candidates? Is it justifiable to choose "the lesser of two evils"? Christians are followers of Christ, among other reasons, because we believe it is the best way to live. Naturally, then, we look for candidates who are intelligent and wise, but also who uphold Christian principles and virtue. It's the best way to conduct society. We seek leaders who embody courage, temperance, justice, fidelity, hope, love, trustworthiness, integrity, honesty, humility, and self-control. We desire representatives who will support the centrality of the family unit as the foundation of society and the protection of innocent life. If you find someone with those qualities, which ought to be commonplace among Christians, then you've found someone you can trust your life to.

Since no government or candidate is perfectly good, any choice for a candidate has always been in some sense a choice between two evils. No candidate and no platform, and not much of anything we support in this life, will ever be perfect. Many important decisions in life involve choices that are less than perfect. My joining the opposition to a transfer station at the garbage dump does not mean that I endorse every opinion expressed against it. My support for Stand Up for Children does not oblige me to inquire about the theological beliefs of every member. The candidate I vote for may not live up to every standard I would prefer. It doesn't mean that no cooperation with a politician is possible or godly.

And this is where responsibility meets risk. As we have noted, sometimes the values of the kingdom of God and of the kingdom of the world track very closely together. At other times, their pursuits diverge, perhaps drastically so. As a post-Christian society, we are now in the latter time. Christians who answer the invitation to participate in a national election have very hard questions to ask themselves. Sometimes a candidate or a movement is so tainted by vice, is so harmful to the public good, that any association is suspicious. In such cases, the burden may be on the Christian to explain his qualified support. At some point, the available candidates or party platforms may be so full of vice that a Christian cannot, with good conscience, cast a ballot at all. Maybe a third party is not available or amounts to voting for one of the two major candidates. If the action is engaged with serious Christian understanding and motivated by seeking the peace of the city, then both options—voting for the less imperfect and refusing to vote for any sinful person or platform—should be respected.

Is civil disobedience ever justified from a Christian perspective? Is it morally permissible for a Christian to disobey the civil government? If so, then under what circumstances? Martin Luther King Jr., channeling Thomas Aquinas and the Christian tradition, said that an unjust law is no law at all.[25] It is a well-established principle that one should obey the civil laws unless they contradict God's laws. Scripture repeatedly confirms that there is a time for civil disobedience. In addition to clear-cut cases where the government commands something immoral, there are also more ambiguous cases in which the government may forbid something good. In Daniel 6, Darius commands no one to pray except to him. Daniel could have prayed to God in the privacy of his own room; he could have been publicly in compliance with the new law, but also without sinning. Yet he continued to open his windows and pray where he could be seen. In Acts 4, Peter and John are forbidden by the Jewish authorities to preach in the name of Jesus. Conceivably, they could have gone back to their corner of Jerusalem and carried on their Christian devotion in silence, preaching under cover. Yet they chose to defy the rulers and evangelize openly. "We must obey God rather than people" (Acts 5:29).

Perhaps the oft-cited principle that "we must obey the civil law unless it contradicts God's law" puts the emphasis in the wrong place, and it should be supplemented with the equally important principle that "our citizenship is in heaven." For Christians, the object of obedience shouldn't start with the government. The primary loyalty of the Christian is not to civil government, but to God. Reversing the emphasis is a subtle point that may be expressed thus: We must obey God; when the civil law is in harmony with God's law, we should obey it too.

In the clear-cut cases, of course, we stand firm on Christian principles and let the chips fall where they may. We will not bow to idols. The civil disobedience of people like the three Hebrew children, Daniel, and the apostles was never violent, and those who disobeyed were willing to suffer the consequences of their disobedience. In cases that involve more gray area, which is probably the majority of cases, wisdom from the Spirit and discernment by a properly trained conscience are necessary. In such instances, we shouldn't stand in judgment against the "Daniels" who openly defy. Neither should we stand against those who are more subtle in their adherence to Christ, who pray behind closed doors and work within their circumstances, surviving today in order to instigate a revolution tomorrow.

CONCLUSION

What does love require of the Christian with regard to political action? As stated already, love of neighbor motivates the citizens of God's kingdom to pray for and actively seek the peace and welfare of the city of the world. This calling requires some level of engagement with and knowledge of the world. In a world of global politics, the task can seem overwhelming because the problems and the proposed solutions are too complicated for amateurs to follow. When we think about politics, our minds most often jump to national and global politics. This fact reflects how inundated we are by national, corporate media and how little we think about our own local communities that affect our daily lives.

I would suggest that, when we think about politics and our involvement in it, we think first about the local community. Start with your neighborhood and move out from there. There are good reasons for this recommendation. First, it may be that, especially on the national level, using political means to influence culture in a Christian direction is no longer effective. Rod Dreher has made the point that the so-called "culture wars" have been lost by Christians.[26] Those who defend the Christian faith and ethics found in this book, once in the majority, are now in the minority. This new situation of Christian principles being unwelcome in public discourse is perhaps a welcome wake-up call to Christians who have too easily assumed the correspondence between the two cities. The primary freedom worth defending publicly is the freedom to practice one's religion. Otherwise, the church's energy and resources should be marshaled to help the church be what it was called to be all along—the body of Christ, a people formed by the crucifixion and resurrection of Christ.

Another reason to stay local is that it is primarily in one's community that a difference can be made. One of the problems with engaging only the national and global news, especially when it is bad, is that one feels helpless about it. What can I do about Trump's latest tweet? What can I do about the coronavirus surge in Florida? Not much. I feel awful about it all, but that news doesn't usually affect my life directly, and there is nothing I can do about it. This common experience leaves us feeling anxious and perhaps even depressed. But I can start in my neighborhood and my city. I can pick up the trash on my street. I can help the sick and refrain from bad tweets. I can meet my local representatives and see what's going on in the schools and community.

What I am recommending here is not political activism that gets caught up in the latest outrage of the moment or consists in shouting slogans on social media or merely carrying picket signs. Rather, it is working for the common, public good to bring peace and joy to our communities. The best way to do this is simply to be a good Christian and love our neighbors, to be salt, leaven, and light in the world. As Origen said, Christians are actually the best citizens of the Roman Empire. "Christians do more good to their countries than the rest of mankind, since they educate the citizens and teach them to be devoted to God, the guardian of their city; and they take those who have lived good lives in the most insignificant cities up to a divine and heavenly city."[27]

In light of Scripture, Christian tradition, and sound reason, it seems that our actions should flow from the following principles. When the government's goals are in line with God's reign, then there is no need to oppose the government as evil simply because it is not God or his church. As with other worldly institutions that lie somewhere on the spectrum between immutably good (God) and entirely evil (nonexistence), we should work to improve it. When an aspect of the government seems irreparably evil, we may need to take leave of it. Good or evil, the present government, if it's like every other human government and institution, will pass away. It is not the kingdom of God and should never be confused with the kingdom of God.

No doubt, we are, first and foremost, citizens of the kingdom of Christ, the true king who lived and died and rose again for us. At the same time, the best citizens of this country are those whose first allegiance is to Christ, who are guided by his Holy Spirit, and who strive to imitate the God and Father of perfect and holy love. So let us make a difference in this world—first, by making a difference in our homes and in our neighborhoods.

DISCUSSION QUESTIONS

1. What are some important similarities between managing a family or homeowners' association and a state or federal government? What are some important differences?
2. Where do you fit on the spectrum between American civil religion and Christian nonparticipation?
3. How have people in general or Christians in particular been unnecessarily disrespectful of and insubordinate to the government?
4. In addition to voting, how have you attempted to persuade politicians or the public to your opinion?
5. Has Christian political involvement ever made the church look bad? What lesson should we learn?

CHAPTER 12

Identity and Race

I have a dream my four little children will one day live in a nation where they will not be judged by the color of their skin but by the content of their character.
—Martin Luther King Jr.[1]

Race and rhetoric have gone together for so long that it is easy to forget that facts also matter—and these facts often contradict many widely held beliefs. Fantasies and fallacies about racial and ethnic issues have had a particularly painful and deadly history, so exposing some of them is more than an academic exercise. . . . It may be optimistic merely to suggest that racial or ethnic issues can be discussed rationally. Evidence to the contrary is all too abundant in the strident and sweeping condemnations directed against many who have tried to do so.
—Thomas Sowell[2]

It is a real challenge—and perhaps impossible—to think of a social issue more fraught with misunderstanding and controversy than that of race, especially in the United States. It is a contentious topic both outside and within the church. History testifies that there is perhaps no issue more divisive than race relations. For these reasons, it is tempting to avoid the topic. For these same reasons, however, it is more important than ever that Christians go to Scripture, not to the extremes of popular culture, to form our thinking about matters related to race and identity.

Limited space here does not allow us to discuss the multiple causes of and proposed solutions to racial inequalities and tensions. The topic is huge, and there is no way to address all the important angles. In this chapter, we will focus mainly on what Scripture has to say about a few issues relevant to race relations, and then we will consider the demands of Christian love from this biblical perspective. Sadly, Scripture is too often neglected in discussions of race, even among Christians.

SCRIPTURE

For our purposes in this study, we can describe racism as the belief that one race is naturally superior to or has more inherent worth than another.[3] Closely connected to this belief, then, is disrespect toward or even contempt for members of races other than one's own. These attitudes may result in hateful behaviors such as discrimination on the basis of race or skin color.

When we go to Scripture with these questions of race in mind, we find strong testimony that racism is morally impermissible. First of all, as with other points discussed throughout this book, the question of racism is decided by the foundational belief that all humans are created in the image of God (Gen 1:27). Scripture recognizes the fact of different tribes and nations, but it nowhere affirms that certain people groups have a greater or lesser share in God's image. The second greatest love command, to love your neighbor as yourself, obviously forbids looking down on or despising another person, particularly for an immutable characteristic such as skin tone. In the parable of the good Samaritan, Jesus made it abundantly clear that neighbor love is not limited to one's own people group, but it extends to everyone.

Many passages indicate that one of God's purposes in creation and redemption is for all people to live together in justice and in harmony, regardless of race or ethnicity. With his blood, the Lamb bought people "from every tribe and tongue and people and nation" (Rev 5:9). The universal intent expressed in the book of Revelation is confirmed elsewhere. God "wills all people to be saved and to come to knowledge of the truth" (1 Tim 2:4). Even when God seemed to favor Israel in the Old Testament, it was so that Israel would be a light to the nations, for the purpose of the world's salvation. Israel was not favored in order to be relieved of responsibility and culpability. Their covenant relationship with God meant more responsibility and greater punishment for their infidelity (Amos 3:1–2). And that covenant was not restricted to physical descent. Rahab the Canaanite was spared for her faithfulness in Jericho (Josh 6:25), and she was included in the covenant and in the covenant people's royal and messianic genealogy (Matt 1:5). By contrast, Achan the Israelite was judged and executed for his unfaithfulness in Jericho (Josh 7:20–26). The difference was spiritual, a matter of the heart—not a matter of race or nation. The New Testament brings the point into focus: God does not show favoritism between ethnic groups (Acts 10:34; Rom 2:11). Part of becoming like God, then, is to imitate him in this respect. That is, if God does not show favoritism, neither should we. Favoritism is explicitly forbidden for God's people (Jas 2:1). Favoritism is called sin (Jas 2:9), whether it is based on race, socioeconomic status, age, or ability.

Christians in the past have used the mark placed on Cain (Gen 4:15) to justify racism. The mark, however, was for one individual, and it was meant to protect him, not to bring him under the dominion and oppression of others. The curse upon Canaan (Gen 9:24–27) has also been used to justify white supremacy as well as slavery. In fact, this passage also has nothing to do with racism, much less racism against blacks. Rather, it is about the enmity between Canaanites and Semites that would play out in Israel's early history. Early Christians also understood that temporary curse to be reversed in Christ, who has brought all people together as one.[4] It is wrong to use Genesis 9 or any other biblical passage to promote favoritism or justify race-based chattel slavery.

THE SITUATION TODAY

Despite the fact that the Christian message of human dignity and equality has permeated Western society, racial tensions persist and have increased to a fever pitch. The grievances of the past figure prominently in the discussion of race. On the basis of the passages surveyed above and others like them, Christians do not hesitate to condemn slavery, the forced segregation of Jim Crow laws, and all instances of legally sanctioned race-based discrimination, common in the United States before the Civil Rights Acts of 1964. But after acknowledging perpetrated evils of the past, it is difficult to know what to do about them in the present. It is undoubtedly true that the injustices permitted under Jim Crow were not sufficiently acknowledged after they came to an end. It is important to recover the true history. How, though, would we now prosecute crimes that are over sixty years old? It cannot be by seeking retribution now, say, by punishing whites who were not even alive. In addition to being simply wrong, it would destroy any semblance of unity that remains in the body politic.

And what about the injustices of today? Tremendous progress has been made since the days of slavery and of Jim Crow. The Civil Rights Act of 1964 made institutional discrimination on the basis of race illegal, and the Fair Housing Act of 1968 further specified fairness in housing opportunities. By all accounts, the phenomenon of conscious or intentional racism has improved over the last half century. These facts, however, do not mean that all personal racism and discrimination ended overnight or that it doesn't persist among some individuals. It also doesn't mean that there aren't lingering effects of racist policies enacted prior to the civil rights acts of the 1960s.

Certain inequalities remain for many minorities in the United States, particularly in areas such as lower education, income, and housing, as well as higher crime. The inequality most frequently cited by the media is police racism and brutality against blacks. When there is racism (again, as defined above), then racists should be held accountable, and Christians in particular should work to make the wrongs right. Inequality of outcome, however, does not necessarily mean that racism is to blame. As a society that seeks effective prescriptions and solutions, then, it is imperative that we have the correct diagnosis. It is likely that the vast majority of people agree on the end—people living together in harmony and with equal opportunities—but disagree on the means of achieving it.

IDENTITY POLITICS

The means that is most prominent in popular culture today for responding to racial tension and achieving racial justice is related to so-called identity politics. In the case of race, people are being trained more and more to see everything through the lens of race. For example, in contrast to the desire to be "color blind" or to judge people only "by the content of their character," as Martin Luther King Jr. urged, many now consider the neutrality and racial equality implied by those phrases to be racist. In the influential book *White Fragility*, Robin DiAngelo speaks of "color-blind racism" and spends several pages arguing that people cannot literally avoid seeing race.[5] Ibram Kendi calls the drive for race-neutrality "the most threatening racist movement."[6] When race becomes the lens for everything, then any inequality or injustice—and life is full of both—can be and often is interpreted as racial discrimination. Anything said or done, regardless of intent, can be taken as a racist microaggression.

In a world ruled by identity politics, we are encouraged to think of ourselves first as a white straight female or a black gay male, and so on, and then to value some of those intersectional identities over others. Our society, after deciding over fifty years ago that it was wrong to discriminate based on physical characteristics that you generally can't help, has recently decided that it's better to prejudge based on these same characteristics. It's hard to fathom, but ongoing discrimination is precisely what some are calling for. As Kendi puts it, "The only remedy to racist discrimination is antiracist discrimination. The only remedy to past discrimination is present discrimination. The only remedy to present discrimination is future discrimination."[7] Kendi promotes discrimination, apparently until there is complete equity—an impossible endeavor to quantify and to satisfy. In effect, it is a call for endless discrimination based especially on the superficiality of skin color.[8]

To be sure, people have always tended to tribalism and finding their identity in external things such as earthly citizenship or economic class. Today's identity politics, however, differs from the tribalisms of the past in at least four ways. First, the identities emphasized are somewhat different from those in ancient cultures, which focused more on civic and ethnic identities. Our culture focuses more than past cultures on skin color, gender, and sexual orientation. Second, the categories and thus the possible intersectional identities are more numerous now than ever before. Our pluralistic, global culture opens up a dizzying array of distinctions to accentuate. Third, the identities and categorizations are often viewed as truly unique and without analogy. Some of these identities are too complex even to be easily spoken or described.[9] Since your intersectional identity is thought to be incommensurate with mine, then mutual understanding becomes impossible, and antagonism results. And finally, the identities that used to shape people have faded, leaving a vacuum to be filled. Identities were once shaped primarily by a sense of belonging to a faith community and a state or country, by being a part of a stable nuclear family in proximity to an extended family, and by having a workplace. But now fewer people belong to a faith community, and a sense of unity or even pride in one's country is no longer a commonly shared value. People now live far away from extended family, and even the nuclear family has broken down dramatically. It is also increasingly rare for a person to work at the same job or company for decades, or people simply work from home in virtual isolation. With the loss of church, family, work, and neighborhood ties, it is no wonder that more people than ever are experiencing an identity crisis. Intersectional identity politics appeals to a culture in an identity crisis.[10]

A CHRISTIAN IDENTITY

This short chapter clearly cannot address all the complex issues related to race. But we can ask whether Scripture has anything relevant to say about it all. First, with regard to the sins of the past, there may be some guidance in the book of Nehemiah. After the return from Babylonian captivity, we are told that the Israelites "confessed their sins and the wickedness of their fathers" (Neh 9:2). The prayer goes on to recount Israel's cyclical history, familiar to anyone who has read the historical books of the Old Testament: God's people fall away, they are oppressed, they cry out to God, God rescues them, they fall away again, and so on. As Nehemiah's community looked back on their own history, it is the continual falling away that they were confessing and their subsequent plight that they were lamenting. The postexilic people saw themselves as part of that cycle, so their own present sins are, in some sense, a reprise of the past sins.

Although white Christians today are not personally responsible for the racist sins of past generations, this account from Nehemiah provides biblical precedent for acknowledging the sins of those who came before us, and this acknowledgment leads those who are white to introspection concerning our own wickedness. Thus, if we find ourselves in institutions that benefitted from slavery or practiced enforced discrimination, then it is appropriate and even necessary to confess those sins. Many Christian colleges and congregations have engaged in just this kind of collective repentance and reconciliation. Once confession and contrite repentance (including restitution, when possible) have been made, then forgiveness can and should follow as a necessary part of reconciliation.

And what about present-day troubles and, what is often seen as the way forward, the current emphasis on distinct racial (and other) identities? When we turn to Scripture to assess the importance of racial categories, we find clear and compelling counsel, especially in the situation of ethnic Jews and gentiles, one that is in many ways analogous to our day. There was no greater threat to the unity of the first-century church than the hostility between Jews and gentiles. Outside of the church, in the Mediterranean world, Jews and gentiles, generally speaking, held one another in contempt. By the first century, the mutual antagonism was already ancient. Gentile pagans had conquered Jews and tried to destroy their culture and sometimes religion, they burdened the Jews with inequitable taxes, and the occupiers commonly treated the Jews as less than human. In turn, the Jews often resisted, sometimes with armed force, and they commonly treated their pagan neighbors as less than human. Each group could point to grievances and annoyances—past and present—to justify their hatred of the other. Besides a forced environment like a workplace, Jews and gentiles generally would not willingly mingle together. That is, except for in the church. The Christian church was the one social body in which Jews and gentiles would voluntarily unite. And even then, it was not always easy, as the New Testament makes abundantly clear.

The churches in Ephesus and Asia Minor were not immune to this struggle, so Paul addresses it in Ephesians 2:11–22. He addresses the gentile Christians first. They are, most likely, "God-fearing" gentiles, that is, synagogue adherents who did not have full membership in the Jewish community. They have been excluded, marginalized, and called "uncircumcision" by those called "circumcision," that is, the "handmade" circumcision (Eph 2:11). Something "handmade" usually has a negative connotation in the Bible, for instance, as a description of idols and of the earthly temple-turned-idol. In other words, Paul is saying that outward circumcision is not the characteristic that really counts; what counts is the inward circumcision of the heart. What Paul describes here is a situation of hostility between two groups, one that is not easily reversed or reconciled. There is bad blood between Jews and gentiles. What possible solution is there?

Paul explains that "now in Christ Jesus you who at one time being far away have come near by the blood of Christ" (Eph 2:13). By abolishing the external marks that divided these groups, he has "create[d] in him, the two into one new man, making peace" (2:15). As he did in the original creation, God makes a new man or group, this time out of two divided groups. In this way, he "killed hostility." How? In Christ (2:16). "Through him, we both have access in one Spirit to the Father" (2:18). Christ has accomplished the reconciliation of humanity to God and to each other. Because of this reconciliation, no one is excluded from citizenship in God's kingdom any longer (see 2:12). Now we are all "fellow citizens" of God's house (2:19). Note the building analogy that Paul uses. We are members of God's house, the building itself. Here, in God's house or household, we belong and find our identity. In Christ, the building is joined together (2:21). Christ is the glue that holds everything together; he is the building's cement and the nails.

We often think about our relationship *with God* being made right and regulated through Christ, the one mediator between God and humanity. And it's true. But we often fail to see that it is Christ who also reconciles *humans with one another*. What does this mean? First, it means that my relationship with you is mediated through Christ. It's not just you and I; it's you and I through Christ. We don't relate to each other, at least not deeply or in an eternally meaningful way, except through Christ. This fundamental belief should affect the way we treat each other. Second, we are not defined or identified by anything other than our union with Christ. He has taken the two old groups and created something new, one new man. In Christ, there is no liberal versus conservative, Democrat versus Republican, black versus white. To Paul, these are "handmade" or external characteristics that some people may notice, but the Lord does not. These categories don't ultimately define us, and they sure don't divide us or create hostility. They are of relative importance. As Christians, we can only get so excited, to a limited degree, about our political party, our sports team, our patriotism, or any of our earthly allegiances or identity markers. We are a new creation.

This grand vision is absolutely contrary to the ubiquitous, dangerous, and destructive ideology of identity politics. Such identity politics should not appeal to those whose identity is found in Christ and who, through Christ, have access to the Father and to one another. Indeed, if you are a Christian who is Hispanic or white or same-sex-attracted or whatever, that is not the extent of your identity; it's not even your primary identity. It all pales in comparison to being in Christ.

It is true that the apostle Paul sees some advantages in being a Jew (Rom 3:1–2; 9:1–5). To be clear, the advantage of receiving God's revelation entails a heavier responsibility and greater culpability, but it is still an advantage. On this one level, Paul seems to have relished in his Jewish heritage. On this same level, then, there is nothing wrong with enjoying and celebrating one's own or someone else's cultural heritage. But when it comes to salvation and one's identity in Christ, Paul's tone changes dramatically. On that level, he does not extol one cultural heritage over another. All are under sin, and all are justified by God's grace alone (Rom 3:22–24). In Christ, "there is no Greek and Jew, circumcised and uncircumcised, barbarian, Scythian, slave, free" (Col 3:11). Such contingencies bow the knee to Christ. Throughout all of Paul's writings, the message is that these things don't matter in Christ, and Paul has a harsh word for people who think such things affect one's worth or treatment. Paul is a Hebrew of Hebrews, yet compared to his identity in Christ, he says it's all dung (Phil 3:4–11).

While the current culture exalts this new, extreme brand of identity politics, a Christian's principal identity is in Christ as a member of God's family. Perhaps we cannot help but be shaped by our embodied circumstances, but these identities are subordinate in Christ. Those identities and loyalties fade from view and are eclipsed by, as Ephesians 2:15 says, the new man, which is Christ. We are in Christ; we *are* his body. We are Christ. Christ is our identity.

This good news—that the gentiles are going to receive the inheritance too—is the mystery now revealed plainly (Eph 3:6).

The reconciliation of those formerly hostile groups is an implausible miracle. As such, it is a sign to the world and to the demons of God's plan of redemption (Eph 3:10–11). The same should be true today. The coming together of all people "in one Spirit into one body" (1 Cor 12:13) is a testimony to the world that harmony is possible. But when Christians join in race politics, our witness is compromised, and we become just another worldly institution divided into irreconcilable parties.

We must not dismiss the good intentions of many who promote identity politics for the goal of seeking justice. We must also not ignore any good messages that we need to hear. We should not be complicit in racism or in any systems that are unfair to people because of their race. We should speak out against it. We should also be willing to take a hard look at ourselves and see if we harbor any negative feelings about others based on their race or ethnic heritage. This introspective work must be done by all people.

Race isn't nothing, but it's also not everything. When people are encouraged to see everything, and especially their human struggles, through a racial perspective, then "the other" is always potentially or even actually racist. According to DiAngelo's *White Fragility*, when a white person denies being a racist, that alone is proof of racism. As many have pointed out, the logic is reminiscent of the water ordeal to determine whether one is a witch—if you float, you're a witch and should be burned; if you sink and drown, then you were innocent. Of course, if everyone is racist, then no one is a racist. Because "racist" has been expanded to include virtually every white person, the word has been effectively watered down and emptied of meaning. Not only has the charge now become meaningless, but its new, expanded use is a genuine insult to actual victims of racism and a minimizing of their experiences.

Healthy introspection is one thing. It is quite another thing, however—and some might say racist—to charge an entire race of people as racists, and the accusation unsurprisingly invites the very reactions of incredulity that DiAngelo claims as proof of racism. Sadly, but also inevitably, being unfairly denounced as a racist could lead some people to react in truly racist ways. In addition, it is equally demeaning and no less racist to categorize an entire race of people or the totality of minority groups as victims who cannot fend for themselves. To tell someone that, because of your skin color, you need to be given a leg up to succeed, is to infantilize them. Sadly, but also inevitably, some will believe the hype and view themselves not as responsible agents but as bound to poverty or incapable of success.

Contrary to the new cultural wisdom, the point of recommending "color blindness" is not to erase individual characteristics, to assimilate everyone to one dominant ethnic culture, or, much less, to claim that one cannot actually see color. The point is to avoid prejudging a person based on skin color, just as we would not prejudge a person for being short or tall. We might notice a person's height or age and therefore help in appropriate ways, but it shouldn't make any meaningful difference to our love for that person, nor should we undermine that person's own dignity, agency, and sense of responsibility by encouraging a narrative of perpetual victimhood. The goal of being "color blind" is absolutely in accord with the truth that, whereas humans tend to look at the outward appearance, "the Lord looks at the heart" (1 Sam 16:7). Our aim should be the same. It is the sentiment that lies behind Galatians 3:28: "There is neither Jew nor Greek." It is not that there are actually no physical differences, but those differences are unimportant when it comes to virtue or to salvation in Christ.

Now, sometimes our diverse perspectives help us see Scripture and life from different angles. Those different angles are beneficial if they are in accord with Scripture and the core teachings of the Christian faith, if they point us to Christ, and if they inspire true love of God and neighbor. The question is whether a given perspective excludes and divides us from other Christians. If our intersectional identity becomes the primary lens through which we see Scripture and one another, then it could lead to marginalizing other voices, presumably the very thing that we wanted to avoid. So we need to be careful when we take over language and thought patterns from the world. We may be bringing in a Trojan horse that will conquer us from the inside.

Make no mistake: our culture today, not unlike the overtly racist cultures of the past, loves to group, label, and divide. And whatever does those things has no place in Christ's one body, the church. Identity politics makes our story—or *my* story—paramount and regulative. The gospel, by contrast, supersedes our story and calls us into another story—the story of redemption—demanding that we die to our old self and rise to a new identity in Christ, the only label that matters. The apostle Paul often addressed people who took notice of their own contingent, earthly identities. His admonition every time was that there is only one thing they should glory in. The Christian faith does not partition us into tribes, but instead brings the tribes together into one body. Here and now, we need, more than ever, to be countercultural. Our faith has a unitive function, narrating a story of unity: one God, creator and redeemer; one Son, human and divine; one revelation, Old and New Testaments; one goal, to recapitulate or unite under one head all creation and all people (Eph 1:10), for there is neither Jew nor Greek, slave nor free, male nor female (Gal 3:28).

CONCLUSION

What does love require? At the most basic level, we must commit to loving our neighbors, regardless of color or race. Such love includes seeking friendships with those from backgrounds different than our own. It means listening to their experiences before judging or dismissing them. It also means that when we hear that people in minority neighborhoods lack educational opportunities and suffer from high rates of violent crime, it should affect us in the same way as if we or our children lived there, and it should move us to act. Love demands that we work, through political processes but also personally, to rectify injustices wherever we find them. Love requires that no one should be prejudged, second-guessed, or pressured to apologize for the color of her skin. When we witness such blatant injustice, we reject it as ungodly.

Love also requires Christian unity. If there was ever a time for Christians to be united with one another, it is now. In a world that is increasingly hostile toward Christians of all nationalities and races, we should be coming together in solidarity with our brothers and sisters of all colors and backgrounds, those to whom we have been reconciled in Christ, in resisting bias and violence against Christians.

Yet the social divisions that plague the world threaten to infiltrate the church and wreak the same havoc among Christians. That infiltration is easily done, for if we are looking for evidence of mistreatment, we can surely find it, even in churches that are populated, as they all are, with the not-yet-perfect. Again, when the injustice is present and real, it needs to be confronted with honest and open conversation, repentance, and forgiveness. But there is only so much that dwelling on past sins will accomplish.

In the first century, did Jews and gentiles have past (and even present) grievances against one another? You bet they did! Did Paul say, let's focus on those grievances and parse them all out? No. If that had been the prerequisite for peace in the church, then peace never would have happened, for past grievances will never be redressed to everyone's satisfaction. In Christ, the hostility is killed. I have heard the following observation attributed to Martin Luther King Jr.: "We may have all come on different ships, but we're in the same boat now." Paul would agree. For Christians, that same boat that we are in is Christ. It matters less how we got here than that we are here together, seeking first the kingdom of God. Racism, whether in the form of blatant racial prejudice or of identity politics, focuses on our differences and obscures our similarities. It is so pernicious in the culture because it divides and is not actually making things better for anyone. It's poison to condemn racism while introducing identity politics. What's poison for society will be even worse for the church.

At the demise of South African apartheid, the Truth and Reconciliation Commission was formed to hear the stories of injustice and violence, allowing the oppressed to confront their oppressors, for the purpose of eventual reconciliation. The truth needs to be sought out and to be heard. One of those truths was famously expressed by Desmond Tutu: "There is no future without forgiveness." In situations of such complexity, this is perhaps the only rule that matters: there must be repentance for real, culpable actions and forgiveness for the penitent.

It is no coincidence that as Christ has faded from public view and the church strives to pursue peace outside of Christ, division is the result. History proves, if nothing else, that humans, left to their own devices, will divide and hate and destroy. Merely human solutions will ultimately fail to unite. Sloganeering will achieve nothing, but if there is a slogan that bears repeating, it is this: We are all one in Christ Jesus (Gal 3:28). Indeed, only Christ can kill the hostility. Only his gospel will accomplish reconciliation.

DISCUSSION QUESTIONS

1. Is racism a difficult topic for you to discuss with others? If so, what makes it so difficult? If not, why do you find it easy?
2. How do you imagine the color of your skin has affected your experience of the world? Has it created privilege and/or hardship for you in various circumstances?
3. What nuances do you think are missing in most discussions of race?
4. In what ways have you seen identity politics infiltrate the church?
5. Has it changed or broadened your perspective to have friends from backgrounds different than your own?
6. What concrete steps can you take to improve race relations in your spheres of influence?

CALLING
PART 3

CHAPTER 13

In the World but Not of It

Simply to say, what the soul is in the body, Christians are in the world. The soul is dispersed through all parts of the body, and Christians through the cities of the world. The soul dwells in the body, but it is not of the body; and Christians dwell in the world, but they are not of the world.

—Epistle to Diognetus *6.1–3*

Vice is a monster of so frightful mien,
As to be hated needs but to be seen;
Yet seen too oft, familiar with her face,
We first endure, then pity, then embrace.

—Alexander Pope[1]

Christian ethics is, of course, primarily for Christians. Because we believe that the moral order taught by the Christian faith is objectively true and universal, we strive to model it, and we recommend this way of life and love—which is to say, the way of Jesus Christ—to all people. We think the world would be a better place if everyone followed this path. At the same time, we do not expect non-Christians to submit to Christian standards. Paul made this clear when he commanded the Corinthian church to discipline their fellow brother for his sexual immorality. The discipline is for the immoral who are part of the church community, "not at all for the sexually immoral of this world" (1 Cor 5:10). He then says, "What is it to me to judge those outside? . . . God will judge those outside" (1 Cor 5:12–13).

Paul's point in 1 Corinthians 5 is not about condemning the world but about maintaining the purity of the body of Christ corporately and our own purity as individual members of Christ's body. As incorporated members of Christ's holy body, Paul expected the Corinthian Christians to follow the moral principles that he had taught them and that were laid out in the Hebrew Scriptures. When they didn't follow those instructions, it was troubling to Paul. The lack of obedience today should be equally troubling to us. This entire book is an exercise in Christian reflection, an attempt to hold a mirror before our own eyes. What do we see?

TWO WORLDS

Jesus prayed that his disciples might not be taken out of the world; they must remain in it. But while they are *in* the world, they must not be *of* the world (John 17:14–17). The ideal status, the sweet spot for all followers of Christ, is to be in the world but not of the world. Taken literally, "in the world" is the easy part. Be physically alive and present, and you are in the world. "Not of the world"—that's the hard part. But perhaps there is a bit more to it. These prepositions—both *in* and *of* or *from*—imply an important distinction that characterizes life in this liminal space between the first and second coming of Christ. Jesus' words suggest that the Christian position in relation to the world is both yes and no.

Indeed, *world* (*kosmos*) is an ambiguous term in the New Testament, and even within the Johannine literature. "God so loved the world" (John 3:16), but we should "not love the world" (1 John 2:15–17). These two verses may correspond to the same basic distinction that the two prepositions indicate in John 17. World in the first sense refers to the inherently good but fallen creation in need of redemption and reconciliation; this is the world viewed from above, from God's perspective. World in the second sense refers to the sinful temptations and rebellious forces of darkness that pull creation away from God—namely, "the lust of the flesh and the lust of the eyes and the pride of life" (1 John 2:16). This is the world viewed from below. These two senses could correspond to the paraphrase from John 17: in the world (sense 1), not of the world (sense 2).[2]

Consider the first sense. If we are to be God's ambassadors of reconciliation, then the disciples of Christ must engage the world at some level. To do so appropriately, we must learn to view the world from above and through God's eyes. This is the world that God so loved and we must love too. We cannot dichotomize God and world in a way that separates God from everything else. The religious life and God himself are not to be compartmentalized. God wants our whole lives—not the separation but the integration of God and all creation.

This world that God loves is broken and in need of redemption and reconciliation. Love means the reconciliation of the world back to God. If love aims at the reconciliation of God and the world that God so loves, then those who practice the ethics of love cannot ignore the world but must see both God and the world at the same time.

In this context, Dietrich Bonhoeffer advocates the idea of a worldly Christian, though not in the sense that one may initially think. The worldly Christian is not meant in the second sense of *world*, but in the first sense. Bonhoeffer explains, "It is a denial of

God's revelation in Jesus Christ to wish to be 'Christian' without being 'worldly,' or [to] wish to be worldly without seeing and recognizing the world in Christ."[3] In Christ, the incarnation of God the Word, we see the reconciliation, the actual joining together, of God and the world for its redemption. The object of our gaze, Bonhoeffer writes, should be simultaneously on God and the world reconciled, which is to say, on the God-man Christ.[4] This is what it means to look to and be transformed into the glory of Christ (2 Cor 3:18). When we follow Christ, formed by his Spirit into his image, we are embodying and imitating the true reconciliation of God and the world.

It is from similar motivations that some Christians speak of the cultural mandate to redeem the world for God. Just as God sent his Son to the world, Jesus Christ has sent his church to the world to proclaim the kingdom and ministry of reconciliation. As Abraham Kuyper affirmed, "there is not a square inch in the whole domain of our human existence" that does not belong to God.[5] Truly, this is our Father's world, the world we are to be "in."

What about the second sense of world, the world that we are *not* to love, the world we are not to be "of" or "from"? Loving the world, in this negative, second sense, is similar to loving this *age*. The Greek word for *age* (*aiōn*) is, in Latin, the source of our word *secular* (*saeculum*). It is a temporal moment, and "this age," in contrast to the coming age, is passing away. One of the greatest pains of Paul's final imprisonment was the fact that Demas deserted him. In 2 Timothy 4:10, we see that Demas, once a companion of Paul (Col 4:14), abandoned Paul. Why? Demas left "because he loved this present age." Paul uses the same word in Romans 12:2: "Do not be conformed to this age." There is no sense in conforming ourselves to a passing fad that will soon be obsolete.

Let us call this love for and conforming to the present age *secularism*. By secularism, I mean that which is "of the world" in the second sense—in other words, whatever Scripture is warning against in John 17:14–16 and 1 John 2:15–16. In this sense, we are to keep ourselves "unspotted from the world" (Jas 1:27). Secularism has to do with the influence of the world that we are not to love.

In its details, secularism will mean different things at different times. Scholars distinguish between different meanings of modern secularism.[6] I propose the following simple description, applicable to our times: secularism is the separation of church and *everything*. You've heard of the separation of church and state. Secularism is not just the distinction but the separation of Christian faith *from* everything else. It is the world that repudiates God and his love. This world is not our home.

This basic description of secularism has many corollaries, all of which may be symptoms and/or causes of this separation. Let us say that these corollaries, some of which we have seen in our previous chapters, are the content of secularism. This content includes the assumption that only the empirically verifiable is real, that there is no such thing as right and wrong, that autonomous choice is the highest good, that toleration should be open-ended, and that diversion (especially in the forms of entertainment, TV, internet, and so on) is the path to pleasure. Above all, if you must be a person of faith, keep it to yourself and keep it separate from the rest of your life.

Secularism is itself a kind of religion. Like a religion, secularism proposes a different value system. And like religious fundamentalists, those devoted to secularism ridicule, pressure, and frequently marginalize those who disagree with them. Secularism is the narrative that drives our modern Western world. It is a different vision of human flourishing. The world values self-centered priorities. Jesus and his followers value *God*-centered priorities, which focus on loving God and neighbor.

Contrary to Jesus' prayer, we Christians are too often in the world *and* of the world. Despite Paul's admonition, the church is being shaped into the world's mold. This mold is secularism. Can we just admit that we are heavily influenced by too many of the negative features of our culture? We tend to pursue the same goals in the same way as the unbelieving world. We have noted how moral relativism, a prominent feature of the secular age, is creeping into the church. Autonomous choice with no restrictions is probably taken for granted by most Christians. There seems to be no quantitative distinction between Christian and non-Christian consumption of diversion and mindless entertainment. So we see Christians who would rather stay home than help the needy, who would rather watch TV than read the Bible and pray, who show their love for this present age by putting money and its pursuit above people. We see Christians who put temporary pleasures ahead of their marriage vows. We see Christians who use their advantages for no good purpose. Some Christians use their intellect to put down others who don't see things their way. Many Christians appear to practice a private faith hidden from public view. Christians often look too much like the world.

In light of these observations, secularism is probably the *greatest* threat to the church in the West, and it has been for a long time. One reason it is so dangerous is that it is difficult to know at what point *in the world* blurs into *of the world*. We want to show love to the world and engage the world in a positive way, but by engaging, we risk being seduced by the world's negative values. Rather than participating in reconciling the world to God, we are pulled away from God toward a godless world.

The Christian's thoughtless engagement with the world results in a moral drift, that is, creeping toward secular values without even knowing it. The modern church, in contrast to the mostly black-and-white morality of the New Testament, has expanded the field of gray area beyond recognition. That is, we have cast into doubt and now regard with uncertainty beliefs and practices that were once easily assessed. The consequence is confusion regarding kingdom values and morality, even within the church. As Alexander Pope observed, when we first encounter vice we hate it, but the more frequently it is seen, we become accustomed to it, then tolerate and pity it, and finally embrace it for ourselves.[7] Or as Isaiah 5:20 puts it, "Woe to those who call evil good and good evil."

As we think about the importance of resisting secularism, we need to seek a balanced understanding and practice. But where is the balance? What does it mean to be in the world but not of it? How can you tell the difference? Can others see the difference in us?

This discernment begins by simply being aware of the distinction between the world that God so loved (sense 1) and the world that we should not love, the age that is passing away (sense 2). Then we might see more clearly when to embrace and when to push back. We should also be willing to ask if we fit in with the world. Are we in tune with the current zeitgeist? If so, that could be a red flag. If secularism, the influence of the passing age, *is* a real concern, then it is important to talk about the desires we value, the things we spend money on, the way we deal with sin, the way we handle conflict, the way we treat one another, the way we behave, the causes that excite us and that we support.

Sadly, much of the Western church has grown comfortable with the world. The church now seems just as likely as any other community to embrace the latest cultural fads. We are in the world *and* of it.

SANCTIFICATION

To return to 1 Corinthians 5, cited at the beginning of this chapter, Paul's moral admonition is directed not to an unbelieving world that fails to live a holy life but to a church that has been excessively influenced by the world. Paul is understandably disappointed, for these saints have not been sanctified. The solution is not to affirm their new standards—which look very much like their pre-Christian standards—but to challenge them to purify the body of Christ. Some might call this moral rigorism. If the rule is an end in itself, then it might be what some call legalism. But for Paul, the rules are never ends in themselves; the point is sanctification, spiritual formation, the means to the goal of becoming like God.

God seeks a holy people who will dwell in communion with him, now and forever, in a mutual relationship of love. Sanctification, therefore, is not an optional menu item for the disciple of Christ. Only the pure in heart will see God. God desires to open and soften our hearts. And he wants us to receive the Spirit's salvation, comfort, and assurance. However, God will not override or compel our wills. He persuades us and draws us in, if we will not resist.

This process of becoming holy, like God, cannot occur without the help of the Holy Spirit. God's presence through the Holy Spirit means our sanctification. Just as we can't pull ourselves up by our bootstraps and save ourselves apart from the Holy Spirit's help, we can't become more like God on our own. The Holy Spirit fills our lives, producing in us the virtues that lead to holiness and helping us carry out those duties that God requires of us. The Spirit places us within a Spirit-filled community and points us to the Spirit-inspired Word of God. The most reliable way to resist becoming too comfortable with vice, being led by fleshly desires, and mistaking evil for good is to return to Scripture and submit to its guidance.

CONCLUSION

The point is not to avoid the world. We cannot avoid culture. As one second-century disciple teaches, Christians are not distinguished from others by clothing, language, nationality, or any other superficial features.[8] As long as the church is in the world, it will be cultural to some degree. The question is, to what degree? In every aspect of the lives of God's people—their knowledge, thought, behavior, proclamation, and even their worship—God's people may be *influenced* by culture, but they must never be radically *determined* and dictated by secular culture. Where is the line? For millennia, the line between influence and determination has been drawn somewhere in a gray area. When it migrates too far in one direction, others are there to pull it back. Wherever that line should be, is it fair to say that modern Christians usually err on the side of capitulating to the world's terms?

So where should we draw the line? We cannot give hard-and-fast answers that address every possible case. But just to ask the question means we are farther along than the many who seem never to give it a thought. We must engage the world, and, as we do so in the world, we cannot help being influenced by culture. But there is a difference between engaging Christ on the world's terms and engaging the world on Christ's terms. May God grant us wisdom to recognize that difference.

DISCUSSION QUESTIONS

1. Give a concrete example of successfully striking the balance of being in the world but not of it.
2. Give a concrete example of losing the balance on one side or the other.
3. How do you think outsiders view the church's relationship to the world?

CHAPTER 14

Engaging the Battle

Lord Jesus Christ, it is indeed from on high that you draw a person to yourself, and it is to victory that you call him, but this of course means that you call him to struggle and promise him victory in the struggle to which you from on high call him, you, the great victor. Just as you keep us from all other error, keep us also from this, that we delude ourselves into thinking ourselves to be members of a Church already triumphant here in this world. Your kingdom certainly was not and is not of this world. The place of your Church is not here in the world; there is room for it only if it will struggle and by struggling make room for itself to exist. But if it will struggle, it will never be displaced by the world either; that you will guarantee. But if it deludes itself into thinking it is to be triumphant here in this world, then, alas, it does indeed have itself to blame that you withdrew your support, then it has succumbed, then it has confused itself with the world. Be, then, with your militant Church so that this might never happen, so that it—and this is truly the only way in which it could happen—would be obliterated from the earth by becoming a triumphant Church.

—Søren Kierkegaard[1]

Milton Mayer, an American Jewish journalist of German descent, was fascinated by the bewildering rise and popularity of Nazism in Germany. After the Second World War, he befriended and interviewed several working-class and middle-class Germans, including former members of the Nazi party, who witnessed firsthand something that, in hindsight, is difficult to comprehend—namely, how it all happened, and with such little resistance within the country. There were many and complex factors, of course, but the accounts recorded by Mayer are noteworthy for their similarities to our own day. The observations of one philologist stand out.

"What no one seemed to notice," said Mayer's philologist colleague, "was the ever widening gap, after 1933, between the government and the people."[2] The Nazis attacked the Communists and Socialists, and then the Jews, but the established church did nothing to resist. "And then they attacked the Church, and he [Pastor Niemöller] was a Churchman, and he did something—but then it was too late." Uncertainty about what to do grows gradually over time. There is little or no public protest over the changes being wrought by the government. If you speak up or protest, "they say, 'It's not so bad' or 'You're seeing things' or 'You're an alarmist.'"[3]

The philologist grants that anyone who pushes back seems to be an alarmist. "You are saying that *this* must lead to *this*, and you can't prove it." So you shrink back. If you're going to do anything to speak up, you know you will be labeled a troublemaker, so you decide to wait for the proper occasion to do so. "So you wait, and you wait."[4]

You wait for others to join the resistance. But, says the philologist, the one great moment when hundreds or thousands have finally had enough and decide to join you never comes:

> If the last and worst act of the whole regime had come immediately after the first and smallest, thousands, yes, millions would have been sufficiently shocked—if, let us say,

> the gassing of the Jews in '43 had come immediately after the "German Firm" stickers on the windows of non-Jewish shops in '33. But of course this isn't the way it happens. In between come all the hundreds of little steps, some of them imperceptible, each of them preparing you not to be shocked by the next. Step C is not so much worse than Step B, and, if you did not make a stand at Step B, why should you at Step C? And so on to Step D.[5]

And then, one day, you wake up and decide to take a principled stand, but it's too late. Some minor incident finally reveals that everything has changed "completely under your nose." For the philologist, that happened when he heard his little boy repeating, "Jew swine." It was no longer the world he was raised in. The outward forms and entertainments of the old culture all remained and were very reassuring—the people, housing, jobs, concerts, cinema, and the like. "But the spirit, which you never noticed because you made the lifelong mistake of identifying it with the forms, is changed." You now live in a world of hate and fear, and the people doing the hating and fearing don't even know it. Now you live in a system that answers to no one, not even to God. "The system itself could not have intended this in the beginning, but in order to sustain itself it was compelled to go all the way. You have gone almost all the way yourself."[6]

BLINDNESS AND REGRET

Mayer's friend's account suggests many analogies to the cultural situation today, but I will highlight only two. First, there is the recurring theme of blindness, willful or not. German citizens didn't easily see what was going on in the moment. They didn't notice how quickly the gap was widening between the ruling class and the people. Cultural changes were quick but incremental and under the surface. The next thing you know, your own children are swept up in the culture's ideology. The philologist's hard look at himself reveals that he had nearly been swept away too.

The second observation is that, for those who did take notice and were alarmed at the changes, there is the recurring tone of regret. The philologist regrets that he and his fellow citizens did not act sooner. There was a kind of bullying against anyone who said anything that questioned the emerging wisdom of the party. So those who opposed the regime waited for the opportune time to speak up. The time never came, and they were too late.

For those who are concerned about the changes we have seen around us and the ones inevitably to come, we, like Mayer's interviewees, are tempted also to wait. Maybe, we think, once the culture gets so absurd things will turn around. So far, this attitude appears to be excessively optimistic. Or we are told, "Things are just too volatile right now to speak up. Let's wait." Wait for what exactly? And the pressure often comes from fellow Christians who ostensibly are on our side!

But things don't turn around and current trends won't stop unless people speak up against them and offer an alternative vision. With moral issues like the kind we have been discussing, I am not even talking about reversing things with federal legislation or with the non-Christian citizenry at large. Instead, I am talking about addressing the church regarding matters of Christian doctrine and practice. But as long as the church is in the world *and* of the world, it is unlikely to seek or even tolerate those conversations.

CHURCH MILITANT

Let's think metaphorically for a moment. How would you describe the course of human life? Life is like . . . what? Forrest Gump said a box of chocolates, but I'm searching for something a bit more thoughtful. When I have asked students this question, someone usually comes fairly soon to the answer I'm fishing for: life is like a journey. I don't have to pull any teeth for the right answer to surface. To see life as a journey down a road, a path, a way, is itself a well-worn path. Everyone has heard this one before. But it is also biblical, so I am not opposed to using it.

Why or how is life like a journey? It takes you from one place to another, it has its ups and downs, you are free to travel along different paths, it can be traveled alone or with loved ones, and so on. Like life, a journey can be long and difficult. So we're not talking about just any kind of journey here. What kind of a journey is life? It is less like the short walk from your bedroom to the refrigerator and more like a long hike up a mountain. Though there may be reward in the refrigerator, it doesn't quite compare with the difficulty and reward that come with the long hike. After obstacles, strain, and pain, you reach the summit. In Scripture, the exodus becomes a metaphor for the Christian life: freedom from captivity to sin, salvation through the water, bread from heaven, a lifetime of testing in the wilderness, and finally crossing the Jordan River into the promised land. It's not a walk across the house. It's not a ten-minute car ride. If it's a race, it is a marathon, not a sprint. It is a long, arduous hike, accompanied by God all along the way.

Now imagine that you have against you not just the length and the steep incline and rough ground and heat and thirst, but there is also an enemy sniping at you, trying to kill you and keep you from reaching the top of the mountain. The hike is now not only difficult but also dangerous. In this metaphor, life is not just a journey; it's now a war. It's serious. You're going to need preparation and a strategy, protection and defense, a weapon or two of your own. You will not survive long without proper training and equipment. So let's allow that metaphor to sink in—life is a journey that is accompanied by God, but also by conflict.

The metaphor I have suggested is inspired by Ephesians 6:10–18. In this passage, Paul exhorts Christians to put on the full armor of God in order to withstand the attacks of the enemy. Paul is not speaking literally, but obviously metaphorically. Life is a struggle not against flesh and blood. We are in a spiritual struggle, a wrestling match, a battle (Eph 6:12). So, it is a hike or journey, but one with enemies. Life is like . . . capture the flag, but with guns. It's not a game. Now twenty-five years a Christian, Paul knows that the Christian life is spiritual warfare. He cannot help but warn his less experienced fellow soldiers.

What is this armor, and why does Paul choose this metaphor?

He writes this letter from prison. He is on the front lines of the battle, near the end of his journey. As he composes and searches for the right words, he sees a Roman guard and runs with it. Here is an apt metaphor. We must fit ourselves with the right equipment to facilitate this battle on the move. A soldier will not survive long without it. We need the full armor, not just part of it—belt, breastplate, shoes, shield, helmet, sword. They are the necessities of spiritual life: truth, righteousness, readiness, faith, salvation, God's Word, prayer. The equipment on which we rely is not something we fashioned. It is the full armor of *God*—all these things are gifts from God to us.

Why do we need these? You cannot read this passage without seeing the reason clearly. The enemy is prominent: devil's schemes (Eph 6:11); rulers, authorities, world powers of this dark age, and spiritual forces of evil (6:12); the day of evil (6:13); and the flaming arrows of the evil one (6:16). Some might call Paul an alarmist. It is definitely frightening.

Now, how often do we think of the Christian life as a battle, a war? I will go out on a limb and say that most American Christians do not. Do you ever wake up in the morning and think, "It's time for battle"? It's time for battling traffic and fatigue, perhaps battling the boss or coworkers, your children or pets. But does it feel like a spiritual battle? If we did consider it a spiritual war, would it change anything about the way we live? Would it affect our decisions? If we are among those who see life from this perspective, then how do our lives differ concretely from those Christians who don't think of life in these terms? Or how *should* our lives be different? How should it affect the way we raise the next generation and pass the faith on to them?

In light of that last question, here's another question. What is boot camp? Even if you've never been to boot camp, you probably have an idea based on movies or on reports from people you know. How would you describe boot camp? What do you expect from it? Boot camp is not for the faint of heart. It is a time of difficult preparation and basic training for the vocation ahead.

What are you doing to prepare for the spiritual battle? What does the armor of God or spiritual boot camp look like in your life? It means guarding our hearts and minds from the inanities of worldly wisdom. It means knowing what we believe and why we believe it. It means filling our lives with the fruit of the Spirit, a regimen of study, prayer, and worship. Putting on the armor of God requires putting the screens away. It means getting to know the older people among us who have survived a long time and have won many victories in the war. It is arduous. It requires practice. Repetition. Training. Do you know how to use the armor of God? What do you actually do to protect yourself from those flaming arrows? If you don't know how to handle a sword, the Word of God, how do you fight back?

To be sure, battle is not the only metaphor for the Christian life, and it doesn't capture the whole thing. Christian life is service to the King. Christian life is friendship with God. It is the love of God's family. It should be joyful and peaceful. Indeed, these descriptions are not incompatible with the battle metaphor. Brothers and sisters in arms wage their battle side by side, facing the obstacles together, and they do it in joy because of their common cause. They show their love for one another as they struggle to protect themselves and their loved ones from the enemy.

Incredibly, with few exceptions, American churches are asleep at the wheel while the road is turning, apparently assuming that the status quo of the past will continue—that people will still attend church, participate, and donate, that children will learn the basics of the faith and be devoted to that faith. Even when churches and their leaders speak about cultural threats to Christian faith and practice, too many of them are on cruise control, neglecting to take the action that is necessary. People won't continue to come to church for second-rate entertainment, theology lite, and cultural fads with Jesus tacked on. The next generation will not become Christian, in any meaningful sense, through osmosis or "moralistic therapeutic deism."[7]

Despite the clear signs, many Christians remain oblivious to the crisis. At any rate, the general lack of action and the outright capitulation to cultural hostility would indicate a lack of awareness or alertness. It's one thing to be in a spiritual battle. It's another and worse thing to be in such a battle without knowing it. To call this a war and to use military imagery is not an overstatement. If the battle is not taken seriously, then we can rightly expect to lose. As long as we are in this life, this time of testing, we are still the church militant, the church at war. And the church militant will survive, by God's help, only if it struggles. But if it remains complacent, the visible church will not long survive in a post-Christian culture.

I imagine that literal boot camp felt a little different in 1943, at the height of World War II, than it does in 2021. The principles may be the same, but there was more urgency then. Everything was at stake. You could be on the battlefield tomorrow, fighting for the survival of civilization. Well, spiritually, it's 1943. The battle is here, whether or not we recognize it. Nothing can be taken for granted. We are long past the day when you could be accepted by popular culture as a Christian. A few subcultures notwithstanding, in most of Western society now, being a Christian is generally a disadvantage. No amount of signaling your love for good secular causes is going to offset, in the world's eyes, the offense of being a devout disciple of Christ. You will be pressured to keep it quiet. It doesn't matter how many people you actually help—if you say that a proper sexual relationship is between a married man and woman, or if you say that terminating a baby before its birth is wrong—you will be ignored, at best, or perhaps ostracized and punished. You may be fired from your job. You will be called a hater, even if you never hated anyone. Are you ready for that? Indeed, this is war. Get ready for it! Don't give in or quit the battle. As Jesus told his disciples, "Get ready to take up your cross." As he prepared them for the battle, Jesus said, "If the world hates you, understand that it hated me first" (John 15:18). We are in good company.

LOVING RESISTANCE FIGHTERS

If we are to press onward as Christian soldiers, what does this journey, this warfare, look like? In the book *Technopoly*, Neil

Postman considered how one should face the technophilia of contemporary American society. He recommended trying to be a "loving resistance fighter," and he described several characteristics of such a person.[8] In light of the situation I have described above, and in light of the Christian ethics I have intended to promote in the preceding pages, I can think of no better image of the church militant than a group of loving resistance fighters. Let me offer a few specific, practical descriptions and suggestions that, although limited in scope, should provide a glimpse of what is needed.

As the phrase indicates, the resistance fighters must be loving. By love, we mean the same thing we have meant all along: holy love. As we have seen, love does not mean catering to anyone's sinful desires. Love always means caring for everyone, being a friend, wanting the best for your neighbors like you would want for your own precious children, and being willing to bear others' burdens sacrificially. Love entails seeking the actual good of others. All of these descriptions extend also to our enemies, whom we are called to love as Christ does for the sake of redemption. The love that we are called to practice is, in imitation of God's love, to work for the reconciliation of the world to God. Without love, the journey and the battle will be aimless and fruitless.

The loving resistance fighter must be alert and awake—both to what God is doing in this world, as well as to the enemy's tactics and attacks. Scripture puts a high value on spiritual alertness over against spiritual slumber. Baptism was the sign of being awakened from a spiritual sleep, enlightened after a state of darkness. "Awake, O sleeper, arise from the dead, and Christ will shine on you" (Eph 5:14). Even physical slumber sometimes symbolizes spiritual apathy, such as when Jesus asks his disciples to stay awake and watch in Gethsemane, but they cannot help falling asleep three times in a row (Mark 14:32–42). Like people on the move in a battle, we cannot afford to be caught sleeping or letting down our guard. We do not have the luxury of living blind, with eyes closed. Our eyes must be wide open to our surroundings. Being alert requires giving attention to our own lives first. It means anticipating the enemy's next move. This requires one to be a student of history and of our own culture, able to read the signs of the times.

Another necessary trait is the willingness to sacrifice in combat. We cannot be among those who look back with regret at missed opportunities. Being a loving resistance fighter is not an easy calling. Christian love is, by definition, self-sacrificial and selfless. It entails stepping out of one's comfort zone. It is not easy to speak the truth in a culture that so often seeks to silence it. The easiest path is to go with the flow or wait until a more opportune time to act. But that is also the deadly path, a sure strategy for losing the battle. The willingness to sacrifice means the willingness to give up everything for the cause.

In addition to these traits, consider a couple of broad suggestions. If the church of travelers and resident aliens is at war, then what should its gatherings look like? Among other things, one might think there would be moments that have the rigor of boot camp or preparation for battle. In many churches, this is simply not the case. Churches could use the existing structures—such as Sunday school—to introduce a little more rigor for those who want it. They might also consider brand-new gatherings and settings with loftier goals for spiritual strength training. The church, the gathering of God's people, needs to be a more integral part of the Christian life, more than one passing hour a week. In a post-Christian and now postpandemic world, the church will need to become a leaner, purer, stronger, more closely knit, and more structurally flexible community if it is going to wage the battle effectively.

The idea of "Sunday school as boot camp" may not be an appealing one. I'm not suggesting that as the marketing slogan. But the impulse is right. We should have more; we should want more. We shouldn't run from the things we need. One of the church's purposes is to make disciples of all nations. The church community is where apprentices learn the discipline. Along with the family unit, it is where virtue is best modeled and passed on to others. The church is the locus of Christ's form, that is, of spiritual formation. It is the body of Christ, where Creator and creation meet. As Bonhoeffer says, "The church is the place where Jesus Christ's taking form is proclaimed and where it happens."[9]

The same goes for Christian schools, often operated by churches. Christian education should fulfill its calling by being unapologetically and uniquely Christian. Christian schools should put as much energy and resources into classical curriculum—especially Bible and theology, languages, and fine arts—as they do into sports. That means hiring and retaining top-notch teachers with the same kind of incentives provided to football coaches. Of course, donors, parents, and stakeholders would need to be on board.

These suggestions and descriptions are only sketches. The point is that the church needs to take its calling seriously in a serious time. At the same time, to take things seriously does not mean that joy is excluded from the journey. On the contrary, joy and peace, even in the midst of trials, are the expected consequences of pilgrim warfare. This joy is possible because the resistance fighters have joined in a common cause. Like boot camp buddies or a platoon that shares each other's successes and failures, happy warriors are joined together by a common desire and bond of love. Joy is present because of the end for which they struggle. That goal is a vision for true human flourishing, which is freedom from sin and death and law. The end for which we were created is the imitation of Christ, the reconciliation of human nature with the divine.

CONCLUSION

What does victory look like? Simply put, faithfulness. Faithfulness to the calling. Success will not be measured in legal victories, cultural approval, money, or packed church buildings. Those never should have been the measure anyway, and they are very unlikely to happen in a post-Christian culture. Rather, knowing goodness, beauty, and truth and seeking the face of God in love—this is the faith that leads to victory. In truth, the victory has already been won. The church triumphant may be an end-time reality, but that eschatological kingdom has already broken through in history, steeling the church militant for the battle that lies before us.

In the meantime, we must wake up from spiritual slumber, realize that we are in a battle, prepare for it, and act accordingly. If we do not, we may not share in the victory that has been won. Our battle plan? To trust in the Father's promises. To be the presence of Christ in a godless world. To rely on the Spirit's strength and peace. To affirm truth and goodness wherever we see it. And to follow our one moral rule: the way of love—love for God and neighbor that translates into action. Not a cheap love that allows sin and harm to run roughshod over those we love, but a real love that models and advocates real human flourishing, in the light of God's grace. That's our job—to be the body of Christ in this world, for his glory.

DISCUSSION QUESTIONS

1. Besides a journey, can you think of another metaphor that describes the Christian life? What does it do better than the metaphor used in this chapter?
2. What are the "flaming arrows" that threaten to kill us spiritually?
3. How can the different pieces of the armor of God defend us against these arrows? Give concrete examples.
4. If you regarded the Christian life primarily as a battle, would it change the way you live your life?
5. What would spiritual boot camp look like? In what ways could our experience of church life be more like boot camp?

For Further Reading

Bonhoeffer, Dietrich. *Ethics*. Dietrich Bonhoeffer Works 6. Trans. by Ilse Tödt and Ernst Feil. Minneapolis: Fortress, 2005.

Budziszewski, J. *What We Can't Not Know: A Guide*. Rev. ed. San Francisco: Ignatius, 2011.

Dreher, Rod. *The Benedict Option: A Strategy for Christians in a Post-Christian Nation*. New York: Sentinel, 2017.

Esolen, Anthony. *Out of the Ashes: Rebuilding American Culture*. Washington, DC: Regnery, 2017.

Hare, John E. *Why Bother Being Good? The Place of God in the Moral Life*. Downers Grove, IL: InterVarsity Press, 2002.

Hays, Richard B. *The Moral Vision of the New Testament: A Contemporary Introduction to New Testament Ethics*. San Francisco: HarperSanFrancisco, 1996.

Kierkegaard, Søren. *Purity of Heart Is to Will One Thing: Spiritual Preparation for the Office of Confession*. Trans. by Douglas V. Steere. New York: Harper & Row, 1938.

Lewis, C. S. *The Abolition of Man*. New York: Macmillan, 1947.

MacIntyre, Alasdair. *After Virtue: A Study in Moral Theory*. 3rd ed. Notre Dame: University of Notre Dame Press, 2007.

Miller, Patrick D. *The Ten Commandments*. Interpretation. Louisville: Westminster John Knox Press, 2009.

Rae, Scott B. *Doing the Right Thing: Making Moral Choices in a World Full of Options*. Grand Rapids: Zondervan, 2013.

———. *Moral Choices: An Introduction to Ethics*. 4th ed. Grand Rapids: Zondervan, 2018.

Smedes, Lewis B. *Mere Morality: What God Expects from Ordinary People*. Grand Rapids: Eerdmans, 1983.

Turner, Philip. *Christian Ethics and the Church: Ecclesial Foundations for Moral Thought and Practice*. Grand Rapids: Baker Academic, 2015.

Wogaman, J. Philip and Douglas M. Strong, eds. *Readings in Christian Ethics: A Historical Sourcebook*. Louisville: Westminster John Knox, 1996.

Wolterstorff, Nicholas. *Justice: Rights and Wrongs*. Princeton: Princeton University Press, 2008.

Wright, Christopher J. H. *Old Testament Ethics for the People of God*. Downers Grove, IL: IVP Academic, 2004.

Notes

Chapter 1: Is There Such a Thing as Right and Wrong?

1. Polycarp, *Letter to the Philippians* 2:1, in Michael W. Holmes, ed., *The Apostolic Fathers: Greek Texts and English Translations*, 3rd ed. (Grand Rapids: Baker Academic, 2007). All quotations from the Apostolic Fathers are taken from this edition. In most cases throughout the book, I have made my own translations of foreign language sources or modified existing English translations based on the original languages. All Scripture quotations are my translations.
2. Georges Bizet, *Carmen*, Act 2, Scene 5: "Pour pays, l'univers, / et pour loi sa volonté, / et surtout, la chose enivrante: / la liberté! la liberté!"
3. John E. Hare, *God and Morality: A Philosophical History* (Oxford: Blackwell, 2007), 196–97, notes that this has been called the "yah/boo theory." As Ayer himself put it: "Thus if I say to someone, 'You acted wrongly in stealing that money,' I am not stating anything more than if I had simply said, 'You stole that money.' In adding that this action is wrong I am not making any further statement about it. I am simply evincing my moral disapproval of it. It is as if I had said, 'You stole that money,' in a peculiar tone of horror, or written it with the addition of some special exclamation marks." He goes on to say that "ethical judgements . . . have no objective validity whatsoever." Alfred Jules Ayer, *Language, Truth and Logic*, 2nd ed. (New York: Dover, 1952), 107–8.
4. I am describing here the default ethic in Western culture. I am not suggesting that this popular ethic is philosophically rigorous.
5. Gabrielle McMillen, "Redskins Exec Doug Williams: Reuben Foster Allegations 'Small Potatoes' Compared to Other Things," *Sporting News*, November 30, 2018, https://www.sportingnews.com/us/nfl/news/nfl-redskins-doug-williams-reuben-foster-allegations-small-potatoes-other-things-domestic-abuse-charges/1rl01t0lld6c61lwqmiw2dtct4.
6. As was said about the president's administration in the film *Clear and Present Danger* (1994).

7. Quoted in Charles Taylor, *A Secular Age* (Cambridge, MA: Belknap, 2007), 596. Taylor calls this way of thinking a "strange inference."
8. Fyodor Dostoevsky, *The Brothers Karamazov*, trans. Constance Garnett (New York: The New American Library, 1957), 534. The dialogue goes on to say that if God "doesn't exist, man is the king of the earth, of the universe. Magnificent! Only how is he going to be good without God? That's the question" (ibid., 538).
9. For helpful reflections on natural law and conscience, see J. Budziszewski, *What We Can't Not Know: A Guide*, rev. ed. (San Francisco: Ignatius, 2011). For an early modern Protestant approach, see Niels Hemmingsen, *On the Law of Nature: A Demonstrative Method*, trans. E. J. Hutchinson, Sources in Early Modern Economics, Ethics, and Law (Grand Rapids: CLP Academic, 2018).
10. This famous analogy is from John Calvin, *Institutes of the Christian Religion* I.vi.1.

Chapter 2: Why Be Good?

1. Gregory of Nyssa, *The Life of Moses* II.320, trans. Abraham J. Malherbe and Everett Ferguson, The Classics of Western Spirituality (New York: Paulist, 1978), 137.
2. Plato, *Republic* II.3, 359D–360D, trans. Paul Shorey, Loeb Classical Library (Cambridge, MA: Harvard University Press, 1982), 1:116–21. This example is also used in Scott B. Rae, *Moral Choices: An Introduction to Ethics*, 4th ed. (Grand Rapids: Zondervan, 2018).
3. Søren Kierkegaard, *Purity of Heart Is to Will One Thing: Spiritual Preparation for the Office of Confession*, trans. Douglas V. Steere (New York: Harper & Row, 1938), 89–90.
4. Cf. C. S. Lewis, *The Abolition of Man* (New York: Macmillan, 1947), 15.
5. The following illustration is inspired by Alasdair MacIntyre, *After Virtue: A Study in Moral Theory*, 3rd ed. (Notre Dame: University of Notre Dame Press, 2007), 57–59.
6. Augustine, *Confessions* I.i.1.
7. Peter Gabriel, "In Your Eyes," on *So*, 1986.

Chapter 3: Ethics beyond Rules

1. Robert M. McCheyne, "When This Passing World Is Done," in *Psalms, Hymns and Spiritual Songs*, ed. John P. Wiegand (Nashville: Praise, 1992), no. 758.
2. George MacDonald, "The Way," in *Unspoken Sermons, Second Series* (London: Longmans, Green, and Co., 1885), 9.
3. Paulina Dedaj, "Utah Teen Attempting 'Bird Box' Challenge Crashes into Another Vehicle, Could Face Charges," January 11, 2019, https://

www.foxnews.com/us/utah-teen-attempting-bird-box-challenge-crashes-into-another-vehicle-could-face-charges.

4. E.g., Irenaeus, *Against Heresies*, IV.xv.1. Cf. idem, *On the Apostolic Preaching* 96, trans. John Behr (Crestwood, NY: St Vladimir's Seminary Press, 1997), 98; and Justin Martyr, *Dialogue with Trypho the Jew* 18–23, in *Writings of Saint Justin Martyr*, trans. Thomas B. Falls, Fathers of the Church (New York: Christian Heritage, 1948), 174–83.
5. *The Rule of Saint Benedict*, VII.67–70, trans. Bruce L. Venarde, Dumbarton Oaks Medieval Library (Cambridge, MA: Harvard University Press, 2011), 54–55 (modified slightly on the basis of the Latin).
6. Romans 13:10 is similar to the first principle of medical ethics: "Do no harm."
7. J. Budziszewski, *What We Can't Not Know: A Guide*, rev. ed. (San Francisco: Ignatius, 2011), 108.

Chapter 4: What Does Love Require?

1. Dietrich Bonhoeffer, *Ethics*, Dietrich Bonhoeffer Works 6 (Minneapolis: Fortress, 2005), 336.
2. "Rick Warren Interview on Muslims, Evangelism and Missions," https://www.christianitytoday.com/edstetzer/2012/march/rick-warren-interview-on-muslims-evangelism-missions.html.
3. Robert Louis Wilken, *Spirit of Early Christian Thought: Seeking the Face of God* (New Haven: Yale University Press, 2003), 289.
4. This central question about the requirements of love follows from the greatest love commands and has been asked by Christians for centuries since. In asking about the demands of love, I am also inspired by Dietrich Bonhoeffer's *Ethics*, which is quoted at the beginning of chapter 4. The question in many ways is an effective summary of that book. However, the precise wording comes from the final stanza of a song that has been one of my favorites for nearly three decades: Sam Phillips and Joseph Henry Burnett, "Same Changes" (1994). I highly recommend the song to readers.
5. Augustine, *Tractates on the First Epistle of John* 7.11, in *Tractates on the Gospel of John 112–24. Tractates on the First Epistle of John*, trans. John W. Rettig, Fathers of the Church (Washington, DC: Catholic University of America Press, 1995), 226. Hebrews 12:5–11 makes the same point.
6. J. Budziszewski, *The Revenge of Conscience: Politics and the Fall of Man* (Dallas: Spence, 1999; repr., Eugene, OR: Wipf and Stock, 2010), xv.
7. Augustine, *Tractates on the First Epistle of John* 7.11, 226.
8. Aristotle, *Nicomachean Ethics* I.iii.1–4, 1094b, trans. H. Rackham, Loeb Classical Library (Cambridge, MA: Harvard University Press, 1956), 6–9.

Chapter 5: The Use of the Bible in Ethics

1. Athanasius of Alexandria, *Festal Letter* XXXIX.6, in *NPNF*, ser. 2, 4:552, translation modified slightly.
2. Richard Hooker, *Of the Laws of Ecclesiastical Polity* V.vii.1, in 2 vols. (London: Dent, 1907), 2:27.
3. Karl Barth, *Church Dogmatics: The Doctrine of the Word of God* I/2, trans. G. T. Thomson and Harold Knight (Edinburgh: T&T Clark, 1956), 502.
4. I do not intend, by this example, to demean Christians who practice footwashing. To my mind, it is an indifferent matter. But the early church certainly did not understand it as a ritual command on par with the other sacraments.
5. Richard Hays describes four modes of ethical appeal to Scripture: rules, principles, paradigms, and symbolic world. My three ways are adapted from his work. See Richard B. Hays, *The Moral Vision of the New Testament: Community, Cross, New Creation; A Contemporary Introduction to New Testament Ethics* (New York: HarperCollins, 1996), 208–9.
6. On the rule of faith and its relationship to biblical interpretation, see Keith D. Stanglin, *The Letter and Spirit of Biblical Interpretation: From the Early Church to Modern Practice* (Grand Rapids: Baker Academic, 2018), 29–36, 44; and Stanglin, "Ecclesial Unity, Biblical Interpretation, and the Rule of Faith," in *Scripture First: Biblical Interpretation That Fosters Christian Unity*, ed. Daniel B. Oden and J. David Stark (Abilene: Abilene Christian University Press, 2020), 77–102.
7. Taken together, these four are known as the Wesleyan Quadrilateral, but they indeed span the history of Christian theology.
8. Hays, *The Moral Vision of the New Testament*, 464.

Chapter 6: Sexual Ethics

1. Pope Paul VI, *Humanae vitae* (July 25, 1986), II.18.
2. Stanley J. Grenz, *Sexual Ethics: An Evangelical Perspective* (Louisville: Westminster John Knox, 1990), 29.
3. Camille Paglia, *Free Women, Free Men: Sex, Gender, Feminism* (New York: Pantheon, 2017), ix.
4. C. S. Lewis, *Mere Christianity*, rev. ed. (New York: Macmillan, 1952), 89. The original talk on sexual morality was given in 1943 (ibid., 5). The fetishizing of food is no longer hypothetical on channels like the Food Network.
5. Quoted in Mark D. Regnerus, *Forbidden Fruit: Sex and Religion in the Lives of American Teenagers* (Oxford: Oxford University Press, 2007), 83.
6. For an insightful discussion of these issues, including the analogy between the reproductive and respiratory systems that follows, see J. Budziszewski, *On the Meaning of Sex* (Wilmington: Intercollegiate Studies Institute, 2012).

7. Portions of the following two paragraphs are based on Allan Carlson, "Meaningful Intercourse," *Touchstone* (Jan./Feb. 2009): 26–31.
8. Quoted in Carlson, "Meaningful Intercourse," 29.
9. See Pope Paul VI, *Humanae vitae* (1968), at http://www.vatican.va/content/paul-vi/en/encyclicals/documents/hf_p-vi_enc_25071968_humanae-vitae.html.
10. For more on this point, see Mark Regnerus, *Cheap Sex: The Transformation of Men, Marriage, and Monogamy* (Oxford: Oxford University Press, 2017).
11. See Irene H. Ericksen and Stan E. Weed, "Re-Examining the Evidence for School-Based Comprehensive Sex Education: A Global Research Review," *Issues in Law and Medicine* 34, no. 2 (2019): 161–82.
12. CDC report, "Teenagers in the United States: Sexual Activity, Contraceptive Use, and Childbearing," http://www.cdc.gov/nchs/data/series/sr_23/sr23_031.pdf.
13. For more on these and related matters, see the rigorous sociological data and analyses in Regnerus, *Forbidden Fruit*; Mark Regnerus and Jeremy Uecker, *Premarital Sex in America: How Young Americans Meet, Mate, and Think about Marrying* (Oxford: Oxford University Press, 2011); and Regnerus, *Cheap Sex*.

Chapter 7: Homosexual Practice

1. Ivan Aksakov, quoted in Vladimir Solovyov, *Russia and the Universal Church*, trans. Herbert Rees (London: Centenary, 1948), 64.
2. I refer to homosexuality as consensual sexual contact with a person of the same sex. That is, unless otherwise specified, it is the practice and not the mere desire that I primarily have in mind here and elsewhere.
3. See the chapter on "homosexuality" in Richard B. Hays, *The Moral Vision of the New Testament: Community, Cross, New Creation; A Contemporary Introduction to New Testament Ethics* (New York: HarperCollins, 1996), 379–406, where he does the same thing. In comparison, my treatment below is necessarily truncated, and I would differ from Hays on certain details, but our methods and results are compatible.
4. For the most comprehensive treatment of homosexual practice in Scripture, see Robert A. J. Gagnon, *The Bible and Homosexual Practice: Texts and Hermeneutics* (Nashville: Abingdon, 2001). See also Hays, *The Moral Vision of the New Testament*, 381–97.
5. Contra Hays, *The Moral Vision of the New Testament*, 381.
6. Hays seems to have a simplistic view of silence, implying that "paucity of texts" means that the question is "a minor concern" or a "peripheral issue." See Hays, *The Moral Vision of the New Testament*, 381. It is as if the quantity of relevant texts alone is decisive. Cf. ibid., 400–401, 445. For

a more responsible treatment of silence, rules, and worldview, see the discussion of Jesus' sexual ethic in Gagnon, *The Bible and Homosexual Practice*, 185–228.

7. Dan O. Via and Robert A. J. Gagnon, *Homosexuality and the Bible: Two Views* (Minneapolis: Fortress, 2003), 93.
8. Luke Timothy Johnson, "Homosexuality and the Church: Scripture and Experience," *Commonweal* (June 11, 2007), https://www.commonwealmagazine.org/homosexuality-church-0.
9. E.g., see Polycarp, *Philippians* 5:3; Justin Martyr, *2 Apology* 12 (FOC, 132–33); Clement of Alexandria, *Paedagogus*, II.x.83–88, trans. Simon P. Wood, Fathers of the Church (Washington, DC: Catholic University of America Press, 1954), 164–68.
10. The first Christian group to approve of same-sex marriage was the Remonstrant Brotherhood in 1986. "Remonstrant Church," https://www.remonstranten.nl/engels/.
11. See William Loader, *Making Sense of Sex: Attitudes towards Sexuality in Early Jewish and Christian Literature* (Grand Rapids: Eerdmans, 2013), 131–40, 146.
12. E.g., see Hays, *The Moral Vision of the New Testament*, 397–98, 405.
13. "Taboo" is a Polynesian term for an ethical prohibition that, at least to outsiders, no longer has any rationale. See Keith Allan, "Taboo Words and Language," in *The Oxford Handbook of Taboo Words and Language*, ed. Keith Allan (Oxford: Oxford University Press, 2019), 1–27, here 3–5; and Franz Steiner, *Taboo* (London: Cohen & West, 1956).
14. See https://www.aclu.org/press-releases/aclu-utah-join-polygamists-bigamy-fight?redirect=cpredirect/16163.
15. E.g., see the CDC press release at https://www.cdc.gov/media/releases/2013/p0125_nisvs.html; and *Sexuality and Gender: A Companion to* The New Atlantis *Special Report* (Austin: Austin Institute for the Study of Family and Culture, 2017), 32. This helpful tool is a collation and distillation of the extensive report in Lawrence S. Mayer and Paul R. McHugh, "Sexuality and Gender: Findings from the Biological, Psychological, and Social Sciences," *The New Atlantis* 50 (2016). Read the executive summary at http://www.thenewatlantis.com/publications/executive-summary-sexuality-and-gender.
16. E.g., see Paul van de Ven et al., "A Comparative Demographic and Sexual Profile of Older Homosexually Active Men," *Journal of Sex Research* 34, no. 4 (1997): 349–60. In sum, about half of homosexual men have had over 100 different sex partners.
17. For more data and analysis of promiscuity rates, see Gagnon, *The Bible and Homosexual Practice*, 453–60.
18. Randy L. Maddox, "The Enriching Role of Experience," in W. Stephen

Gunter et al., *Wesley and the Quadrilateral: Renewing the Conversation* (Nashville: Abingdon, 1997), 121.

19. On these points, see *Sexuality and Gender*, 8–23.
20. Maddox, "The Enriching Role of Experience," 107, quotes a letter to the *United Methodist Reporter* to this effect: "I'm tired of having my interpretations of Scripture dismissed simply because they aren't orthodox. Everyone interprets Scripture from his or her experience, study and reason. Are we supposed to turn off our minds and let traditionalists think for us?"
21. Johnson, "Homosexuality and the Church."
22. For the specific claims and data, see Mark Regnerus, *Cheap Sex: The Transformation of Men, Marriage, and Monogamy* (Oxford: Oxford University Press, 2017), 22–28, 36–37, 91–92.
23. For a concise summary of the basic vocabulary and issues, see Mark A. Yarhouse, *Understanding Gender Dysphoria: Navigating Transgender Issues in a Changing Culture* (Downers Grove, IL: InterVarsity Press, 2015), 13–27. See also the summary presentation in Mark A. Yarhouse and Julia Sadusky, "A Christian Psychological Assessment of Gender Dysphoria," in *Cultural Engagement: A Crash Course in Contemporary Issues*, ed. Joshua D. Chatraw and Karen Swallow Prior (Grand Rapids: Zondervan Academic, 2019), 93–97.
24. Yarhouse, *Understanding Gender Dysphoria*, 19.
25. *Diagnostic and Statistical Manual of Mental Disorders*, 5th ed. (Washington, DC: American Psychiatric Publishing, 2013), 451. For an exposé and critique of the processes and principles behind *DSM-5*—and, by extension, of the APA—see Gary Greenberg, *The Book of Woe: The DSM and the Unmaking of Psychiatry* (New York: Penguin/Blue Rider, 2013).
26. https://abcnews.go.com/blogs/headlines/2014/02/heres-a-list-of-58-gender-options-for-facebook-users. Many of these options overlap or at least appear to be different ways to identify the same thing. But the point remains that one may choose from a multitude of gender options.
27. This example is raised in K. J. Zucker, "Children with Gender Identity Disorder: Is There a Best Practice?" *Neuropsychiatrie de l'enfance et de l'adolescence* 56 (2008): 358–64, here 359. He advocates addressing the underlying issues that make persons uncomfortable with their actual ethnic or gender identity.
28. See https://www.welcomingschools.org/resources/definitions/youth-definitions/.
29. E.g., see https://www.welcomingschools.org/pages/looking-at-gender-identity-with-childrens-books/.
30. http://www.genderbread.org/resource/genderbread-person-v3-3.

31. This statement was in the draft comprehensive sex education curriculum for sixth graders distributed by Austin (Texas) Independent School District in 2019.
32. E.g., see https://www.nbcnews.com/feature/nbc-out/boy-or-girl-parents-raising-theybies-let-kids-decide-n891836.
33. For a response and an alternative to the transgender agenda, especially as it affects young people and their families, see *Parent Resource Guide: Responding to the Transgender Issue* (Minnesota Family Council, 2019), https://genderresourceguide.com/.
34. See https://tavistockandportman.nhs.uk/about-us/news/stories/referrals-gender-identity-development-service-gids-level-2018-19/. See also the report in "Gender Identity Clinic Services under Strain as Referral Rates Soar," *The Guardian*, https://www.theguardian.com/society/2016/jul/10/transgender-clinic-waiting-times-patient-numbers-soar-gender-identity-services.
35. See the excellent resource for parents at https://www.parentsofrogdkids.com/.
36. *DSM-5*, 458, 344.
37. Sabine Müller, "Body Integrity Identity Disorder (BIID)—Is the Amputation of Healthy Limbs Ethically Justified?" *The American Journal of Bioethics* 9, no. 1 (2009): 36–43, here 37.
38. Müller, "BIID," 37.
39. Müller, "BIID," 37–38.
40. Cecilia Dhejne et al., "Long-Term Follow-Up of Transsexual Persons Undergoing Sex Reassignment Surgery: Cohort Study in Sweden," *PLoS One* 6, no. 2 (2011), at https://www.ncbi.nlm.nih.gov/pmc/articles/PMC3043071/. Cf. Mayer and McHugh, "Sexuality and Gender," 108–13; *Sexuality and Gender*, 53.
41. Mayer and McHugh, "Sexuality and Gender," 112. Cf. *Sexuality and Gender*, 53.
42. *Sexuality and Gender*, 58–59. Cf. Peggy T. Cohen-Kettenis et al., "The Treatment of Adolescent Transsexuals: Changing Insights," *Journal of Sexual Medicine* (2008): 1892–97, here 1893: "80–95% of the prepubertal children with GID [Gender Identity Disorder] will no longer experience a GID in adolescence."
43. For an informed discussion of transgender ideology, its effects on the medical community, and the medical harm being done, see Marcus Evans, "Why I Resigned from Tavistock: Trans-Identified Children Need Therapy, Not Just 'Affirmation' and Drugs," *Quillette* (January 17, 2020), at https://quillette.com/2020/01/17/why-i-resigned-from-tavistock-trans-identified-children-need-therapy-not-just-affirmation-and-drugs/.

44. Camille Paglia, *Free Women, Free Men: Sex, Gender, Feminism* (New York: Pantheon, 2017), ix–x.
45. Paglia, *Free Women, Free Men*, ix–x.
46. For a brief analysis of this contrast, see Stanley J. Grenz, *Sexual Ethics: An Evangelical Perspective* (Louisville: Westminster John Knox, 1990), 29–30.

Chapter 8: Abortion

1. Karl Barth, *Church Dogmatics: The Doctrine of Creation* III/4 (Edinburgh: T&T Clark, 1961), 416.
2. George Orwell, *Nineteen Eighty-Four* (New York: Harcourt, Brace & World, 1949), 303.
3. Orwell, *Nineteen Eighty-Four*, 281.
4. See Centers for Disease Control and Prevention, "Abortion Surveillance—United States, 2008," *MMWR Surveillance Summaries* 60, no. 15 (November 25, 2011): 1, 3–5, 15. These totals exclude California, Maryland, and New Hampshire.
5. https://www.cdc.gov/reproductivehealth/data_stats/abortion.htm (accessed before the new, updated page).
6. For 2015, see https://www.cdc.gov/mmwr/volumes/67/ss/ss6713a1.htm. For the report's homepage, see https://www.cdc.gov/reproductivehealth/data_stats/abortion.htm. For 2018, see https://www.cdc.gov/reproductivehealth/data_stats/abortion.htm (accessed January 2, 2021). Note well that the US government does not require clinics to report any data and some states are excluded, so the actual numbers are higher.
7. Nick Brown, "Abortion," in *Discerning Ethics: Diverse Christian Responses to Divisive Moral Issues*, ed. Hak Joon Lee and Tim Dearborn (Downers Grove, IL: IVP Academic, 2020), 108–24, here 108–9.
8. See https://www.cdc.gov/reproductivehealth/data_stats/abortion.htm. This percentage is up from 28 percent in 2016. The percentage of medical abortions is increasing versus a decreasing percentage of surgical abortions.
9. *Didache* 2:2, in Michael W. Holmes, ed., *The Apostolic Fathers: Greek Texts and English Translations*, 3rd ed. (Grand Rapids: Baker Academic, 2007). The same instruction appears in the *Epistle of Barnabas* 19:5, in *Apostolic Fathers*.
10. Kurt Niederwimmer, *The Didache: A Commentary*, trans. Linda M. Maloney, Hermeneia (Minneapolis: Augsburg Fortress, 1998), 89–90.
11. Tertullian, *Apology* IX.8 (FOC, 31–32). Cf. Clement of Alexandria, *Paedagogus*, II.x.97 (FOC, 174).
12. Tertullian, *Apology* IX.7 (FOC, 31).
13. Justin Martyr, *First Apology* 27 (FOC, 63).

14. Margaret D. Kamitsuka, *Abortion and the Christian Tradition: A Pro-Choice Theological Ethic* (Louisville: Westminster John Knox, 2019), 17–47.
15. Kamitsuka, *Abortion and the Christian Tradition*, 34.
16. For an accurate treatment of Jewish and early Christian prohibition of abortion, see O. M. Bakke, *When Children Became People: The Birth of Childhood in Early Christianity*, trans. Brian McNeil (Minneapolis: Augsburg Fortress, 2005), 110–39.
17. *Hippocratic Oath*, in Steven H. Miles, *The Hippocratic Oath and the Ethics of Medicine* (Oxford: Oxford University Press, 2004), xiv.

Chapter 9: Wealth and Consumerism

1. *Shepherd of Hermas* 51:5, in Michael W. Holmes, ed., *The Apostolic Fathers: Greek Texts and English Translations*, 3rd ed. (Grand Rapids: Baker Academic, 2007).
2. Sam Eaton, "Church Rejects $600,000 Donation from Lottery Winner" (Aug. 14, 2008), at https://www.wltx.com/article/news/local/fyi/church-rejects-600000-donation-from-lottery-winner/101-381020247.
3. The news report does not indicate the reason for the church's decision. The church did not seek publicity—the pastor declined to comment on the case. Presumably, it was Powell, the rebuffed donor, who sought media attention, which does imply something about his motives.
4. William T. Cavanaugh, *Being Consumed: Economics and Christian Desire* (Grand Rapids: Eerdmans, 2008), 36–47, 52.
5. Brad S. Gregory, *The Unintended Reformation: How a Religious Revolution Secularized Society* (Cambridge, MA: Belknap, 2012), 235.
6. Cavanaugh, *Being Consumed*, 53.
7. Bede, *Ecclesiastical History* III.5, in *Baedae Opera Historica*, vol. 1, trans. J. E. King, Loeb Classical Library (Cambridge, MA: Harvard University Press, 1954), 346–49.
8. In Hosea 6:6, the Hebrew *hesed* (loyal love) is translated into Greek as *eleos* (mercy).
9. Gary A. Anderson, *Charity: The Place of the Poor in the Biblical Tradition* (New Haven, CT: Yale University Press, 2013), 33–34.
10. Anderson, *Charity*, 25. Much of Anderson's book is devoted to describing the theology of a treasury of merits in Second Temple Judaism and ancient Christianity.
11. *Didache* 4:6–7. This section of the *Didache* was part of typical early Christian catechesis. The same instruction appears in *Epistle of Barnabas* 19:10–11.
12. *2 Clement* 16:4.
13. Polycarp, *Philippians* 10:2.
14. *Shepherd of Hermas* 51:5.

15. *Shepherd of Hermas* 51:5–7.
16. *Shepherd of Hermas* 51:7.
17. *Shepherd of Hermas* 51:10.
18. Quoted in Anderson, *Charity*, 25.
19. See 2 Corinthians 8:1, 4, 6, 7, 9, 16, 19; and 9:8, 14, 15.
20. Anderson, *Charity*, 59.
21. Clement of Alexandria, *Who Is the Rich Man That Shall Be Saved?* 1–3, in *ANF* 2:591.
22. Clement, *Who Is the Rich Man?* 11 (594).
23. Clement, *Who Is the Rich Man?* 13 (594).
24. Clement, *Who Is the Rich Man?* 15 (595).
25. Clement, *Who Is the Rich Man?* 16 (595). See a similar sentiment in Clement's contemporary, Marcus Aurelius, *Meditations* VII.27, trans. C. R. Haines, Loeb Classical Library (Cambridge, MA: Harvard University Press, 1987), 177–78.
26. John Wesley, "The Use of Money," sermon 50, in *The Works of John Wesley*, vol. 2, Bicentennial Edition (Nashville: Abingdon, 1985), 266–80.
27. Anderson, *Charity*, 36.

Chapter 10: The Use of Technology

1. Aldous Huxley, foreword (1946) to *Brave New World* (New York: HarperCollins, 1946), xvii.
2. Michael Crichton, *Jurassic Park* (New York: Ballantine, 1990), 318, spoken by Ian Malcolm.
3. Plato, *Phaedrus* 274C–277A, trans. Harold North Fowler, Loeb Classical Library (Cambridge, MA: Harvard University Press, 1914), 560–71. Plato uses the Hellenized names of the two characters, Theut (for Thoth) and Thamus (for Ammon). Neil Postman uses this same story to great effect in *Technopoly: The Surrender of Culture to Technology* (New York: Vintage, 1992), 3–20. My subsequent discussion of technophilia and technophobia is inspired by Postman's treatment.
4. Kevin Binfield, ed., *Writings of the Luddites*, foreword by Adrian Randall (Baltimore: Johns Hopkins University Press, 2004), xiii–xv.
5. Cf. Gen 6:1–5, 11–12, with 1 Enoch 7–8.
6. Luke Clossey, "Relevance of Things Past: Contemporary Applications of Early Modern Studies," *Sixteenth Century Journal* 50, no. 1 (2019): 141–47, here 147.
7. Michael Crichton, *Jurassic Park* (New York: Ballantine, 1990), 318.
8. E.g., see Susan Pinker, *The Village Effect: How Face-to-Face Contact Can Make Us Healthier, Happier, and Smarter* (New York: Spiegel and Grau, 2014), 184–96; James M. Lang, "The Distracted Classroom,"

The Chronicle of Higher Education (March 13, 2017), https://www.chronicle.com/article/the-distracted-classroom/; Lang, "The Distracted Classroom: Is It Getting Worse?" *The Chronicle of Higher Education* (April 17, 2017), https://www.chronicle.com/article/the-distracted-classroom-is-it-getting-worse/; Carrie B. Fried, "In-Class Laptop Use and Its Effects on Student Learning," *Computers & Education* 50, no. 3 (2008): 906–14; Paul A. Kirschner and Pedro de Bruyckere, "The Myths of the Digital Native and the Multitasker," *Teaching and Teacher Education* 67 (2017): 135–42.

9. Although such evaluation is rarely carried out in popular discourse, "technology assessment" is a recognized discipline especially in the fields of business and politics. It is, in the words of Ernest Braun, "a systematic attempt to foresee the consequences of introducing a particular technology in all spheres it is likely to interact with." Quoted in Brian Brock, *Christian Ethics in a Technological Age* (Grand Rapids: Eerdmans, 2010), 13. Technology assessment is aimed at giving the most accurate picture possible of the future impacts of new technologies (ibid., 14). Brock's book offers a critical analysis of technology assessment from a theological perspective.
10. Jacob Shatzer, *Transhumanism and the Image of God: Today's Technology and the Future of Christian Discipleship* (Downers Grove, IL: IVP Academic, 2019), 1.
11. Shatzer, *Transhumanism and the Image of God*, 2.
12. See *Deep Shift: 21 Ways Software Will Transform Global Society*, Survey Report, November 2015, World Economic Forum, http://www3.weforum.org/docs/WEF_GAC15_Deep_Shift_Software_Transform_Society.pdf.
13. This is no doubt named for the ancient Vedic priestly drink that produced a high.
14. See https://www.bbc.com/news/technology-44640959.
15. See https://www.businessinsider.com/silicon-valley-parents-raising-their-kids-tech-free-red-flag-2018-2.
16. John S. Hutton et al., "Associations between Screen-Based Media Use and Brain White Matter Integrity in Preschool-Aged Children," *JAMA Pediatrics* 174, no. 1 (2020): 1–10.
17. See https://www.cdc.gov/mmwr/volumes/67/wr/mm6722a1.htm?s_cid=mm6722a1_w.
18. Elroy Boers, Mohammad H. Afzali, Nicola Newton, and Patricia Conrod, "Association of Screen Time and Depression in Adolescence," *JAMA Pediatrics* 173, no. 9 (2019): 853–59. See also Cal Newport, *Digital Minimalism: Choosing a Focused Life in a Noisy World* (New York: Portfolio/Penguin, 2019), 105–6; Pinker, *The Village Effect*.
19. See Newport, *Digital Minimalism*, chapters 2 and 3.

20. For a good discussion of technology in the home, see Andy Crouch, *The Tech-Wise Family: Everyday Steps for Putting Technology in Its Proper Place* (Grand Rapids: Baker Books, 2017).

Chapter 11: Politics

1. *Epistle to Diognetus* 5:5, 9–10, in Michael W. Holmes, ed., *The Apostolic Fathers: Greek Texts and English Translations*, 3rd ed. (Grand Rapids: Baker Academic, 2007).
2. Origen, *Contra Celsum* V.37, 40, trans. Henry Chadwick (Cambridge: Cambridge University Press, 1965), 293, 296.
3. As Justin Martyr takes it in *1 Apology* 17 (FOC, 52). After quoting this saying of Jesus, he addresses the emperors thus: "Only God do we worship, but in other things we joyfully obey you."
4. See Aristotle *Politics* I.i.1, trans. H. Rackham, Loeb Classical Library (Cambridge, MA: Harvard University Press, 1932), 2–3.
5. Augustine, *The City of God against the Pagans*, XIX.24, ed. R. W. Dyson, Cambridge Texts in the History of Political Thought (Cambridge: Cambridge University Press, 1998), 960.
6. Jon Butler, Grant Wacker, and Randall Balmer, *Religion in American Life: A Short History*, 2nd ed. (Oxford: Oxford University Press, 2011), 162–65. See also Gary Laderman, *American Civil Religion* (Minneapolis: Fortress, 2012). The concept was given famous expression in Robert N. Bellah, "Civil Religion in America," *Daedalus* 96, no. 1 (Winter 1967): 1–21.
7. As John Winthrop described the new world in 1630. See Butler, Wacker, and Balmer, *Religion in American Life*, 48.
8. See John Howard Yoder, "Constantinianism Old and New," in *Revolutionary Christianity: The 1966 South American Lectures*, ed. Paul Martens et al. (Eugene, OR: Cascade, 2011), 135–45; Yoder, *Christian Attitudes to War, Peace, and Revolution* (Grand Rapids: Brazos, 2009); and Yoder, *The War of the Lamb: The Ethics of Nonviolence and Peacemaking* (Grand Rapids: Brazos, 2009).
9. These points are my summary of David Lipscomb, *Civil Government: Its Origin, Mission, and Destiny, and the Christian's Relation to It* (Nashville: Gospel Advocate, 1889). Lipscomb was a prominent defender of this perspective in late nineteenth- and early twentieth-century American Churches of Christ. According to Lipscomb, one should not even vote to prevent war, for one never knows for sure whether that vote will help prevent it (ibid., iv). Moreover, a Christian "may work as an employe [sic] of the government but may not be an officer or supporter." The difference he has in mind is in the oath of office taken by officers (ibid., 142).
10. Lee C. Camp, *Mere Discipleship: Radical Christianity in a Rebellious World*, 2nd ed. (Grand Rapids: Brazos, 2008), 253 n. 4.

11. Which is qualitatively different from saying it "was" or it "should be" God's country.
12. Sydney E. Ahlstrom, *A Religious History of the American People* (New Haven: Yale University Press, 1972), 2.
13. The contrast between the city of God and the city of the world is concentrated mostly in books X through XXII.
14. See Paul Tillich, *Systematic Theology*, vol. 1, *Reason and Revelation, Being and God* (Chicago: University of Chicago Press, 1951), 11–15.
15. Letter of Hosius to Constantius II, in Athanasius of Alexandria, *History of the Arians* 44, in *NPNF* 2nd ser., vol. 4:286. Cf. Peter J. Leithart, *Defending Constantine: The Twilight of an Empire and the Dawn of Christendom* (Downers Grove, IL: IVP Academic, 2010), 186. Leithart's book is, among other things, a thorough critique of Yoder's historiography and many of its consequent theological conclusions.
16. Contra Camp, *Mere Discipleship*, 253 n. 4, cited above.
17. Again, the language in Camp, *Mere Discipleship*, 45–46.
18. *1 Clement* 55:5–6.
19. Justin Martyr, *1 Apology* 1–3, in *Writings of Saint Justin Martyr*, 33–35.
20. Justin Martyr, *1 Apology* 68 (107).
21. Athenagoras, *Plea for the Christians* 1, in *ANF* 2:129.
22. Athenagoras, *Plea for the Christians* 37, in *ANF* 2:148.
23. See Irenaeus, *Against Heresies* V.xxiv.2.
24. For more detailed discussion of Christian engagement in a liberal democracy, see Francis J. Beckwith, *Politics for Christians: Statecraft as Soulcraft*, Christian Worldview Integration Series (Downers Grove, IL: IVP Academic, 2010).
25. Martin Luther King Jr., "Letter from Birmingham City Jail," in *Readings in Christian Ethics: A Historical Sourcebook*, ed. J. Philip Wogaman and Douglas M. Strong (Louisville: Westminster John Knox, 1996), 345–58, here 349.
26. Rod Dreher, *The Benedict Option: A Strategy for Christians in a Post-Christian Nation* (New York: Sentinel, 2017).
27. Origen, *Contra Celsum* VIII.74 (509–10).

Chapter 12: Identity and Race

1. Martin Luther King Jr., "I Have a Dream," speech, Washington, DC, August 28, 1963.
2. Thomas Sowell, *Black Rednecks and White Liberals* (San Francisco: Encounter, 2005), ix.
3. The definition of "racism" is, perhaps not surprisingly, one of the many contested issues related to race. The term is fluid, and its referent is increasingly broad and vague. See John McWhorter, "The Dictionary

Definition of Racism Has to Change," *The Atlantic* (June 22, 2020), https://www.theatlantic.com/ideas/archive/2020/06/dictionary-definition-racism-has-change/613324/.

4. For a typical early Christian interpretation of the curse on Canaan, see Justin Martyr, *Dialogue with Trypho* 139–40 (FOC, 361–63).
5. Robin DiAngelo, *White Fragility: Why It's So Hard for White People to Talk about Racism* (Boston: Beacon, 2018), 40–43.
6. Ibram X. Kendi, *How to Be an Antiracist* (New York: One World, 2019), 20. Kendi denounces color blindness in ibid., 10, 159–60, 166, 178–79.
7. Kendi, *How to Be an Antiracist*, 19.
8. For further analysis, see critical reviews of *White Fragility* by John McWhorter, "The Dehumanizing Condescension of *White Fragility*," *The Atlantic* (July 15, 2020), https://www.theatlantic.com/ideas/archive/2020/07/dehumanizing-condescension-white-fragility/614146/; and by Matt Taibbi, "On 'White Fragility,'" https://taibbi.substack.com/p/on-white-fragility. For a critical review of *How to Be an Antiracist*, see John McWhorter, "The Better of the Two Big Antiracism Bestsellers," https://www.educationnext.org/better-of-two-big-antiracism-bestsellers-kendi-how-to-be-an-antiracist-book-review/. For substantive analyses of the intellectual side of these movements, see Christine Rosen, "You Will Be Re-educated," https://www.commentarymagazine.com/articles/christine-rosen/you-will-be-re-educated/; and William Voegeli, "The Bigotry of Social Justice," https://americanmind.org/essays/the-bigotry-of-social-justice/.
9. One typical example recently brought to my attention is the category of "~~LatinoXa~~" theologies. As one author explains, the "a" and the "o" are gender inclusive, whereas the "X" reflects gender fluidity beyond the need for a gender binary. The strikethrough line indicates that no descriptor can "fully engage/reveal the complexity of realities." The author then notes her preference for showing the word in multiple colors, giving "particular attention to race, ethnicity and sexuality." See Neomi de Anda, "Latina Feminist and *Mujerista* Theologies as Political Theologies?" in *T&T Clark Handbook of Political Theology*, ed. Rubén Rosario Rodríguez (London: T&T Clark, 2019), 271–83, here 274, 281–82 n. 13.
10. For an insightful account of the origin and nature of identity politics, see Mary Eberstadt, *Primal Screams: How the Sexual Revolution Created Identity Politics* (West Conshohocken, PA: Templeton, 2019).

Chapter 13: In the World but Not of It

1. Alexander Pope, *An Essay on Man*, epistle II.5, in *The Complete Poetical Works of Alexander Pope*, Student's Cambridge Edition (Boston: Houghton Mifflin, 1931), 144.

2. This language, derived from John 17, is made famous in the second-century *Epistle to Diognetus*: "Christians dwell in the world, but they are not of the world." *Epistle to Diognetus* 6:3, in Michael W. Holmes, ed., *The Apostolic Fathers: Greek Texts and English Translations*, 3rd ed. (Grand Rapids: Baker Academic, 2007).
3. Dietrich Bonhoeffer, *Ethics*, Dietrich Bonhoeffer Works 6 (Minneapolis: Fortress, 2005), 58.
4. Bonhoeffer, *Ethics*, 82.
5. See James D. Bratt, ed., *Abraham Kuyper: A Centennial Reader* (Grand Rapids: Eerdmans, 1998), 461.
6. For example, Charles Taylor describes three different types of "secularity." Taylor's analysis is insightful, but for our purposes, I do not want to focus on one type to the exclusion of the others. See Charles Taylor, *A Secular Age* (Cambridge, MA: Belknap, 2007), which is the most exhaustive account of the origins and nature of secularity. For a more accessible introduction to Taylor, see James K. A. Smith, *How (Not) to Be Secular: Reading Charles Taylor* (Grand Rapids: Eerdmans, 2014).
7. Pope, *An Essay on Man*, epistle II.5 (144), quoted at the beginning of this chapter.
8. See *Epistle to Diognetus* 5.

Chapter 14: Engaging the Battle

1. Søren Kierkegaard, *Practice in Christianity*, trans. Howard V. Hong and Edna H. Hong (Princeton: Princeton University Press, 1991), 201.
2. Milton Mayer, *They Thought They Were Free: The Germans, 1933–45* (Chicago: University of Chicago Press, 1955), 166.
3. Mayer, *They Thought They Were Free*, 169.
4. Mayer, *They Thought They Were Free*, 169–70.
5. Mayer, *They Thought They Were Free*, 170–71.
6. Mayer, *They Thought They Were Free*, 171.
7. On moralistic therapeutic deism, see Christian S. Smith and Melinda Lundquist Denton, *Soul Searching: The Religious and Spiritual Lives of American Teenagers* (Oxford: Oxford University Press, 2005). See also Kenda Creasy Dean, *Almost Christian: What the Faith of Our Teenagers Is Telling the American Church* (Oxford: Oxford University Press, 2010).
8. Neil Postman, *Technopoly: The Surrender of Culture to Technology* (New York: Vintage, 1992), 181–99.
9. Dietrich Bonhoeffer, *Ethics*, Dietrich Bonhoeffer Works 6 (Minneapolis: Fortress, 2005), 102.

Index